MORE PRAISE FOR *SPIRIT HEALS*

"*Spirit Heals* is deeply touching, beautifully written, profoundly and positively life changing. This book has the power to significantly impact the way you view the world and your life. Be prepared for a powerful healing and uplifting of your own spirit." — Peggy McColl, author of *Your Destiny Switch*

"If your eyes have found *Spirit Heals*, you have probably been guided by your inner knowing. Don't miss this golden opportunity of synchronicity. This book is not just another intellectual self-help book that leaves you wondering. It is an eminently practical guide that will quiet your mind and awaken your spirit to guide you on your healing path. You will indeed experience the power of Spirit to heal." — Robert Lang, MD, associate clinical professor, Yale University

"A true gift to womankind, from a wise and wonderful spiritual teacher. Each chapter sparkles with valuable, insightful information on the dynamics of health, illness, and healing. This life manual should be placed in every woman's hand as a helping tool to navigate the currents of our often challenging lifestyles. It is a wellspring of life-altering awareness." — Kim Makris, certified classical homeopath

"In over twenty-five years of working with patients with chronic illness, I have not found a book that so perfectly describes the core understanding of successful physicians and healers: that a patient's sense of possibility is the key factor in creating a positive outcome. Meredith Young-Sowers teaches powerful tools for accessing the inner knowing that makes healing possible. Her insightful, inspired words empower women to step into the wholeness of who they are, to tap their inner wisdom and take charge of their healing journey. I will use *Spirit Heals* as a resource in my practice and recommend it to my patients."
— Dr. Linda Haltinner, chiropractic physician
and founder of Sojourns Community Health Clinic

"Meredith Young-Sowers is a pioneer in health and spirituality. What impresses me most is her ability to bring life's challenges into focus through the lens of love in a simple yet profound way. She does this by skillfully weaving questions and concepts that allow women to unlock hidden beliefs and find their own truth. Both personally and professionally, I highly recommend Meredith's insightful work." — Dr. Diana Cable, holistic family practitioner

"On each page of *Spirit Heals* Meredith Young-Sowers lifts the veil of illusion, offering the power of grace and healing that is our birthright. Hers is a clear, practical, and amazing bridge over the chasms of physical, mental, emotional, and spiritual illness, as she calls us to the unfolding of our natural balance and harmony. Through her book's insights and reflective guidance, we are invited to renewal and wholeness. During times when fear and pain can seem so isolating, Meredith's words offer us back our community of Spirit, self, others, and creation."

— Yvonne Brandenburg, pastor, the Church Within, Indianapolis

PRAISE FOR OTHER BOOKS
BY MEREDITH L. YOUNG-SOWERS

"*Wisdom Bowls* is a blessed addition to the healing knowledge coming forth from the heavens. I encourage you to let Meredith's wisdom guide you through the pages of this remarkable book."   — Caroline Myss, PhD,
author of *Sacred Contracts* and *Anatomy of the Spirit*

"*Wisdom Bowls* offers us powerful and effective ways to remember our inner fullness and use it to fill the emptiness in our outer lives. A must-read for anyone who dreams of living life as if it were a spiritual practice."

— Rachel Naomi Remen, MD, author of
Kitchen Table Wisdom and *My Grandfather's Blessings*

"*Wisdom Bowls* is an inspiring book of life-changing insights. Based on a powerful but simple intuitive process, it offers imaginative ways to see into your true spiritual nature and heal at the deepest levels."

— Sue Bender, author of *Stretching Lessons*,
Everyday Sacred, and *Plain and Simple*

"*Spiritual Crisis* explores in a beautiful and almost poetic fashion the awakening of the human spirit within the luminous web of love in which we live and move and have our being. This is a book that will offer the reader substance and solace in the often difficult journey toward renewed self-worth and spiritual awakening." — Joan Borysenko, PhD, author of *Minding the Body, Mending the Mind*

Spirit heals

Also by Meredith L. Young-Sowers

Agartha: A Journey to the Stars

Angelic Messenger Cards

*Wisdom Bowls: Overcoming Fear and Coming Home
to Your Authentic Self*

Spirit heals

Awakening a
WOMAN'S
INNER KNOWING
for Self-Healing

MEREDITH L. YOUNG-SOWERS

New World Library
Novato, California

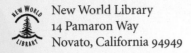
New World Library
14 Pamaron Way
Novato, California 94949

Stillpoint School of Integrative Life Healing™ and Stillpoint Model of Integrative Healing™ are trademarks of the Stillpoint Foundation.

The material in this book is intended for education. It is not meant to take the place of diagnosis and treatment by a qualified medical practitioner or therapist. No expressed or implied guarantee as to the effects of the use of the recommendations can be given nor liability taken.

Text design and typography by Tona Pearce Myers

Library of Congress Cataloging-in-Publication Data
Young-Sowers, Meredith L. (Meredith Lady).
Spirit heals : awakening a woman's inner knowing for self-healing / Meredith L. Young-Sowers.
       p.   cm.
Includes bibliographical references and index.
ISBN-13: 978-1-57731-577-3 (pbk. : alk. paper)
1. Mental healing. 2. Spiritual healing. 3. Mind and body. 4. Women—Mental health. 5. Self-actualization (Psychology) I. Title.
RZ400.Y686 2007
615.8'51—dc22   2007025603

First printing, October 2007
ISBN-10: 1-57731-577-4
ISBN-13: 978-1-57731-577-3
Printed in Canada on acid-free, partially recycled paper

g New World Library is a proud member of the Green Press Initiative.

10 9 8 7 6 5 4 3 2 1

To my darling daughter, Melanie — now all grown up.
I send you my love and appreciation
for being the wonderful daughter you are.

Contents

Foreword

*I*n *Spirit Heals,* Meredith Young-Sowers guides us through the important considerations that we encounter during life's crises, including illness. In my seventeen years as a gynecologic oncologist, I have observed that cancer diagnoses are life-altering events. On the pathway to wellness, the body must navigate many changes, and these changes influence all aspects of our lives — our physical stamina as well as our mental attitudes. In fact, these changes — and the choices made for treatment and healing— seem to redirect our entire lives.

Of course, all of life, not just cancer treatment, is a series of choices. As obstacles rise in our pathway, we continually consider which course to pursue. Do we react or retreat? Do we select another course of action? This dilemma becomes even more problematic if the obstacle is a serious illness. This book helps us explore our options and identify which behaviors might have contributed to our current predicament and which choices might steer us toward a healthier future. Meredith helps us understand how we might avoid future problems. More important, she gives us practical steps to take now that the situation exists.

Hippocrates, who lived from BCE 460–377, said, "The natural healing force within each one of us is the greatest force in getting well." Although we often sense that central force, many of us do not understand or accept its role in the healing process. Without some guidance, we may not recruit that energy, that "healing force," to help us heal.

In my work, I routinely discuss cancer diagnoses with patients and families. To move past the initial shock of the diagnosis, most patients ask the following questions: *How serious is the condition? What course of treatment is recommended? And what is the prognosis for survival and healing?* They want accuracy, honesty, and encouragement, but most of all they want to know what they can do. They take a proactive approach, asking questions and enlisting the help of professionals and loved ones to aid their healing. Routinely, cancer treatments require some combination of surgery, chemotherapy, and radiation. Often these therapies last for many months or in some cases even years. All individuals undergoing treatment must also, as Hippocrates suggests, seek out and enlist their own natural healing force.

The textbook definition of *healing* includes "to restore to spiritual wholeness." Indeed, we must understand and address all the dimensions of healing — spiritual and mental as well as physical. None of these dimensions can be ignored or forgotten. In *Spirit Heals*, Meredith Young-Sowers explores the mental (mind), physical (body), and spiritual connections to our natural healing force, whether we are healing from cancer or from some other illness or disease. She leads us through each area and explores how these interwoven energies affect our daily health and wellness. Meredith takes us by the hand and gently, lovingly walks us through a series of real-life scenarios. *How are we living? What behavior choices are we making? How do we deal with illness? What can we do to improve our current situation? What changes can we make to move toward a more wholesome, balanced lifestyle?*

These questions and scenarios remind us that healing is both an art and a science, and they prepare us for our journey to wellness. Meredith guides us to remain open to the moment and to choose healthier possibilities within each moment while we rebalance our lives and bodies. She reminds us to seek spiritual nourishment by filling each day with a positive, hopeful, loving perspective. She encourages us to walk with the right intention for healing and living: "Be the loving mentor instead of the punishing taskmaster." All of these choices will support the healing force within and can lead us to a more balanced, healthy life.

Drawing on twenty-seven years of experience, Meredith provides powerful tools such as "intuitive perceptions" that are available to each of us in the process of healing, and she demonstrates how to fully engage them. She gives us valuable mechanisms and specific activities and exercises to help restore ourselves to a stronger, more connected life. Using personal and client examples, she provides a blueprint for building a unique, individualized plan for recovery — that is, for feeling well, functioning at home and work, and interacting positively with family and friends. Meredith encourages us toward that wellness. She arms us with the wonderful skills and tools we need to reach the life we want. As Meredith writes, "Healing is what we are doing all the days of our life."

This is a book to be read again and again. As we step into our lives and incorporate Meredith's wise words, we can continue to use them for support, encouragement, and illumination. I will recommend *Spirit Heals* to my patients, as I am recommending it to you as the beginning of your journey to Spirit-driven wellness.

— Dr. Allan Mayer, codirector of gynecologic oncology,
Saint Francis/Mount Sinai Regional Cancer Center

PREFACE

On Healing

*I*n *Spirit Heals,* healing is more than a physical experience. I use healing in a different way, and I want to share that with you as we begin the book.

Healing means coming into wholeness by simplifying our thoughts, finding peace within the circumstances we face, and opening our deep heart and Spirit to mend our disconnection from the essence of all life — Love.

Love is the energy of Spirit, the Great Mystery, God, the Tao, the Source of all life and beyond, that is meant to blossom our life.

Our healing is a continuing process, as our physical health waxes and wanes and our mental and emotional well-being rises and falls. Healing means we become more aware of when we feel off-balance and then become equally present to the practices and shifts in behavior and attitude that return us to balance. Balance is obtained only when our life is in alignment with our inner still point.

Our physical healing is promoted as we shift our perspective from pain, fear, and loss to inner strength, joy, and opening to Grace.

Our mental and emotional healing comes from rebalancing our thoughts and feelings to be in touch with our wisdom mind rather than our self-critic. Through this process we become more aware of the true power and presence we possess. We recognize that we are completely safe and have the authority to be fully engaged in our life journey.

Our spiritual healing comes from opening our deep heart to love, joy, and meaning, which allows us to love all and to serve all.

All healing is a process of waking to our innate goodness, our potential, and our means of living a complete and fulfilling life.

Healing is what we are all doing — all the days of our life.

Introduction

My experience over the past twenty-seven years has shed varying degrees of light and understanding on the unknowable, mysterious world of Spirit and the guidance that directs, inspires, motivates, and informs our life.

My life seems strange in retrospect because I didn't end up where I imagined I might. Perhaps we never do. My life is very different today from when I first noticed my spirit light. My life is better, more fulfilled, and much more involved with other people's spiritual growth and healing than I would ever have imagined.

Most significantly, it seems that I have developed courage in putting forth what I know to be true from direct experience with Divine Love. Each of us is destined to awaken our spirit light, and as this happens we have a responsibility to share our experience and to help and support others on their own path to awakening.

Many years ago, my own spiritual journey and experience of guidance from Spirit began when I discovered that there is in fact an inner, invisible, spiritual world. Through a deep and meaningful soul opening, I learned that we are guided by teachers both around us and within us, and they represent Spirit in whatever forms we most easily recognize and trust—our beloved grandmother who has passed over, an angel, or any cherished form of God in human form. While Divinity is the Source within every form, the point of our waking up is to draw us ever closer into alignment with the Source of Love within — our true Self, or spirit.

I now think of Spirit, or God, as both Divine Mother and Divine Father, as the presence and great unknowable mystery. I have realized, slowly, over all these years that life really has to do only with loving — with how we love, why we love, and whom we love; with the ways we love when it's hard and the ways we love when it's easy; with how we love ourself, our life, and each other when we can't grasp or control what is happening to us; and finally, with discovering that the reason we love is simply because we can.

TRAVELING THE SPIRITUAL PATH

You've no doubt found your own sources of love and inspiration, and call God by whatever name you hold dear. As you read you'll notice that I reference many spiritual traditions: Western Christianity, Native American beliefs, Buddhism, and Hinduism, among others. This is truly a time of unity. By blending cultures, it helps us to expand our spiritual understanding by shedding new light on familiar struggles.

I've also included in this book the exquisite teachings of the Indian holy man Sri Sathya Sai Baba. His life and teachings — that you are an embodiment of Divine Love, the stuff of stars and stardust — is a profoundly meaningful and enlightening message for our troubled times. My husband, Errol, and I have had experiences with Sai Baba, and I've shared some stories that I hope will be as meaningful to you as they are to us.

Any and all of these guides can help you as you travel your spiritual path, and because you are motivated to read *Spirit Heals*, it is also right for you. Trust your guidance that *Spirit Heals* has come into your life for a reason; we are led to books that are intended for us. This book can assist you in finding the best ways to direct your life in a safe and meaningful way.

You're being led to more fully appreciate the courage and tenacity you've already shown in your life as well as toward a new willingness to learn and grow. You'll find within these pages many ways to become your own best friend — how to generate support and positive feelings even when no one else seems to be offering them. This book is intended to be both a resource for learning how energy moves in the body and how it impacts your health as well as a spiritual resource you can return to over and over for information, guidance, and renewed trust in your life path.

I share what I've learned from clients and been taught by Spirit about the relationship between healing and our spiritual journeys, and I make special note of our reproductive system as women: breasts, ovaries, uterus, and vagina. I discuss imbalances within this system and ways to rebalance what needs healing. I also write about our heart: physical, emotional, and spiritual. Our heart holds the key to many levels of our healing. For instance, we can minimize our risk of heart attack and stroke as we understand how our heart thinks and what it needs to be healthy.

GETTING TO KNOW SPIRIT

While your body and your thoughts are more obvious than your relationship with Spirit, nevertheless, it is time to come to know what your spirit is all about. It is the supreme energy of Divine Love that rests within and all around you. Spiritual energy extends beyond you, becoming the one universal soul that fills life everywhere.

Your inner knowing is what comes from your connection with Spirit. Inner guidance for your health and well-being makes itself known to you in many ways: through synchronicities, daydreams, night dreams, meditations, prayers, walks in the woods, and even in the most unlikely and mundane moments of your life — perhaps as you round the corner from your favorite hot dog stand and head back to your office after lunch.

Inner guidance shows you what to do and how to do it when you're lost. It also gives you confidence to think big when it comes to your passion and the contributions you wish to make in your life. Your inner channel is always available, and as you open up and listen more intently for your own healing guidance, you will know more clearly what to do and how to respond to life's challenges and joys.

This book covers a great deal of territory, providing specific advice as well as broad understanding that I hope will help you on your healing journey — whether that means physical healing, rebalancing your emotions, recharging your spirit, or stabilizing your lifestyle. The book contains aspects of the Stillpoint Model of Integrative Life Healing and the Path of Inner Knowing that has and continues to be my life work. This work has helped many, many people. Let it help you, too.

Stay with me as we turn the pages together and discover the invisible world of subtle energy and the guidance from intuitive perception. These can show you what you need to find within yourself and how to use it to enhance your life force and the power of Spirit to bring you into greater health and happiness.

HOW TO GET THE MOST FROM THIS BOOK

As we explore our individual healing journeys, I will periodically ask you to take time to reflect on our discussion. I will ask you to be an active participant in your healing and rebalancing journey.

Each chapter contains several sections that guide you in this reflection and participation. One is called "Ask Yourself," which is a series of questions to ask yourself about how a particular topic applies to your life. As you ask the questions, I suggest you write your responses in a journal. You may want to buy a beautiful journal book or resurrect that special one you put aside for just the right time. Write your thoughts, draw pictures, make notes, or just enjoy having a secret and private space in which to express your feelings.

Each chapter also contains important healing practices called "Activities." By doing these practices on a regular basis, you create a daily plan for staying steady and enhancing the flows of subtle energy that support your body. A little effort every day makes all the difference. Some days you'll have more time than others, but try to do at least one activity daily — whether a meditation, breath awareness, and/or the Healing Art of Loving Touch.

Perhaps most significant are each chapter's "Attitude Shifts." These are listed at the end of each chapter, and each one is indicated by an image in the margin next to sections that are especially important for you to consider. These flag important points to reflect on. As you incorporate these attitude shifts into your healing journey, you immediately lessen the energetic burdens carried by your body and mind. It is important for your healing that you take in the energy of these experiences rather than only storing more information in your head.

Whether you seek physical healing for a present imbalance, want to hold strong to prevent illness, or need a more enduring connection to Spirit, all the ideas in *Spirit Heals* can help.

ACT AS IF IT WERE TRUE

Our mind works in interesting ways when we are learning new material. Sometimes our thinking plays to our advantage and sometimes to our disadvantage. Our mind can react cautiously or suspiciously to new information, particularly if the information raises questions about the way we see the world and ourself. We need to enter new ideas slowly and openly, without our mind jumping in first to judge, argue, or prove what's true. To help keep your thinking from getting in the way, and to help you proceed at a pace that is comfortable for you, I suggest that you practice this material *as if it were true, and to keep doing so until you're certain what is true and most applicable for you.*

As you read, listen inside, and practice the work, you will find whatever value and worth it has for you. By telling yourself that you're only practicing these suggestions *as if* they were true, you circumvent your mind's need to prove the work to be right or wrong at the onset.

The work can take flight within you and aid your journey only if you find the threads that make sense, that feel useful and fulfilling. Proceed knowing that you are in charge of your own destiny. And yes, you do have a destiny, and you are not limited by fate. You are making important decisions, and you can learn to listen inside for what is best for you.

Ultimately, healing — and for that matter, entering into any worthwhile undertaking — requires personal confidence and faith in yourself. This work will open your mind and heart to the very depths of potential and possibility for your healing and for your life's direction.

You don't need to be fearful or anxious about exploring the way you see, sense, and experience yourself, your partnerships, your friendships, and the world — for that is what makes you wondrously unique and precious. There is only one of you — there will never be another. How you see and contribute to the world is entirely your own, while your desire to be happy and healthy and avoid suffering is shared by all peoples and creatures everywhere. Even as we heal ourself, our attitudes, beliefs, and actions have a direct influence on the health and happiness of others: we are each an integral aspect of the total web of life.

Welcome to *Spirit Heals*.

PART ONE

The Art and Science of Healing

My dear, this world, its laws,
Our perceptions,
Are such a minute part of existence.

Should not all of our suffering and sadness
Be like this:

As just dropped from an infant's palm
That is asleep against the breast
Of God?

— Hafiz

CHAPTER ONE

Giving Ourself the Best Advice

All living entities and all energy fields
understand the frequency of love,
and activating this frequency is one of the greatest treasures we can possess.
— Mikio Sankey, PhD, LA

*H*ealing is both an art and a science. In our Western model it is easy to focus exclusively on the science of healing — the treatments, practices, medicines, surgeries, radiations, and chemotherapies. These are important, but not exclusively important. The essential companion to the *science of healing* is the *art of healing*, which, as it suggests, is more focused on our creative, intuitive, psychological, emotional, and spiritual selves.

Thousands of years before Christ, the early Taoists, who were healers, were also mystics and philosophers. They believed that to heal the body one needed to rebalance one's life. A person needed to be in harmony with Heaven and Earth — in other words, to renew one's sense of a spiritual connection and rediscover one's true destiny to find the optimum way of living in one's physical environment. They believed that the rebalancing process allowed the body to right itself, thus enhancing the flows of energy that support the physical organs and systems.

As we focus on the *art of healing*, we become aware of the subtle energy shifts that can support our ability to heal ourself from the inside out — from our spirit to our body. Just as a wound must heal from the inside out, our lasting healing arises first from what is invisible to our physical eye.

It is sometimes difficult to believe that the *invisible* world has as much power for healing as the visible one, but the evidence surrounds us every day. We can't see electricity, for example, but we see the result when we turn on the light. We can't see protons, electrons, or neutrons with the naked eye, but we see the physical desk in front of us. We can't see love, but we feel it.

What we can't see is often even more powerful than what we can see. Just because we can't see attitudes, beliefs, emotions, assumptions, and assertions does not mean they aren't acting on us — just that we're not yet aware of their impact.

Healing requires us to enter a meaningful self-discovery and rebalancing process, one in which we discover many influences we haven't been aware of before. This learning will add new, positive components to our life and our healing journey.

The essential thing to remember as we begin is that this process of self-discovery is not meant to make us feel bad, about either what we've done or what we didn't know up to now. Life is a journey, and at any point in our life, we can only remind ourself of the truth: I did the best I could, given what I knew and understood at that time.

BLAME HAS NO PLACE IN HEALING

It is extremely important that we take a moment to reflect on blame and how it puts us at a disadvantage in our healing. We want the best for ourself, and so we can begin right here, right now, by promising to give ourself only the best advice. Healing has nothing to do with blaming, but with taking responsibility for our life and finding the ways that we can grow in understanding and wisdom.

There is no one right way to live, to feel, or to heal. Each of us finds our own way by being as true as possible to the best of who we are and what we know about ourself. Rebalancing our life and body is not about identifying what we've failed to do in the past; it's about recognizing what is available to us in each moment.

Opening ourself to wisdom, learning, and insight is central to healing. As human beings we always do our best to provide comfort and happiness for ourself and those we love. We all want to avoid suffering and enjoy happiness. But as we learn more about life, we make different choices.

The choices we made at fifteen are probably not the ones we would make now. The same is true about the ideas and feelings we experienced with such passion at age twenty that may not be the same ones that are important to us now. We change and renew our thoughts and emotions just as our cells and organs renew themselves. We must learn about and understand the invisible world of feelings and spirit — the art of healing — as well as the visible world of treatments and procedures — the science of healing — so that we can combine them and benefit from the best of both worlds. The art and the science of healing are like two halves of an apple — both are essential to create the whole.

ASK YOURSELF

How can I keep from blaming myself or others for being sick physically, being scared about what has happened or what might happen again, or being simply out of sync with my life and the people in it?

What can I do to help myself when I find myself in that place of self-blame?

And yet, even knowing this, it can still be easy to fall into blaming ourself or others. We can't help but say, if only. How can we counter the unwanted and continual tirade that goes around and around in our head?

The answer is that we must become more selective about which of our thoughts we listen to. It is like choosing a healthier diet for our body, only we are choosing healthier thoughts and feelings. Do we listen to regret, blame, shame, and criticism, or do we listen to comfort, friendship, caring, and loving? This is our continual choice, which, though we may not have stopped to realize it, is always posed by our two inner voices — the inner critic and the inner healer or spirit.

Later in *Spirit Heals*, we'll explore further the ways we process our thinking; right now, it is enough to begin our healing journey by simply becoming more aware of our assessments, judgments, and assumptions and the feelings that they generate. We'll need to pay close attention to even recognize some of them because, almost by definition, our assumptions are those thoughts we rarely stop to reflect on, but which still solidify in our body and our life. For example, I may assume that my partner will never understand my needs, or that he will always understand my needs. These types of absolute positions are dangerous, for they don't give me or my partner space to move.

Imagine we took a jar, and as we recognize our various positions, opinions, assumptions, and judgments, we place them inside. We don't need to argue with the attitudes we observe, we just pick them up — one at a time — and put them in the jar and put the lid back on. Put the jar on a shelf out of immediate sight. We can come back to them when and if we choose.

By setting aside our upsetting and negative feelings, we find space to breath, giving ourself wiggle room to reconsider our life and how we want to spend our precious energy. If we don't, if we instead hold on to old reasoning and assumptions about the possibilities or lack of possibilities for our healing, we will always be looking backward. Imagine driving down a road, stopping your car, getting out, and studying only the road you've just traveled.

The art of healing begins by being open to the present moment and looking forward to where we want to be. Looking back at our life doesn't tell us what the road ahead will be like. Even if we feel we have been lost up to now, that doesn't mean we won't still find our destination. The questions we need to ask ourself are: What destination do we have in mind when we step on the gas? And are we willing to do whatever it takes to get there?

How we respond to the events and circumstances in our life right now sets the course and determines the destination toward which we are heading. Actions speak louder than words — but the words we tell ourself can have a real say in whether we reach that destination. They can generate or diminish the healing energy we need to restore our body, mind, and spirit.

If we want more from life, a greater quality of life, we must consider those various aspects of healing that move us toward greater awareness and inner knowing. When we operate from inside our deep heart and spirit, when we make decisions from our core of wisdom and compassion, we move successfully out into the various relationships in our life. When we do this, the difference in the outcome can be astonishing.

When clients ask me whether I think they will heal and overcome what is dragging them down, I tell them the truth of what my experience has shown me: when we allow today to be as meaningful as possible and fill it with a positive, hopeful, and loving perspective, then we are much more likely to have a tomorrow, and it is more likely to also be good and healing.

FINDING WHAT WE LOVE NOURISHES US

In addition to putting aside blame, we need to do what nourishes us and gives us the courage to believe in our life, our inner knowing, our assessment of circumstances, and our willingness to change our mind and our heart. Healing is all about nourishment.

Nourishment is essential to our emotional, intellectual, physical, social, and spiritual lives. Each person is nourished in various ways that are also individually satisfying. One person may seek emotional nourishment by planting a row of pansies in the spring and social nourishment by browsing a boutique. Reading a travel book on touring the French countryside may fill one person with delight and intellectual nourishment, while another finds the same by studying the mechanisms of a German race car. Praying quietly in the back of a great cathedral may be spiritual nourishment for one person, while chanting in a group may be essential for another.

It isn't so much *what* nourishes us, rather that we may appreciate that many kinds of nourishment are essential for a good life. Think of the search for nourishment as "finding what we love," because in doing what we love, we feel valuable and valued and create a self-generating sense of inner delight and warmth. Finding and following the threads of our life through the various veins of nourishment are requirements for a meaningful life and thus for healing.

We will continue to explore the various ways we nourish ourself in the rest of part 1. Before continuing, however, I'd like you to begin by doing the following practice, which is easy and very rewarding. It is called the Healing Art of Loving Touch.

ACTIVITY
The Healing Art of Loving Touch

As you follow the practice of placing one or both hands over the center of your chest — that is, over your heart center or fourth chakra — you are nourishing every level of your being. You are disconnecting from your thinking and reconnecting to your inner knowing, the quality of intuitive awareness that opens doorways to useful guidance and understanding. This practice also speaks directly to your physical heart's health, supports your immune system, and energizes your ability and desire to circulate the positive and loving feelings of healing through your life and the lives of others.

1. Place your hands, palms against your chest, in the center area of your chest.
2. Close your eyes, or otherwise soften your gaze, and shift your awareness from thinking to knowing, which is a product of your intuitive perception and comes from deep heart or spirit.
3. Feel the energy in your hands, the warmth of connectedness to your physical heart, your emotional heart, and your deep heart or spirit.
4. Take several slow breaths and focus on feeling connected to Spirit. As you hold your hands in this position, you are regenerating your energy, your spiritual will, and your love and compassion for yourself and others. *You are charging your battery from God's.*
5. Ask to be guided, helped, or supported in whatever way seems most appropriate.
6. When you are finished, open your eyes, and after giving yourself several moments, return to whatever you were doing.

This practice is like mother's chicken soup, a hug from the person you care most about, and a love letter from God — all rolled into one. It works as physical, emotional, and spiritual support, reminding us of what is really important.

❧ ATTITUDE SHIFTS ❧

1. There is both a science of healing and an art of healing, and both are available to me.

2. I now recognize that blame, my own and that of others, is unproductive and has no place in my healing journey.

3. I can choose the thoughts I listen to, whether they are positive or negative. Choosing the positive enhances my healing.

4. I can make my new way of knowing a reality by understanding that what I love nourishes me.

CHAPTER TWO

Emotional Nourishment — Expressing the New Season of Our Life

Be content with what you have;
Rejoice in the way things are.
When you realize there is nothing lacking,
The whole world belongs to you.

— Lao-Tzu

Feelings are an important part of the journey to wholeness as we allow ourself to reframe our present circumstances toward more specific body, mind, and spirit nourishment. We express feelings through our words, whether we say them out loud or only in our mind. The words we choose are important because they bring back the memories and feelings associated with the events of our life. The more vivid the words or images we absorb, the greater the impact on our whole being — for good or ill.

The media, for example, is expert at painting pictures through their commentary and images that elicit powerful responses in us. These "high shock and impact" messages stay with us and resurface every time we repeat a tragic or upsetting story.

We experience similar "high shock and impact" messages every time we imagine or relive traumas in our own life, such as the feeling when we realized we had cancer, the loss of a mother or father, or a missed career opportunity. We may repeat these stories many times, and become accustomed to hearing ourself talk about what happened, but while the feeling of disaster and dread may lessen some, the pain remains and continues to register in our body.

We may think we have gotten used to hearing these high-energy negative, sad, or worrying feelings over and over, but our body has not. We feel words in our gut, in our heart — and these impacts influence our mood, our sense of safety and well-being, and our sense of being loved and of being worthy of love.

WORDS THAT INSPIRE, HEAL; WORDS THAT DIMINISH, DEBILITATE

Normal conversation tends to focus more on what is wrong than on what is mending, growing, and improving. This leads us to reflect more on the struggle than on the healing in our life. Feel in your body, for example, the difference between these two statements: *What a stupid thing to do — can't you ever get it right?* or *Thank you for helping me with this.*

Our feelings are powerful re-stimulators of our past experiences, but they can also be powerful stimulators of our progress, growth, development, and faith in ourself.

Emotional nourishment means making choices all through our day to hold steady to the awareness that tomorrow is being written as we speak. We are, in essence, expressing the new season of our life with each intention.

Whether we feel we're about to drop into the dark hole of anger and despair or we feel lifted into enjoyment and pleasure, both are calls to take a breath, put our hand over our heart — the place of spiritual connection and sustenance — and say to ourself, *steady, steady, steady.* Repeating this phrase allows us to stay in touch with what's going on inside, while also expressing our trust that there is a greater goodness always at work within us even when we can't see, prove, or understand it.

Healing comes from really knowing ourself. When it comes to our emotions, that means allowing ourself to feel what we are genuinely feeling, but at the same time supporting and nourishing our emotional self so we can move into healing and rebalancing our body and our life.

Our past, though imperfect, holds valuable learning. In healing we're not trying to create a perfect life or even undo what has been done. We're seeking to come to peace with what has happened in order to direct our life in a more positive direction.

Old feelings that come back to haunt us are like food that offers no nourishment; they reinforce our emptiness and sorrow. Instead, in healing work, we look to provide ourself with solid and enduring emotional strength that is balanced with the truth of what we feel, but isn't weighted only toward the pain. For example, positive emotional nourishment may sound a lot like this: *I've always done the very best I could even if I can't let myself completely believe that yet.* Or, *My life is about learning, and I'm no longer afraid to learn more about myself because I'll find the value inside that I've never fully seen or appreciated.*

OUR NATIVE AMERICAN VISION QUEST

Emotional nourishment can also come from experiences in which we are pushed to our limits and find something within us to hold true to. In Native American traditions, young people were given a designated period of time in which they were sent out to find their vision of what the Creator intended for their life. The elders realized that in order for young people to find the deep resources within their hearts and souls, they needed to be pushed beyond their normal physical, mental, and emotional limits. This test of stamina allowed these people to tap into their internal wisdom — their spirit, the sacred nature of their journey, tor, and the voices of their ancestors — which would then guide them through the larger ordeal of life.

We, too, may feel we've been sent on a vision quest — pushed to our limits. Even if we've not developed cancer, heart disease, or any other physical malady, we may still feel pushed to discover our true vision. By listening within, we can garner the courage to walk with the right intention for healing and living.

As on a sacred vision quest, the anger and pain we feel when things fall apart can be a doorway to transformation. We can't complete the ordeal of any illness or life disaster without looking differently at ourself, our life, our circumstances, and our resources. The outer world offers no true and lasting solace when we hurt inside. But once we taste the freedom of connecting to a greater power, we find it easier to take the next steps toward living more fully. Our vision quest can bring us to a place of renewal, from where we can decide what we want from life and what we want to give back.

On this journey of finding emotional nourishment, we begin by not defining ourself by the disease or challenging circumstances we may find ourself in. Instead we define ourself as we choose by the quality of spirit with which we enter each day.

This is the pearl of great price — *truly defining ourself comes only from within*. We begin by shaping our life toward quality rather than quantity, reframing our experiences right now and finding a newness within. To polish this pearl is to trudge through some mighty rough terrain, but in the end we discover more than if we'd never walked that path. It is the quality of our life and our personhood, our "spirit-hood," that we must find and value.

We write the story of our life every day, through every emotional response. Every moment is an invitation to look at things from within rather than from what others will think, feel, or say about us. Ultimately, it is our own opinion that weighs in most heavily toward our healing.

ASK YOURSELF

Do you feel as if you have been or currently are on a vision quest?
How have you begun to redefine yourself as a result of the
challenges you've faced?

ILLNESS OR CHANGE ALLOWS US
TO SET NEW PRIORITIES

The reality that disease or imbalance can offer us something important is perhaps why so many women tell their stories with the "illness-
as-a-gift" theme. We know that the treatments are extremely difficult
and that the terror of having a cancer diagnosis or of having a stroke
or heart attack can weaken whatever inner strength we thought we had.
But the truth is, just as in a vision quest, when we finally recognize
what is important to us, we can clear the clutter from our life — the obligations and fears of others' opinions — and rise like the phoenix (the
mythical bird who rises from the ashes) to experience our own true
Self. And, of course, this feeling of authenticity, of having something to
hold on to — resources that no person or life scenario can ever take
from us — is deeply freeing. It is the gift that can be gleaned from a serious diagnosis.

As we take stock of our life and practice saying kind and forgiving
things to ourself for nourishment, we may sense a confidence and
inner knowing taking seed. We begin to trust our perspective on
things. Rather than trying to change other people, we put our efforts
into enhancing ourself. In healing, we benefit from putting ourself at
the center of our life right now, no matter how strange and uncomfortable this feels. We learn to pay attention to our feelings, thoughts,
and attitudes: what we do and why, who pulls our strings and how we
react, what makes us feel overwhelmed, and what to do when we hit
bottom.

We learn to direct our thoughts and feelings toward opening the inner resources of lasting strength, courage, joy, and love for ourself and others. We can't give in a healthy way when we're on empty. Sometimes illness and disillusionment show us we've been trying to run on empty for a long, long time.

❧ ATTITUDE SHIFTS ❧

1. My body hears my words and accepts them as truth, so the words that I use are vitally important.
2. Learning to stay "steady, steady, steady" allows me to be open to new possibilities at the same time that I reflect on the lessons from the past.
3. I can use positive emotional nourishment to reframe my past and chart my new future.
4. My diagnosis, like a vision quest, can play two roles in my life — pushing the limits of my endurance and becoming a place of discovery.
5. I am more than my diagnosis. Yet it affords me the opportunity to craft a new and expansive definition of myself.
6. I can consider that through my illness or life struggles, I'll find things to learn.
7. Now is the time to put myself at the center of my life.

CHAPTER THREE

Intellectual Nourishment —
Doing It Our Way

There is more to life
than merely increasing its speed.
— Gandhi

*L*earning is important to our healing. Typically, we explore what has immediate relevance for us. If we are pregnant, we track the developmental stages of the fetus in our uterus; if our children are born, we learn about and encourage the development of their minds, senses, and hearts. If we are pursuing career goals, then we're taking courses, networking with friends and colleagues, learning the ins and outs of the business. In other words, we go where our interests lie.

Having a diagnosis of cancer, having a family member diagnosed with cancer or heart trouble, or feeling the weight of undue stress on our life instantly moves us to explore methods of healing and the many paths that are offered today in the rapidly emerging world of integrative medicine. Integrative healing combines Eastern and Western methods to create a healing plan that represents both aggressive and nonaggressive treatments and approaches.

These are also called "complementary healing practices," and we may have already experienced the benefit of them if, say, we treated back pain by taking medicine prescribed by our family doctor while also getting a massage or acupuncture treatment. Perhaps we've already been inspired to learn about the human energy field, chakras, and meridians, or we have already tried hypnotherapy, relaxation and breathing techniques, yoga, tai chi, or chi gong.

We begin our healing journey by learning about the various treatments that are available for healing, and then creating an artist's palette of various life-enhancing practices, healing methods, and treatments, some of which we may continue throughout the changing course of our life. A client recently told me about an experience in which complementary practices were the key to relieving the severe abdominal pain she was experiencing as a result of adhesions from surgery. She had been told that nothing could be done to eliminate the pain. Not accepting that she was helpless, she tried a few energy healing practices that she had learned, using them with love and trust that some manner of help would be forthcoming — and it was. Within an hour the pain was gone.

Just as we've come through the Industrial Revolution, we have entered the Healing Revolution. Today, it is possible to explore the many facets of subtle energy healing. Subtle energy healing isn't a New Age approach, but rather an ancient and time-honored way to rebalance our body and realign our emotional and spiritual energies so we can recreate greater health within us and around us. The early healers were indeed spiritually minded, realizing that the body exists not by itself but in relationship to one's complete life. Today we are reconnecting with the truth of this awareness.

THERE IS NO ONE MAGIC PATH TO HEALING

There are as many ways to heal illness as there are people wanting to feel better about their bodies, lives, and futures.

Because there are so many variations in our healing journeys, we are bound to ask ourself why one woman heals breast cancer with chemotherapy, and another without chemotherapy; why one woman with surgery, and another without surgery; why one woman benefits from herbs and acupuncture, and another doesn't. Why does one woman hike a mountain to lessen her fear and anger, and another tattoos her chest with a glorious nature scene, flaunting her now flat chest? Why does one woman recover fully from a stroke and another only partially? We ask ourself, What way will work for me?

We want a single way to move toward healing. But there isn't one path. We can't even hitchhike on someone else's path, though it's helpful to know about others' successes. While there will be similarities, what we believe in and what holds love, power, and healing energy for us will be different than for anyone else.

Healing isn't a group experience but a very personal and intimate individual experience. We must find what makes us unique and beautiful and how we can enhance our own sacred connection, thus amplifying our way of being with ourself and others.

For each of us, there is only *our own* path in healing, and it continues over the horizon into the new seasons of our thoughts and feelings. We aren't talking about reaching some imaginary goal and then feeling we're finished with our healing. Instead we're becoming more aware that healing from cancer, heart disease, stroke, and every other disease — including major shifts in life circumstances — requires us to see healing as a lifelong journey rather than an immediate goal.

As our life journey takes us down unanticipated roadways, we really do become more than we've allowed ourself to be before. For instance, we may have been consumed with our own life, but as we go in for treatment, we may become more aware of other women and their pain, too.

The problems we have faced in the past may seem less than the ones we face at present, but up to now we've managed to negotiate the boulders in our road to happiness, joy, love, and meaning. As we remember to place our hands over our own wise, precious heart, we can know for certain that we are still finding our right way. That right way may change, but if we continue to stay in touch with our deep heart, we can shift directions and adjust as need be. The journey continues and we're okay.

At the start of our healing journey, we may feel like we've entered a great dark, dangerous forest. Now pretend we look down at our feet and see a nourishing bread crumb. Our job is to follow the bread crumbs through the forest to find our way to the open sunny meadow. The bread crumbs represent the heart and soul of our renewal, which comes from within us, around us, and through friends and family and those who listen to us, love us, and respect our opinions. We're being guided by an unseen hand. We're okay, and we're on track. Even though we don't know what will come next — right now — we don't need to know in order to be happy.

OUR WONDERFUL MIND

Orienting ourself toward the invisible world of energy healing may be good news for those of us who dwell more comfortably in our creative right brain. If touching, feeling, and intuiting are our strengths, we may find it easier to enter the invisible world of inner power and spirit — for that is where lasting healing originates. For those of us who are more aligned with our concrete left brain — for instance, if we feel we need to chart every turn in our healing journey before we take the first step — then we may find it challenging to explore this art of healing.

Concrete thinking helps us figure out how to manage the details of our life and translate them into appropriate actions. But the insight into what healing methods to explore requires different skills — for this guidance, we need help from our intuitive right brain and our sacred heart.

When we balance our checkbook, for instance, our left brain is essential. But the logic of the balance sheet is not enough when we're making decisions about our caregivers. We must consult our deep heart and right brain to know how we feel about the people we're approaching for treatment, for we need to choose people who are not only skilled but who will listen to us and respect our feelings and opinions. Those we go to for treatment are partners; there needs to be mutual respect and appreciation for our combined efforts to find and follow the right healing path. The right caregiver will recognize and support our innate spiritual guidance, helping us to trust the path to our greatest healing.

Our left brain also contains our self-critic, the one who is always poking us with what we should do or should have done. Quieting this loud voice can be quite a challenge; we do so by deciding to listen to different inner feedback. Learning to quiet our inner critic is part of our healing journey. It is essential as we battle the fear and depression that can come as we seek to round the corner from our pain and anxiety into the light of our new life.

ASK YOURSELF

What is the way I frame my sense of my inner voice?
What do I need to do to remember to listen more deeply than my concrete left brain allows?
How easy is it for me to recognize my creative right brain?

Gradually, through practices like the Healing Art of Loving Touch in chapter 1, we quiet our incessant and useless repetitive worries, we gently slow down unwanted messages, and we replace them with life-affirming beliefs and attitudes that lead us in positive directions and encourage us to find what we love and live it now.

Ultimately, exploration and learning are essential and necessary for our healing journey. We need all our gifts — our right brain, our left brain, and our deep loving heart — that together offer us the essential guidance we need on our path of healing and spiritual awakening.

Pursuing the art of healing means evaluating what is most important to us and what about us is most noteworthy. Healing asks us to reevaluate our interests, yearnings, desires, fantasies, and opportunities so that we can freely satisfy our own needs and those of others. We don't experience freedom by becoming independently wealthy or by living on a tropical island. We feel free when we choose a course for our life that moves us into greater happiness and meaning.

This new view of what is possible for us emerges from our nonrational thinking, our intuitive voice. This may take some getting used to for those more comfortable with linear and deductive approaches to learning. But the symbolic, metaphoric, and artistic approach is a good balance for all of us, since most of us want to think our way to solutions.

In fact, when we ask deeper questions, ones that require more than mere rational analysis can answer alone, the results are quite interesting. When we take the time to ask more deeply, no matter what we call this contemplation, we engage our deep heart or soul. The creative intuitions of our right brain flow into the left brain, where they become data that can be articulated and explained whenever we are ready to do so.

❧ ATTITUDE SHIFTS ❧

1. I can create a pallete of options for my healing.
2. Healing is a specific journey. One size does not fit all, and I am in charge of making my own fit me.
3. I can understand that the healing journey I am undertaking is lifelong — because this is about healing my life and all its various fractures, not just a disease. As I heal my life, I heal my body.
4. I can learn to quiet my critical mind in order to hear my deep inner knowing, which I can use to guide me.
5. I am learning to balance my heart and my mind; both are important and need to be in balance to give me the most useful options.

CHAPTER FOUR

Social Nourishment —
Finding Our Community

Act as if everything depended on you;
trust as if everything
depended on God.

— Saint Ignatius

*P*eople and community are important to our healing; they provide social nourishment. At the heart of healing is our heart aligned with other hearts and the ways we share our biology, our memories, and our interests. Community is based on having things in common that are important to us. It is where we feel we fit and belong and feel safe.

Social and family structures in America have shifted, often creating more distance between us. Instead of extended families living together and ethnic communities providing familiar settings, we more often live as individual family units, many with only one parent. If we have pursued careers, we may have sacrificed family or not maintained a closeness with others, and we may not even recognize that we feel like a fish out of water at many gatherings.

The art of healing requires us to take stock of our community and whether we find in it the support and connection we need, both during and after our healing. Whom do we socialize with, and are these times with friends and family enjoyable and meaningful? Of course, many of us have wonderful friends and loving people who will stand with us in our present situation, and it is important to identify and gather with these people regularly. And yet, as we heal we are in fact changing; we are growing in our view of ourself, the community around us, and the world at large. We will not be the same person coming out of an illness or life-changing event that we were going into it. Many times these changes are subtle and go undetected until our life has returned to normal — only to realize that our *normal* is no longer the normal it was before.

We find ourself in a quandary: How can we clue in the people we love that we are different? We may feel stronger, with new ideas, and a greater confidence in sharing them, or we may feel more patient and compassionate, less driven by old priorities. We may find ourself in a period of adjustment, as we assess how we are different and as our community reacts and responds to that difference. Indeed, we may need our old community, in whole or in part, to shift and re-form to create a new community.

A number of years ago a strikingly beautiful women in her mid-forties with big olive eyes and shoulder-length brown hair came to see me. She was living with stage IV colon cancer and undergoing chemo every day. When I asked how long the treatments would continue, she said indefinitely, since they were the only thing keeping the cancer at bay. As we talked she spoke of how she loved her small son and how he was the apple of her family's eye. Then she described her husband's extended Italian family, which was very "old school." In spite of her illness, she was still expected to host all their large family gatherings, and she confessed that she couldn't imagine telling them that she was too exhausted and that someone else needed to take over for a while. She was certain no one would understand, and she would be seen as a bad daughter.

I was taken aback to realize that this woman felt she had no choice — and maybe she didn't. Maybe her husband's family would have rejected her, but maybe not. Sometimes we have to consider what is more important: the status quo, or the changes that we need to make to save our sanity or our life.

As this woman's story makes clear, healing may mean we must take stock of how we fit with our family of origin — our mother, father, siblings, aunts, and uncles. Do we have anything in common with them besides the Thanksgiving turkey? Can we share our thoughts as equals or at least with respect? Do we know why we were born into our family, or is that still a mystery? Or, can we show up at family events and have a strong enough sense of ourself and our journey, so that we're not swayed by their questions or criticisms?

Only we can feel inside what the truth is for us. As we consider our communities, consider how we behave within them: Do we slip into the river of mud, doubting our choices, or do we stay on the sunny banks and watch the water — our own negative opinions and those of others — float past?

Our healing asks us to question our social interactions and find those places that provide positive nourishment as well as those that are in need of transforming — or leaving.

FINDING OUR NEW COMMUNITY

Finding our new "normal" and establishing a new community that understands us is perhaps one of the most difficult aspects of healing. We long to remain the way we were before, and it is hard to feel that we are the ones pulling away from old friendships, careers, or even extended family. I've found, however, that it is really our spirit that pulls us away, and it does so not with malice but with kindness, as if to say, you can still linger here, but it's important to find your way with additional friends and support.

ASK YOURSELF

Where do I fit?
Do I feel harmonious with my family, extended family, work colleagues, and friends?
Who are my closest friends that I consider my community?

We alone are the ones who can say what we need to fill and nourish us, and there are no right or wrong answers. In fact, feeling off-balance emotionally or facing a difficult diagnosis that means physical limitations can actually create a space in which we solve problems that we weren't able to figure out or address before. Our illness may create a "time out" from our daily routine, or from our everyday stresses and worries, that provides an opportunity to make longed-for changes that will benefit our body and our mental health right now.

A woman who was hoping to heal liver cancer was working with me. She was an artist, and she continually expressed how she wished that she had taken the time to travel to Europe and soak in some of the great art of Florence, Milan, and Rome. Although she was physically unable to make such a trip, I suggested that she plan for the trip in the future and that she begin now by gathering copies of the great works she wanted to see. This process enhanced not only her painting but also her healing.

LOVING OURSELF IS THE KEY

Loving ourself isn't a new idea, but managing to do it is something else. How can we love ourself and others, fit into social and community settings, and still be true to ourself? This is clearly the challenge in sustaining meaningful relationships. But the relationships we choose need to come about as a result of our caring for and loving ourself. Caring for and loving ourself also includes being aware of our flaws and edges — those aspects of ourself that are weak or undesirable but that we are healing.

Indeed, we can love ourself because of our flaws, just as we recognize that others also are not perfect and that everyone needs kindness and attention. We are a work in progress. We can change only what we realize originates within us. Rather than seeing the world around us as causing the problem, if we can focus on our reactions and see what happens when we change our behaviors, we can learn a great deal about how to enhance every manner of relationship — and further our healing.

Finally, it's true that social nourishment can also mean meeting the needs of others before meeting our own. While we keep in mind that our needs are not the only needs of our family, still we must take our own needs seriously. Focusing on ourself is not selfish or inappropriate. Sometimes our very life depends on taking the time we need for treatment, recovery, and renewal of our spirit.

LIFE THE WAY IT WAS

It is easy to believe that once treatment is over, we can get back to life the way it was.

But we don't want to go back — we want to go forward — which means educating our friends and family about what we can do and what we can't. This isn't the time to be heroic in caring for others. It's more heroic to do what we need to do so we'll be around for those we love.

We need to care enough about ourself and our needs to seize hold of our opportunities to be free — free to enter into relationships that sustain, brighten, and enhance our inner self.

❧ ATTITUDE SHIFTS ❧

1. Community is a great source of nourishment, and in order to place it effectively within my healing journey, I must understand how and why I fit in.
2. I will not be the same person coming out of a major illness or life-changing event as I was going into it. My "normal"

will be different. I will need to find activities and relationships that reflect the new me.

3. Illness or other changes in my life can act positively as a
"time out" to reassess my relationships and give me the im-
petus to make beneficial changes.

4. I can expand my current community in creative ways that
don't necessarily involve drastic changes.

5. The relationships I choose must come about as a result of
caring and loving me first.

6. I also have to be responsible to my community regarding
my own flaws, which may not always be easy to deal with.

7. Although balance in my relationships is the goal, I can also
claim that at this moment in time I must take my own
needs seriously.

CHAPTER FIVE

Physical Nourishment —
Believing in What Sustains Us

*The art of medicine consists of
amusing the patient
while nature cures the disease.*

— Voltaire

*E*very healing path is a singular journey into greater personal clarity and spiritual authenticity. Many people write about healing with the same basic attention to body, mind, and spirit. But what is important is to find a path that helps us internalize not only what others are saying about healing but *what we are feeling*: about our own state of wellness and growth, about our own emotional and mental resources, about what and whom we love, and about our dreams, interests, and desires for our future.

Supporting what our body requires for healing is an obvious and important part of the journey. We are the most comfortable in this aspect of our nourishment because we can touch, taste, and experience the healing results of many of the remedies we are taking. This is also the arena that our present Western health-care environment is the most comfortable focusing on. When we're diagnosed with cancer, for example, immediately a giant established process swings into place, one we can feel helpless to influence or slow down. However, while it is important to act, it's more important to act from a place of inner belief when choosing our treatment.

Our healing is enhanced when we believe in the treatment we're getting. And herein can be a twofold struggle. First, we often want to believe that if we do all the right things for our body, then our responsibility for our healing is complete. And second, we often trust that our doctors or others in positions of authority have all the answers to make us healthy — they know best, and we may be reluctant to disagree, or even be discouraged from doing so.

But the same treatments don't benefit all clients in the same way, as every true physician and healer will tell you. We are each individuals, and the program components that we choose need to be tailored to our needs and beliefs. We should undertake healing strategies we believe in and choose people to treat us that we trust implicitly. If we're not completely satisfied, we should ask for a second opinion or change physicians, nurse-practitioners, or any other helper who feels out of alignment with what we need.

We obviously want to make clear decisions based on accurate information. We need to know what our medical team is doing and how they are thinking about our case. However, their assessments and advice often come solely from a linear, Western perspective. Considering only the limited "truth" of their diagnosis may not be helpful, especially when the diagnosis is very bad. We may hear and believe that there is no hope and that the end result is inevitable. Our mind is a finely tuned energy instrument, and we want it to be directing us toward healing.

Because our body hears every word that we say and that is spoken to us, we need to learn to balance the "truths" of the left-brain science of healing with those of the right-brain art of healing. We may well have a real physical challenge in front of us, yet hope and possibilities for healing always exist. We hear every day of remissions, healing, and recoveries that medically shouldn't happen, but do. The truth we need is support for making the most of today and knowing that tomorrow will likely be a positive day as well.

THOUGHTS AND WORDS AFFECT
OUR HEALING ENERGY

Healing means clearing the flows of energy that support our physical organs and systems to help them do their work well. Chinese medicine and the Indian system of Ayurveda — both developed over five thousand years ago — are greatly respected systems for dealing with the energetics of the subtle body (through "meridians" in Chinese medicine and "chakras" in Ayurvedic medicine). Both theories are founded in an understanding of the body and mind as a vibration field extending and interacting with the universe. The role of the healer in both traditions is to monitor and clear energy pathways to keep the flow harmonious and tied to the universe.

In these systems, physical nourishment involves helping the body unload old emotional messages as well as unwanted physical toxins to make way for increased absorption of the healing foods, ideas, and feelings that we're now filling ourself with.

Tending to the body's needs includes a variety of elements, many we already know about: energy work for continually rebalancing the body, eating nutritionally, getting plenty of sleep, engaging in creative movement and some kind of exercise, finding interests that suit our new views, and enjoying the people we love and who love us.

Many energy-enhancing healing modalities are available to us. We can try different ones and find what suits us: for example, massage, polarity, cranio-sacral, reiki, therapeutic touch, shiatsu, kinesiology, acupuncture, energy-based chiropractic, reflexology, guided imagery, meditation, biofeedback, and more.

Perhaps the most important component to our healing is that

inner spiritual belief that comes from doing the things for our nourishment that are satisfying and nurturing. As we feed ourself on all
levels, we are being the loving mentor instead of the punishing taskmaster and finding our way into the new territory of rebalancing and
healing.

❧ ATTITUDE SHIFTS ❧

1. It is paramount that, while acting quickly once I am diagnosed, I make sure I am acting from a strong inner place of
   belief and knowing.
2. Once I choose a direction for my change or healing, it is
   important to believe in my treatment. When I do, the treatment will have the most positive impact.
3. I must choose only healers that I trust, and I must give myself permission not to act until I find them.
4. I must recognize that truth is relative. It is important to
   know the specifics of my diagnosis and treatment plans,
   but it is equally important that I hold to my belief in my
   ability to heal.
5. Healing means cleansing my energy fields because my
   body holds all the old messages. Cleansing makes way for
   the new story.

CHAPTER SIX

Spiritual Nourishment — Aligning with Love as the Source of Life

He makes me lie down in green pastures;
He leads me beside still waters.
He restores my soul.

— Twenty-Third Psalm

*T*he world of spirit means many different things to each of us. It can mean a traditional religious path or a spiritual path crafted from a variety of meaningful influences. We can have a daily practice of meditation and prayer, or we may feel connected to the Creator when we're weeding our garden or listening to the birds calling "good-night" to each other.

It doesn't matter so much what we believe, but that we have some way of accepting that we are inside — not outside — Spirit's larger plan. In healing we need to know absolutely that we have a link to our deep heart, where we experience a genuine and lasting connection to Source.

We may come to this through our affiliation with a church, syna-gogue, or mosque — or we may simply know that, separate from any organized belief system, we are a precious aspect of Divine creation. We have within us the knowing of our Divine spark, and we trust that there is a divine order, though we can't grasp its intricacies intellectually.

Spirit-directed healing, which is what we are exploring in *Spirit Heals,* helps us coalesce what we know logically and deductively and emotionally into our best plan and then to hand it over to Spirit. We ask Spirit to invigorate our efforts with love to generate real power. The power we ask for is to recognize and receive all that contributes to our greatest good.

We don't need to understand in our mind how the art and science of healing come together. It is enough to appreciate in our deep heart that we are an essential and important part of creation, and that all factors of benevolent action — whether we believe in angels, guides, spiritual way-showers, gurus, or teachers — offer invisible ways to work for our healing.

The Source of Life, God, is love, and it is from this love that we need to nourish ourself in order to produce positive energy that flows into our mind and emotions, our intellect and body, and our various social and community relationships.

WE ARE SPIRIT

We are spiritual in nature, coming from the One Source of Love and receiving grace and support as we ask, pray, and allow its presence to be known to us. Imagining that we are kin to a Loving Source around us and in our deep heart encourages our healing; we find greater comfort in our quiet times, our prayers and meditations, our walks in the gar-

dens, and our acceptance of what is at hand. We are empowered spiritually to face whatever we have to face and come out a winner. The core values of our life form a strong and comprehensive safety net from which our body can heal.

Our mind is able to listen to our deep heart's wisdom — because we are in this life at the pleasure of our Spirit. Spirit has the final word on our healing. Our thoughts and feelings may shift with the unpredictable results of every blood test, every ache and pain, and every perceived slight or injustice — unless we have something bigger and more trustworthy to hold on to that balances our emotions.

What do we take hold of when we're in trouble? The awareness that we are held in Love, and we can feel that reassurance and support when we put our hands over our own heart — the center of our chest — and tap into the power and love of Spirit.

OUR INNER FLAME

We need to nourish our body with food, our emotions with positive feelings, and our spirits with belief in our true Self. In additional to recognizing our connection to Spirit, spiritual nourishment requires us to take care of our inner flame. We can reach for this spiritual nourishment by experiencing high points of loving God through devotion as well as through service to others and service to ourself.

Service to ourself requires slowing down our hectic daily activities so we can reap the benefit of the positive and nourishing elements that are part of every day: filling the bird feeder, watching the grandkids unwrap gifts, sitting on the grass with a glass of something wonderful, smiling that we are alive right now. Nourishing ourself spiritually comes from the little things that carry great impact. When we feel happy, our thinking softens and our deep heart expands. We are then running on the strongest possible energy — the energy of Love.

Finding our own sense of the sacred, or Spirit, is an essential component in our healing. Together we'll explore the many ways to understand and integrate our attitudes and beliefs about the sacred into our daily living. Slowly, we find Divinity, Spirit, showing up in all aspects of our life, from the smallest incident to the monumental shifts that sweep us into a new direction.

We are a part of a unifying field of love and acceptance. We have a purpose — we fit with the sacred even if we don't seem to entirely fit with the people around us. Our needs are important in the grand scheme of things. We're not forgotten — nothing is forgotten or left behind.

ACTIVITY

Write a Personal Sketch

As you consider your life in smaller detail, sketch a picture of yourself. For many, writing will be easiest and most comfortable, but also consider sketching your portrait using clay, paint, or a collage of images from magazines. Use any medium that seems to express something about yourself — what is most important right now — or that embodies a challenge you are facing or have solved. If you feel a little self-conscious at first, remember that no one is watching, so give it a try.

To begin, set aside at least half an hour for you and your healing. Write several paragraphs describing yourself and how you feel right now. If you are using another medium, reflect on what the pictures and images you choose say about you. Include anything about yourself, your life, your family, and your health that feels meaningful and appropriate. Try not to listen to the critical voice in your head that would belittle your efforts. Treat this as if you were having a friendly chat with yourself, conversing as you might with a trusted friend — because in addition to your inner critic, you do have an inner friend and helper, your true Self.

Here are two real-life sketches from women I've worked with; details have been changed to maintain their anonymity. The first sketch is from a woman who had received a diagnosis of breast cancer. The second is from a woman who had recently had surgery to repair a hole in her heart. Finally, I've added my own personal sketch.

Personal Sketch 1: Geneva

My name is Geneva, and I am a fifty-nine-year-old married mother of two and grandmother of three, a family business owner, and an aspiring part-time health educator and counselor. I love physical activity, aerobics, water aerobics, and nature walking.

I've realized lately that fear has had a big impact on my life. This constant state of fright has led me to count on others for safety, support, and approval. I have only recently turned inward to discover my own source of strength. Being indispensable to others was so important to me — I struggled attempting to say I couldn't do something for someone or, worse, that I didn't want to. Focusing outwardly on pleasing others has left little room for exploring my own wishes and desires, and they still remain somewhat hidden. *Where have I been all my life?*

I'm now under the worst stress of my life — family, business, and the breast cancer diagnosis. My other stresses have pushed the breast cancer to the side. I think I have been pretending something — I don't really have it? It's a mistake? It's all gone? But radiation begins tomorrow (Tues. — the pretending is over. I can't stay suspended in space anymore — down to earth for me.). I need to learn more.

Personal Sketch 2: Suzette

My name is Suzette. I'm forty-seven years old and live in Buffalo, New York, where I share a home with my husband of six years and our adorable four-year-old golden retriever. I am also blessed with a lovely twenty-year-old daughter who currently spends most of her time at college, although she is home with us for the summer and working.

Let me humbly acknowledge that I've come through this traumatic surgery but am not sure what it all meant. I'm still recovering, but I'm afraid all the time, as if another hole will appear even though the doctors assure me that this is the only hole and that I was born with it.

I also have some very real challenges in my life right now, both with the person I'm living with and with feeling inadequate, because even though I'm trained as a business consultant, I can't seem to make ends meet financially, and my bills just keep piling up.

My journey to wellness recently led me to this work, and I feel that it is my good fortune to be learning how to help myself and others. After spending a lot of time, energy, and money looking to outside sources for answers to all my ongoing problems, I am finally grasping the concept of looking within myself.

Though still very much in the beginning stages of understanding what this process is all about, I have a strong sense that a different approach to living is required if I'm to really heal my heart. I think the surgery performed the mechanics of healing, but the true healing is up to me.

My Personal Sketch: Stranger Than Fiction

We may find our genuine awareness of and connection to Spirit in ways we never imagined. When in 1981 Spirit showed up dramatically in my life, not only did I feel unprepared, I wasn't even sure what was happening — yet perhaps this is as it should be. We're never prepared, nor can we be, because the experience is so much beyond normal parlance.

For many years my challenge was figuring out what to think of this powerful and beautiful inner voice of love that I could hear but I couldn't seem to assimilate. I tell this story in my first book, *Agartha: A Journey to the Stars*: I woke up one day to the reality of a God that lives not just outside us but within our heart. I heard a voice that I couldn't identify as my own, and so I was left with the quandary: Whose voice was it? Was it an angel, spirit guide, teacher — God? And what or who was God, anyway, that I could know through this extraordinary line of spiritual teaching, which I'd never before heard or been trained in?

After writing *Agartha*, I traveled for years, talking and teaching about the nature of this inner voice, this teacher and mentor, without allowing myself to fully appreciate what the experience was all about. It does take years on our spiritual journey to come to terms with the mystic within us.

I knew from the very beginning that sensing Mentor (the name I used to refer to this voice of Love) as something outside myself was somehow incomplete. And yet I was plagued by the feeling of *Who am I to speak from such a voice?* Of course, we all have this wondrous energy of God within us; we just find it hard to imagine that it is real and that it can be available to an ordinary mortal like ourself.

For years I agonized over how to express this deep knowing in ways that felt appropriate. I couldn't figure out whether to keep writing books that separated Mentor's words from my own (called channeling) or to allow the process that wanted to happen to indeed happen — to bring my personality self up under my greater self, which of course is the way the mystical path draws us home to our true identity.

How much easier my path seems now to no longer struggle with those early questions. I use what comes to me from this inner voice with gratitude and humility because I know it directly carries God's love to me and others. That is why I talk about Love and God's Love as if it is so real — because I know it is.

AREN'T WE ALL THE SAME?

We all have had times of deep inner knowing, special gifts that we can rightly call mystical — meaning directed by Spirit — and yet we are afraid. We wait upon the will of God for guidance, and also for our own maturity, so we can ultimately decide to be completely who we are at every moment and to know that this is more than enough.

The spiritual doesn't take us out of life but more fully bring us into life as we learn to embrace the magnificent joy of having a physical existence and as we realize that we do not need to waste our time making war on our ego — our personality self. Instead we can make it an ally.

Spirit is waiting to guide us, and we have but to put down our fears and say *yes. Yes,* I'm ready to know more of my life and its purpose. *Yes,* I'm ready to feel more aligned with love and joy and to know that I can heal what needs to be healed and find good ways to live with the rest. When all is said and done, it comes down to saying *yes* instead of *no.*

Life is not monochrome — it is a vast array of hues. Some are dark and some are light. This mixture can propel us toward loving ourself with all of our quirky idiosyncrasies, even as we also accept that there is an aspect of ourself that isn't influenced in the least by what we think about the world around us — our Spirit. It, instead, is the influencer of our thoughts and feelings, our attitudes and beliefs.

We are mystical by nature — entrenched in the mystical, that which is of the great mystery — and we recognize it most clearly in healing. We are in a whirlwind of pain, anger, love, and acceptance much of the time during our healing and even after the diagnosis has long since been put to bed. What we feel and the attitude shifts that we're making are the basis of genuine, long-lasting life healing.

It isn't a problem that we have many imperfections and unresolved issues. The challenge instead is to accept our unfinished business — to pay attention to it — while at the same time understanding that we're a work in progress. And in spite of all the aspects of us that aren't yet fully polished, we can remember to guide ourself into still waters by staying steady within and by embracing the possibility of what can happen if we refuse to run away.

ATTITUDE SHIFTS

1. How I believe and worship is not as important as knowing that I am already aligned with Spirit.
2. I don't need to understand how the art and science of healing work together; all I need to know is that I am an essential and important part of Divinity.
3. Spirit is my safety net for this journey.
4. Setting a spiritual context for my healing, seeing myself aligned with Spirit within my deep heart, is the most crucial part of this journey.
5. The spiritual attitude shifts I make now will create the basis for my long-lasting life healing.

PART TWO

Mind as Healer, Mind as Critic

If we want stillness of mind — "so that
something of God can enter us" — we must
learn how to hold off those conditioned responses.

— Carol Lee Flinders

CHAPTER SEVEN

Our Search for Meaning —
The Cornerstone of Wellness

May I be filled with loving kindness
May I be well
May I be peaceful and calm
May I be happy
— A Buddhist meditation

*W*hen we are diagnosed with cancer or heart disease, or when we are recovering from a stroke or in any acute or chronic mental, emotional, or physical situation that seems to spell disaster, life suddenly becomes even more precious. We may believe that life is a gift, but as we plow through each day's activities and demands, we tend to forget the gift until we are reminded that it will one day be taken away from us. Everything seems to suddenly become more beautiful and breathtaking when bad news strikes. Our family and our friends, our work, and even those who cause us consternation and struggle seem to fade in favor of the exquisite pleasure of simply being able to draw a breath on our own.

So many clients have told me that they took life for granted, as if they and it were permanent fixtures. When a diagnosis of trouble pulls us out of our everyday thinking or when an unforeseen challenge arises, we are shocked by the reminder that we won't be on Earth forever, even though we may well heal from the cancer or heart problem.

This realization plays an important part in healing and spirituality. Because we won't be on Earth forever, and because we don't know when or how we will leave, we need to be doing and practicing what is important to us right now and not putting it off. We have no idea whether tomorrow will come for us. We are all in this particular life temporarily.

The truth of these thoughts is sobering indeed, but they lead us to a greater determination to make the most of what we have and who we are today. The search for meaning is clearly what we're after in our busy life, as we try to fit in more and remake ourself to be more of what we value. Yet meaning comes from the way we live with ourself and in the community of life around us, right now.

ASK YOURSELF

Where have I assumed greater meaning would come from?

What would happen if I stopped pushing this agenda and found easier means to a similar end?

What feelings come up when I consider shifting from grander to simpler?

Human beings have the extraordinary ability to register beauty and meaning. Along with many of our animal allies, we recognize that life is more than eating, drinking, having sex, and dying. We are a species in search of meaning, whether or not we recognize this as the driving force behind our ambitions and our search for lasting relationships.

Meaning comes from engaging in life fully and enjoying and embracing the experience of living, even when our earthly dreams are tossed this way and that. Life lived only on the surface won't really create lasting meaning. One's social status — too much or too little — makes no difference. Nothing prevents life from happening; there is no insurance policy that can keep us safe. So how do we continue to find meaning when things take an unexpected downward turn? We draw from what we've laid in or put aside.

In other words, what inner reserves do we have? We fill these reserves by doing more of what fills us and less by rote or obligation. These are the treasures we can store up, which we can bring out one shiny bauble at a time — when we are sitting in a hospital bed recovering from a mastectomy, learning how to function again after a stroke, or managing our way through a day of depression or sadness.

Our shiny trinkets are the books we treasure, the people who make us smile, the love letters from our children (or their children). We find comfort in the things that inherently represent the people and experiences in which we've mattered, in which we've been loved and been the carriers of love to others.

Our extraordinary existence offers us much that is beautiful and exciting. The trap is to think we can control events, that with just a little more effort we'll finally have everything we need — a permanent plateau of happiness derived from doing more or accomplishing more.

It isn't what we do but whom it helps that generates meaning. It isn't what we get but what we contribute that counts most in the long run. Our hopes and dreams will be like bubbles blown from a child's wand, here today and gone tomorrow — unless they arise from something solid that we believe in.

DOING THE WORK WE LOVE

We can find meaning by doing the work we love rather than looking for work to love. A client of mine struggled for years to complete a book of poetry. She imagined that as soon as it was published she would be recognized as having something to say that contributed to the collective voice of peace, which was something she was passionate about. But book never seemed to land in the hands of the right agent or publisher. After a bout with cancer, she finally put aside the idea that the only way she could really feel complete was to have her work published.

Instead she began to share her poetry in a more casual way with family and friends and through local outlets where she was already known. Of course, as soon as she stopped pressing, the poetry was picked up by a publisher. But although the book was available to many and she enjoyed seeing it in stores, she realized the meaning for her was in her personal sharing of the work with individuals — reading a poem aloud, for example — because she could then share in people's reactions of delight. She learned that the meaningfulness of being a writer for her existed in her love of poetry and the immediacy of sharing; she didn't need an official invitation or external validation to finally see herself as a real author.

THE POWER OF FAITH

Meaning comes to us in many ways: through our relationships, our work, our efforts to improve the plights of others. All these efforts are spiritual if we connect them to our faith in God, in Spirit, in Love. Believing that we are part of something magical and benevolent keeps us steady through dark times. As our healing energy expands, so does our awareness that our healing energy is really the energy of love and self-acceptance.

Healing meets spirituality for many of us when our belief in a higher power becomes our major source of strength — such as in the twelve-step program of Alcoholics Anonymous. When this happens, our personal connection to Spirit informs all our daily behaviors as well as becoming our means of addressing illness, health, and even death.

We live in a larger web of life — the great mystery — and rather than having that be fearful, for many it is supremely comforting. The truth is that our body, mind, and spirit are interwoven energies all related to the larger scheme of things — the universal energy of Divinity. *You can't take the sacred out of healing any more than you can take the seeds out of an apple. One grows the other.*

Just as they say there are no atheists in foxholes, so there are probably no atheists who have come through treatment for a major illness. It is just too scary to think about life without a greater guiding force. It seems impossible that a loving God would have just dumped us on this Earth and then forgotten about us. And so we find our way to faith, whether it's a strong belief or a tentative acceptance that there must be more to life and more to come in our life.

Our faith is usually strengthened during crises, but it can also evolve. At least, we find out how much we truly believe what we say we believe. Our faith changes as life happens to us. We are no longer the same person, and so our faith shifts, too — in order to accommodate whom we're becoming and the way we now see the life in front of us.

SPIRIT POWER

We must give our faith a new direction after difficulties or illness — and a new energy source. Our willpower alone is no longer enough; we must shift to *spirit power*. We must align our faith with the faith of a creative and ever-changing Universe where all of us are cared for. We are not alone in our struggle, or in overcoming struggle. We are held firmly in the arms of a great love and compassion.

Our faith seems to change as we heal, as we age, and as we face difficulties that seem unsolvable. Our faith actually gets condensed when we're in the most serious trouble. At these times, we focus on exactly what we most believe in and what we know will keep us alive and bring us through whatever we are facing.

Our faith expands after the crisis has passed to allow us to return to our life and our family, our career and our interests. Sometimes we may want to put the struggle behind us and return to our life as if nothing had happened. Yet that is not possible because so much has changed inside us. Our faith is now a different color and texture; we have found something solid to hang on to, whatever form that takes. Our life has a new meaning not only because of our survival but because of the quality of human being we recognize we are becoming.

If God had a formula for pointing us in the right direction to find meaning, it might go something like this: look around and follow what leads to lasting happiness, not away from it; generate your own path and trust it. We are free, we may finally realize, to decide what we believe will ultimately bring us happiness.

Meaning from our healing journey comes from connection to Spirit. We want our healing process to work for us and to redirect our life toward more positive feelings and health. In spirituality we want to know and trust that we are safe in a world that is anything but safe. We want to be convinced of an inner world that we can touch even in our darkest moments.

Trying to arrive at lasting meaning without engaging the sacred reminds me of a telling comment made by a traffic cop as I was desperately trying to find a way through a cordoned-off construction site. I was trying to get to a building where I was to give a workshop, and he nonchalantly leaned in my window and said, "Sorry, ma'am, you can't get there from here."

ANCHORING OUR LIFE FORCE

We can heal faster, overcome recurrences, and beat the odds against living longer than predicted when we anchor our life force in the search for greater meaning. First, we benefit from realizing the ways we have already contributed to those around us. Then we must remember to continue to intentionally contribute our insight, love, compassion, and appropriate efforts to our community and the world. If we haven't yet embraced this in our life, then we are clearly alerted that we need to do so now. The reality that we no longer have all the time in the world is an amazing motivator — whether we have active disease or not. Our clock is ticking.

The idea that our life is about making a contribution is empowering, and our efforts can take any shape. Whether we carry water and sweep out our hut as our daily contribution to our family, or we direct the Gates Foundation, funding megaprojects to serve humanity — we are contributing to the welfare of others. By contributing, I mean helping others in a way that in turn fills us — we can all find things to do that are available to us right now to make life better, and in so doing we find inner satisfaction that makes us whole.

Finding meaning in our life, then, is a cornerstone in our call to wellness. For without a true reason to heal, we won't. Sometimes the thought of going back to the way life was before treatment fills us with complete sadness, or the feeling that we have nothing to give or receive, no matter our degree of material ease, closes down our body. *We need hope and a means of realizing that hope in order to heal.*

ATTITUDE SHIFTS

1. I can expect that often with a diagnosis comes the first real understanding that my physical life is indeed temporary.
2. While it is scary to recognize that I don't know how long I will live, it allows me to pause long enough to decide what is truly important and to live each day more fully.
3. I can recognize that meaning comes from how I value myself and my relationship with all life.
4. I need to build up my reserves of good, meaningful memories so that I can draw upon them when I need them most on my healing journey.
5. Illness or trial can open me to the truth that my body, mind, and spirit are all interwoven energies and that energy is Divine Love.

6. I can expect that just as I will change through illness or dif-
    ficulty, my faith will grow and change as well.
7. God has given me the right to always head toward hap-
    piness.
8. I need hope and a true reason to heal to produce positive
    outcomes.

CHAPTER EIGHT

Our Believability Factors

*Freedom is the basic concept and construct of life everywhere,
because freedom is the basic nature of God.
All systems which reduce, restrict, impinge upon, or eliminate freedom
in any way are systems which work against life itself.*

— Neale Donald Walsch

We need to merge our inner and outer resources for healing and life advancement. The thing that does this, that helps us turn the corner into a healthier and happier life, is belief.

A "believability factor" refers to anything, whether a person or a treatment or an idea, that we have a deep belief in to help us. Through our belief in this other power, we believe more in our own. Our belief in our doctor or acupuncturist, for example, not only gives us courage to face various treatments or physical limitations, but it encourages us to believe, through their attitude, in our own potential for healing. We absorb quite invisibly the attitudes and beliefs of those around us. Like a sponge we become what others expect.

We need to identify the people or things that are our believability factors. It can be a local healer or helper or a motivational personality.

It can be our mother or father or Aunt Mary. It can be God in the form of Jesus Christ, Buddha, or Sri Sathya Sai Baba; it can be a spirit guide, an animal guide, or an angel. Focusing on someone or something we trust, admire, and believe in helps us awaken these very same qualities within ourself. In other words, we accept deep within our mind and heart that we can overcome. We've given our left brain something to hold on to.

OUR MIND NEEDS REASSURANCE

Our logical mind needs to find reassurance in a believable way in order to turn the physical mechanisms of our body on and keep them on. Thoughts, the mind's energy, directly influence the way the physical brain controls the body's physiology.

As we gain permission to heal from our personality self, the home of our everyday thinking, the familiar self-critic — we tell the body that in fact it is healing or will heal.

Many years ago, a report was published of a man who entered a hospital with a large cancerous mass. He was thought to have only a short time to live. His doctor told him about a new experimental drug that could help him. The doctor began the drug treatment, and the tumor went away, much to everyone's amazement. Then the man read a review in the newspaper that debunked the drug, saying it was useless. The man's cancer returned. Desperate to help his patient, the doctor told him that a newer version of the drug was now available, and after being given the new drug, the man's tumor again disappeared.

Eventually, the man discovered that there wasn't a newer version of the drug; he was taking the original drug. He died shortly thereafter. This incident demonstrates both the amazing power of the placebo or belief effect and the devastating impact of negative beliefs, which is referred to as the nocebos effect.

Our mind and what and whom we trust make all the difference in our healing and in our belief in ourself — whether we're applying for a new job, writing a book, or raising money to do research in the Congo. We often assume that other people who seem so confident and put together just came into the world that way. Actually, it's my experience that everyone struggles with issues of self-esteem and self-worth; it is just that some people's struggles are more obvious than others. Only by being taken under a stronger and more knowing *wing* do we begin to develop the wonderful qualities we see in others. Confidence, self-assurance, true inner power, and compassion live within all of us, but only through our belief are they activated, becoming aspects we can count on as part of our physical healing or life-healing regime.

Change is inevitable — and we usually dread it. We like things the way they are even if they are disagreeable. As one of my students suggested — everyone wants transformation, but no one really wants to change. Yet our healing journey is all about change, and to handle the various upsets and plateaus we are facing, for them to make sense, we need to believe deeply in our efforts.

NOT THE PLACEBO EFFECT — THE BELIEF EFFECT

Much research is presently being done on what is called the placebo effect. A placebo refers to a nonchemical, harmless pill or process that is given to patients to test the healing that is possible when the patient merely believes the pill or procedure is true medicine. The findings are startling. A person who takes a simple sugar pill believing it to be medicine often achieves the same or better results than those who take a drug designed to accomplish the same thing.

Rather than the placebo effect, I think we should call this the belief effect. A placebo refers to something that is fake, but belief — whether in the medicine or the doctor prescribing it — is real, and it inspires real results. A Baylor School of Medicine study, published in 2002 in the *New England Journal of Medicine*, evaluated the placebo effect in patients with severe, debilitating knee pain. Two of the patient groups underwent different kinds of arthroscopic knee surgery, while a third group went through the process of having a surgical procedure — incisions were made and all the same protocols where followed in the operating room — except no surgery was performed. The people who believed they'd had the surgery, even though they had not, displayed the same healing as those who actually had the procedure.

This study demonstrates the power we have to facilitate healing through our beliefs. What we believe to be true is or can become true. Clearly, we need to assess what we believe, not only consciously but unconsciously (such as beliefs instilled in us from childhood), because what we accept to be true and what we allow to be true makes all the difference in our healing.

It is important to realize, however, that while we all have the potential for healing, the goal isn't to reach an imagined pinnacle of healing success or else to feel like a failure. Healing is a process. The more we work with our feelings, both positive and negative, to achieve balance, to steady our emotional reactions, the more we'll make friends with our body and with our life and achieve the real goal — which is to be happy right now, right here, with everything that is going on inside and outside us.

❧ ATTITUDE SHIFTS ❧

1. The tool of a believability factor allows me to merge my inner and outer resources and gives my journey hope and power.
2. I can choose anyone I have deep faith in to represent my believability factor. Accepting their power gives me power.
3. My body's healing power is turned on when my left brain has some reason to believe in my healing.
4. Scientific research on the placebo (or belief) effect confirms that I do have the power to create heightened healing for myself when I trust my believability factor.

5. I need to hold my healing journey gently and understand that there will be times when it might not go as well as I had hoped. I should not feel like a failure. Attaining balance in the present moment, regardless of what is going on, is success.

CHAPTER NINE

Intuitive Perception — Our Channel to Spirit

You are a human being. What does that mean?
Mastery of life is not a question of control,
but of finding a balance between human and Being.

— Eckhart Tolle

*I*ntuition is generally referred to as our sixth sense; it is a way of arriving at information without any observable or rational basis for our knowing. We usually use intuition more than we realize, allowing it to guide us in the decisions we make. As women, for the most part, we have a well-developed intuition, which alerts us to what we need to know: for instance, when our kids say one thing but really mean another, when the baby is sick although there are no visible symptoms, when we sense a family member is in need of a friendly phone call, or when we know where to look for the cat that has been hiding all day. This is probably where the idea came from that *Mom has eyes in the back of her head.*

Intuition is a natural state that alerts us to information before we ascertain it through our five physical senses. We use intuition in all situations, casual and serious. When things are serious, when we need to know how to proceed when there seems no opening or the way is dark, we often call on our intuition intentionally: to know how we can heal, to know if our loved ones who have passed over are okay, to figure out where to find the money to pay the mortgage, to find meaningful work, and to know how to develop our connection to Spirit. *The intentional ways that we receive help from Spirit are called guidance.*

Our guidance is the energy channel between our spirit or deep heart and our mind or personality self. We use the term *guidance* because we find ourself guided in love from our deep heart, since it cares about our welfare and is the source of well-being. Spirit is also our inner healer, inner helper, or true Self. Other ways to think of Spirit are as the God within, our spark of eternal light, our soul, or our link with Divine Intelligence. Our deep heart is also the source we draw from when we use our expanded intuition, which I call *intuitive perception.*

Intuitive perception is a tool that we need to use on our healing journey, which is full of serious questions and the need for reassurance. We open this inner passage so that we can find the energy to sustain us, the love to hold us when we're scared, and genuine direction for how to proceed for the best results.

Intuitive perception works because our individual spirit is connected to all life force energy. Our spiritual energy radiates from our deep heart, expanding like a huge bubble out past our physical body, and merges with the spiritual energy of all other life forms. Spiritual energy knows no physical boundaries; our spirit is both within us and without, which provides us with an ample supply of spiritual energy. We are not limited to what we know or can generate exclusively through our own efforts. Spiritual energy is available to anyone

who asks.

How do you access intuitive perception? You ask, and then allow guidance to come to you: it can arrive through synchronicities, unlikely occurrences, inner awarenesses that push their way into your conscious mind, information that comes to you in unusual ways, a piece of information that is repeated by various people or sources, and information or feelings that come to you in prayer or meditation.

God is undifferentiated energy — like the ultimate stem cell energy — and it can take any shape that we require for our health and well-being. This powerful energy of the Universe is the great expander — which means that whatever we need is available to us when we allow it to come to us and expand our circumstances. We must only remove the obstacles in our thinking that keep what we need at arm's length.

Imagine right now that we are plugging our single battery into God's battery — the greatest source of usable energy there is. And imagine that the energy we need for our healing and happiness is beginning to flow right now into each of us and through each of us to all who need it.

ASK YOURSELF

As I imagine plugging into the Universe's battery of love and help, what specifically do I need to ask for?

As I listen for my special guidance from Spirit using my intuitive perception, what is it I sense, feel, or just know when I put my hands over my heart?

THE MOST IMPORTANT SENSE

Our intuitive perception — or channel to Spirit — has a Divine purpose, which is to give us the support and assurance that we need, providing us with the ability to trust what we can't in the moment prove.

Past memories and long-buried experiences live within our energy fields, as well as potentials and untapped emotional and spiritual resources we've not yet discovered. All these factors are extremely significant for us in regaining our health and deepening our sense of meaning.

I first became aware of intuitive perception early in my own discovery process concerning Spirit. Why was Spirit in my life, what did it mean, and how could I know this ineffable and mysterious force of love? I had much confusion at first in believing in my guidance and experiences of Spirit because they didn't arrive in the obvious way, as input from my five everyday senses. They came to me through a series of extraordinary spiritual encounters.

Slowly over the years, I've realized that what we sense with our deep and true inner knowing holds the real directional signals for our life. While our understanding seems to come from what we see, hear, touch, smell, and taste, the actual meaning of these experiences is governed by our inner knowing, not our ego or personality self. Our inner knowing is different than our thinking, which guesses or speculates based on surface impressions. Our intuitive perception leads us to inner knowing that confirms what we sense with our hands and eyes.

ACTIVITY

Inner Guidance through Symbolic Interpretation

This is a practice for receiving useful direction and guidance from Spirit. I teach this everywhere I go because it is incredibly powerful. It's a right-brain exercise, rather than a left-brain one, because it asks you to think symbolically, which is the language of Spirit. In this simple practice, you ask for and receive guidance. The information you receive may be specific or general, and you can ask any question you want as many times as you want. The power is in the interpretation, so keep practicing until you are getting important guidance.

1. Close your eyes. Think of a question, any question, concerning a specific worry or need, and say the question to yourself. Make sure that what you are asking for is clear but open-ended: it is better to say *What do I need to know to earn more money?* rather than *What job should I apply*

for? Your answer will most likely relate to a process, not be a specific name.

2. Open your eyes and pay attention to exactly what you observe and sense, even though you may have looked at the same scene many times. Every tiny detail counts: a breeze blowing a tablecloth, a bug crawling across the window, a light turned on or off, the edge of a counter, the flower pattern of a lampshade. Stay focused on the exact images that catch your attention, and explore what they might mean on a symbolic level. You'll feel inside, with practice, which directive is most accurate. For instance, a table isn't just a table, but perhaps a surface on which to lay out new ideas. A light that's turned off may be telling you that you need energy to shine; a wilted flower may tell you to reconnect to beauty.

Here's an example. Say my question is: *What direction do I need to go to find my most perfect work and how to do it?* I open my eyes and see the side of a clipboard. It has an indented line that runs all the way down the side. The indentation feels significant. I realize that I'm being guided not to abandon my present work but to go more deeply into what I'm doing. I'm being advised to literally make a new cut, open a new way, go more deeply into what I've only seen on the surface.

At this point, I can continue to ask questions based on the answers I'm discovering to deepen the guidance, or I can work with the first interpretation I get.

THE BRIDGE BETWEEN SPIRIT AND ENERGY

Intuitive perception is the mainstay that guides our healing journey. Intuitive perception provides a bridge that allows us an understanding of the world not just beneath our feet but inside our heart — in our soul. The language of intuitive perception gives us a connection between God, as Source, and humanity, between the unknown and the known, between the invisible and the visible, between energy and matter.

Indeed, matter is made of energy. If we want to make tangible changes in our circumstances, we must change our energy, which creates their external physical manifestation. In terms of our healing, I'm suggesting that our belief in ourself and our willingness to surrender to the process of learning has direct impact on the physical nature of our disease.

As we change what we imagine can become true, we create a workable language of spirit that carries us between our inner knowing and the tangible world around us. Rather than being a victim, we become victor. As one woman who was healing from rheumatoid arthritis told me, "I'm no longer just going to survive, I'm going to thrive."

ASK YOURSELF

Am I ready to sense and listen inside for my guidance from Spirit and so ask my deep heart the questions to which I need answers?

Will I be patient but persistent, insisting on finding the way to live my best life?

Can I put my hands over my deep heart, ask for a moment, then go about my normal day expecting an answer within the next twenty-four to forty-eight hours?

WAYS OF THINKING

To understand the process of intuitive perception, we need to look at the way we think and how we process information. We want to be able to shift our attitudes, so we need to understand our thinking mechanisms. Let's first consider the roles of the left brain and the right brain.

Our left brain gathers information using logic and analysis. It can take an idea and break it down into its parts; it approaches the big picture in a step-by-step, logical fashion. Our left brain is deductive, concrete, and rational.

Our right brain collects information by focusing on aesthetics, feelings, intuition, and creativity. The right brain does not use a step-by-step approach when conceptualizing, but instead captures everything all at once in a gestalt fashion. The right brain expresses itself best not in words but through art, music, dance, or other expressive modalities. The right brain is emotional, innovative, and abstract.

Many of us are dominant in either our left brain or our right brain, but each of us possesses both, and we need both to realize the gifts of intuitive perception.

The third aspect of our reasoning anatomy is our deep heart or spirit. As we understand from the picture (on the next page), our deep heart responds to deeply felt emotional questions as well as to more linear, left-brain queries. The process by which we understand our deep-heart conversations is intuitive perception. For example, suppose we're upset, feeling sick, or are just sick and tired of what is happening in our life. When we ask, pray, or meditate with an intention, that intention is heard loud and clear in our deep heart, and information is forthcoming through our intuitive perception. However, even when we do not specifically ask for help, if we need help, it is forthcoming. Our spirit will click into gear as a result of our anxiety level, guiding us into a better frame of mind and a more effective path of action.

Much of what originates in our deep, spiritual heart deals with understanding our role in life, our purpose, and our soul's intention, as well as how to avail ourself of spiritual information that can improve our life and ways to be more closely linked with our original nature as Spirit.

When we ask, for example, *Can I heal?* or *How can I heal?* the only place that accurate feedback can come is from our deep heart. The powerful energy impressions generated in response to our question pass from our deep heart to our right brain, where we recognize the symbols or impressions, and then play with the images in a free-form way to find how they fit together. Once we have a sense of what the impressions mean to us, we move the data into our left brain, where we develop the words and perhaps a specific application for our new thoughts.

This is a creative, dynamic process. It is not about reasoning out the solution to our problems, as software companies encourage their designers. We must learn to think outside the box — that is, we need to take away the restrictions and the boundaries imposed by our left brains or by others. Only then will we understand the response of our intuitive perception and discover new designs for our life.

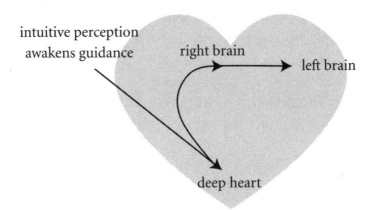

ACTIVITY
Thinking Outside the Box

How do you "think outside the box" to discover greater healing and happiness? Quite simply, you free yourself of all that you think you know and visualize a different path.

Whether you admit it or not, you have already accepted many elements of your current situation to be "true" or "real," and your mind is working from this accepted blueprint of the situation. Your awareness of your situation includes what you know or believe is wrong; the information that you've been told by experts and that you've discovered through your own research; the reactions of friends and family to your situation; and your spoken or unspoken assumptions of how logically you think your situation adds up. In other words, you've decided already where you stand in your healing, whether the situation is a broken love affair or a struggle with cancer.

Now, store away for a moment your understanding of your current situation and imagine this scenario: you are sitting at a table filled with fun, creative toys and interesting photographs. Visualize each item; pick it up, play with it, feel it, smell it. Perhaps as you randomly sift through these colorful objects, you notice some pictures from someone's travel adventures. You find yourself daydreaming about visiting one of these beautiful places, and for an instant you can imagine yourself looking and feeling great. You absentmindedly look out the window at a bird soaring over some blueberry bushes and think about calling your friend and telling her of your idea to go away on a trip together.

You decide that you need to take a trip with her in order to soar like a bird over or through your treatments so that you can laugh from deep within and trust that creative energy is working on your healing as you lighten up.

Your deep heart is at work in this scenario, helping you plumb the depths of your true creative nature — Spirit — in order to send you ideas that you can use to refocus your healing journey. Once you receive these intriguing thoughts, your task is to winnow them down to a workable, doable, and meaningful plan.

When you do this, you are changing the way your mind is handling your healing. You're creating another plan that is stronger and more meaningful than sitting around the house or going immediately back to your old job. Even if your circumstances won't allow you to take an actual trip, you can still create an equally useful alternative — perhaps visualizing a new destination each night. More important than what you do is that you open up your mind to possibility. You're allowing for healing without making any heavy-duty thing out of it. This is why visualization is so powerful. This is why we get so engrossed in reading a novel or watching a movie, because we can identify with the characters and the story.

What you're really doing is creating a new movie of your life and becoming so intrigued with it that you forget the old story and align with the new one, in which you have solved your problem and you are opening to a new, healthier, and happier future.

USING THE RIGHT LANGUAGE

As I've said, some of us are left-brain dominant and some are right-brain dominant. We need to be aware of our own tendencies if we want to hear what our deep heart is telling us. Our deep heart speaks a symbolic language that the right brain naturally understands but that the left brain can struggle to decipher. If we're left-brain dominant, we won't receive the data because the information is being transmitted in a language that our logical thinking self doesn't recognize or value; it's as if we are a computer that hasn't downloaded the correct software program to open the files generated by our deep heart. We need deep-heart software in order to understand and interpret the language of Spirit.

Our deep heart offers guidance, which our intuitive perception turns into symbolic language that our right brain interprets and gleans for meaning. This meaning is then passed to the left brain for understanding and comprehension in everyday language. From the left brain, the information can either be acted upon, kept in one's active mental file, or relegated to the unconscious for storage. If the data we receive from our deep heart through the conduit of our right brain is perceived as interesting and useful, then we use it; otherwise, we store it in the unconscious or toss it into the circular basket in the corner of our mind.

Here's an example. Suppose we have a night dream in which a glorious and powerful fire-breathing dragon lands on a rock near where we are standing. We awake with a very strong feeling that the dream is telling us something.

If we have a well-developed right brain, we'll latch onto the images and decipher their meaning. We might conclude that the dragon represents our own inner power, and the rock indicates how steady we now feel within ourself. The images might suggest that we can believe in ourself and can feel encouraged to go ahead and apply for the job of our dreams.

If we're a left-brain dominant person, we might not even remember our dreams, considering our weak connection to the inner language of symbols. But if we did, we might be more inclined to think of the dragon literally — wondering what kind it was or where it came from — or simply shrug it off with a smile, thinking we probably had too much dessert the night before.

ACTIVITY
The Breath of Oneness

This activity is a short and simple but very meaningful way to experience how your spirit senses all life — as one. This practice allows your heart to open for your own healing and increases your joy and your willingness to receive joy as you appreciate that you are interconnected with all life.

Take a breath; slowly inhale and slowly exhale. As you do, become aware that you are breathing in harmony — one breath at a time — with all living things. You breathe with a tree frog in Tanzania, a leopard in Africa, an eighth-month-old child just diagnosed with AIDS, a woman drawing her last breath, a baby drawing her first breath, a butterfly on its flight to Guatemala. We breathe as one life because at a subtle energy level we are connected by the same threads.

When you tap into this ever-present current of thought, information, inspiration, and true and lasting connection to love, you have used your intuitive perception. When you've finished, pause to consider the experience. Ask yourself: What results from this experience? What have you received, and what have you shared?

THE POWER OF BREATHING WITH OUR HEART

When we put our hands over our heart, we are activating our spiritual heart and its guidance for life. We often find new ideas and important revelations when we do this over extended periods of time, whether we're using the Healing Art of Loving Touch or the Breath of Oneness. These practices feed data to our right brain.

Days or hours after doing these meditations, we may be dancing around the living room having fun with our daughter when we suddenly have a great idea or know exactly how to better approach a long-standing struggle in a creative fashion. Unless we understand the process at work within us, we will think the important idea just popped in all by itself, when really it came from Spirit. Spirit is the originator of great ideas as well as what to do with them.

ATTITUDE SHIFTS

1. I naturally possess the gift of intuition that exists beyond my five senses and intellect; this is my guidance from Spirit.
2. My intuitive perception is an important tool for my healing journey that can guide and comfort me because it is connected to all life-force energy.
3. The intuitive guidance I ask for will not come through my linear thought but rather through a variety of other symbolic messages.
4. I can learn to deepen my intuition by actively practicing and learning how it speaks to me.
5. I can change the energy of what I believe, and that will positively impact my healing journey.
6. I can learn to engage my deep heart. My deep heart is my conduit of intuitive guidance. Intuitive guidance received through my deep heart can be processed through

the creative language of my right brain and then transmitted through the specific to-do list of my rational left brain.

7. Thinking outside the box allows me to create a stronger,
   more workable, and meaningful healing and life path.

8. Each time I use the Healing Art of Loving Touch, I open
   myself to deep-hearted guidance and to the beauty and potential of my healing.

CHAPTER TEN

Personality Mind Is the Critic

*If in the past you haven't experienced love's purity
and understood its innocence,
then the foundation of relationship hasn't been laid.
Longfellow spoke truly when he said, "Love gives itself; it isn't bought."*

— Deepak Chopra

As I began my spiritual journey in 1981, I assumed that what I felt — my attitudes, assumptions, and projections — was simply who I was. We all start in this place, but I found that our personality is like the clothes we put on: today an orange dress, tomorrow a beige pantsuit. We can take on new ways of thinking and of understanding events, and we can leave behind ways of listening to ourself and interpreting the world that create only pain and suffering.

Happiness and healing are in our perspective rather than in events themselves. What a startling revelation. We have a choice of what our experiences will mean to us and how we will grapple with difficulties. This is not only about the spiritual path; it is about the healing path. Our life can come to feel weighed down with opinions or thoughts telling us in no uncertain terms that we're clearly inadequate in some essential way. If this isn't true, and we are adequate, then who tells us that we are incomplete or damaged? And more to the point, why do we believe them?

The answer is that these thoughts come from ourself, from our own mind. Our mind contains both our greatest self-critic and also our most empowered wise counselor. In this chapter we'll explore how this can be so.

OUR PERSONALITY SELF

Our personality is a framework that develops for us to use in this lifetime. It holds all the personal identification tags that we associate with ourself as an individual: how we look, how smart we are, who our parents are, how many kids we have, in which country we live, our religious affiliation, our sexual preferences, our economic status, and so on.

Our personality — or our ego, as it's also referred to — gives us a perspective of our life only from our individual vantage point. It's like reading a newspaper that only carries news of ourself rather than the world. To get a worldview, we need to read a different paper, one written by what we can think of as our true intelligence, our wisdom mind.

Our personality can be thought of as our "lower mind" because it is our self-critic. It is called the self-critic because it generates our reactionary and oppositional attitudes and behaviors. When we're feeling angry, jealous, envious, unjustly accused, and invisible to those with authority, money, and position, we're looking at the world from our individual needs or from the perspective of our self-critic.

We can choose, however, to listen to our higher mind, or wisdom mind, so called because this is our intelligence, which is kin to our deep heart. Intelligence leads our thoughts toward love and compassion, and toward God.

Our wisdom mind leads us to find greater value in our work, to make better friends and lovers, to be more fun, to avoid being caught in our own fear. When we are in our wisdom mind, we have greater empathy and compassion and are more appreciative of life. All the values we're addressing in this book only register in our wisdom mind. The self-critic laughs at the very ways of loving and sharing that our wisdom mind encourages.

As long as we are in our wisdom mind, we can offer guidance, comfort, friendship, and support to others regardless of their reaction to us. We are not being kind because we expect kindness in return. We're being kind for its own sake. But as soon as we fall back into our self-critic, we begin to struggle with others in life's unending dramas. We not only make situations worse, but we get lost in the process. It can take weeks to dig out of the dark ditch of fear, lack, and worry that our self-critic would have us believe is all there is.

Continually, we flip-flop between the two perspectives — critic and wise counselor. Which is it going to be today? All the time, every moment of every waking hour, we are making decisions, either at a conscious or unconscious level, as to how we will respond. One of our tasks for healing is to learn to distinguish our self-critic from our wisdom mind and choose more wisely.

ASK YOURSELF

I know the people or types of people who get to me and rock my boat.

Can I remain steady if I realize they are operating out of their self-critic?

What can happen to the relationship if I refuse to get attached to their velcro?

Am I prepared to be in relationships that are without drama?

OUR SELF-CRITIC STORES ANGRY THOUGHTS

Our personality self stores the feelings of irritation, inadequacy, and injustice — perhaps because we feel they can be used as ammunition at a later date, or perhaps we're just used to all our negative self-talk so we no longer think it's unnatural. When we're having a bad day, out come feelings that reinforce our struggle and make us feel more and more deprived and hopeless — if we keep listening to our self-critic.

But where does it say in our life contract that we have to keep listening? It's like continuing to watch a horror movie that we find disgusting; it's as if we've forgotten that we can push a button and turn it off. When the tone of our inner dialogue becomes critical and judgmental, stop listening. Turn off the voice. How do we do that? We put our hands over our heart, which lets us change the dial to our wisdom mind.

From the perspective of our wisdom mind, we can then reflect on what we've just experienced and what it may mean, since we won't be sucked back into the negative dialogue. In this way, we don't run away from our feelings, but we're not getting hopelessly lost in them, either.

Once we stand outside our self-critic, we can understand this personality component, which we all have, and learn to make friends with it. Much as we wouldn't expect a two-year-old who is screaming for what she wants to suddenly be reasonable and understand Mom's point of view, we can't expect our self-critic to appreciate our healing per- spective. We understand and have a meaningful conversation with our self-critic only from our wisdom mind.

ACTIVELY ACCEPT OR REJECT THOUGHTS

For the most part, we don't consciously choose which thoughts to accept, let alone where we'll file them in our thinking. All the thoughts that we accept either consciously or unconsciously become part of our body-mind memory patterns. We take the energy of words directly into our cells as surely as if we were receiving an injection. This includes all words: those we think, those we say, those that are said to us, and those we hear others saying to others. We need to wake up and say to ourself: *I accept this thought* or *I reject this thought.*

For instance, consider how tired we feel after a fight with our spouse or our kids. When we are around arguing people, we get sick easier, we're more irritable ourself, and we find ourself having a harder time pulling up from our own emotional nosedives. By contrast, when we're in a positive environment, our troubles seem smaller, and we are drawn to happier and more positive thoughts. We resonate with the energetic environment around us. We want to make our environment as positive as possible because that enhances our health.

ASK YOURSELF

Can I be responsible for accepting or rejecting the words (and thus the energy) that I or others say?

For the next ten minutes am I willing to pay attention to what I think and say and what others say so I can practice saying, "I accept that thought" or "I reject that thought," and see what happens?

THE FOUR STAGES OF BECOMING AN INDIVIDUAL

Our personality, while critical of us and the world, nevertheless serves a genuine purpose, which is to allow us the experience of being an individual. Here are the four primary early stages of emotional and spiritual development that form our personalities. These discoveries and assumptions begin immediately after birth and continue for the first six years of life.

Stage One

Shortly after we're born, we realize that when we cry for Mom, she doesn't always respond in exactly the way we want or need. We conclude that we are separate from Mom and Dad and from all other beings.

This must be a frightening revelation because before entering this particular incarnation we've been rocked in the truth that we are in fact spiritually connected to all life in all forms.

Stage Two

Because we now appear to be separate from others, we become aware of a spatial relationship with time. We accept — because we are separate from others — that there is a spatial relationship that comes into play. In other words, there is a before and an after. Everything is no longer happening in the present. With the birth of our sense of time, we come to the unassailable conclusion that there is a death, and so we begin to fear and anticipate that one day we will die.

For our personality self, the product of only this incarnation, there is, of course, a death and an end to this experience. We fail to connect, however, with the truth that our universal intelligence, our sacred nature, doesn't die, but provides the continuity between lifetimes.

Stage Three

Now that we feel entirely separate and unsettled by the knowledge that we are finite, we realize that there is much around us — both in our body and in our environment — that we can't control and that doesn't respond to our wishes. Bad things happen as we fall and hurt ourself; we can get sick or develop diseases; our best friend can become our worst enemy; friends can break our toys and gang up against us. We recognize that thinking about things is safe while experiencing them is risky. We enter the perceived safety of the ivory tower of our personality's thinking, never again to venture out into the world of feelings and sensing. While we think we've figured out how to stay safe, we've actually only succeeded in cutting ourself off from all meaning and intimacy with ourself and others.

Often a person presents herself to me with a challenge, in which, energetically, she lives so completely in her head that the energy seems to form two bodies — one of her brain and one of the rest of her. However, we can't isolate ourself in our thinking and hope to have a meaningful life or to heal physical imbalances. The sacred lives within our body, and all around us.

Stage Four

The final stage of development of our personality comes as we concretize what we know and believe from our personality's perspective. We forget that we have our true worldview in our wisdom mind and in our deep heart. Carl Jung referred to our personality as our persona. In this final stage of our young development, we identify completely with our persona — the opinions and assumptions we've developed — and become ready to defend them to the death.

The extent to which we become lost in our personality's assumptions and opinions, the ones that we believe define us and that we vigorously defend and guard, demonstrates the power of our personality self. Whenever we hear ourself proclaiming that the world is a scary and fierce place, we are looking at the world through our personality and not our wisdom mind. Whenever we respond to trouble by becoming defensive, to protect ourself or our way of life, we are operating from our personality. If we stop and listen instead to our wisdom mind, we will hear it telling us that defending ourself isn't as important as helping whomever we are struggling with to move into their wisdom mind, rather than staying in their self-critic. When we make war, we do so because we're operating from our personality's defensive posture. When we make peace, we do so from our wisdom mind, which tries to bridge differences.

Whether we're talking about war or our struggle with a raging disease, the same understanding applies. We need to move to our wisdom mind to explore options, seek meaningful approaches, feel comfortable in asking questions, and be sure we get answers. The wisdom mind allows us to grow our power and our capacity to heal our body and whatever is out of alignment in our life.

ASK YOURSELF

*What opinions do I feel the most certain about regarding politics,
sexual orientation, religion, world events, and society?*
What if I relaxed or even let go of these certainties?
Which would be easiest and which hardest?
What anxiety or fear shows up?
What is the fear connected to?

WHEN OLD STORIES ARE NO LONGER USEFUL

Our old stories are based on those behaviors that we have used in the
past, consciously or unconsciously, to help us solve situations that
seemed otherwise unsolvable. Our old stories are the product of our
personality, or lower mind, while our new stories are the products of
our wisdom mind.

As a child, we learned to act in certain ways to survive or at least
keep out of harm's way. As we grow up, we forget that that old story of
how to behave may no longer be appropriate for who we are or what
we need. Old stories often reflect a lack of confidence in ourself along
with impossible expectations for how we must or should behave.

Old stories often take the form of "the way things are." When we
shrug and say that we'll never get the job or the relationship we want because "that's what always happens to me," we are telling our old story.
Usually, we cling to these old stories because we're afraid to risk being visible, vulnerable, or losing control. An old story can also take the physical form of a recurring illness. For instance, we may develop a digestive
problem that, conveniently, always crops up whenever we really want to
leave a job or situation that we dislike but are too afraid to quit.

The illness, in this case, serves the purpose of helping us solve a
problem. Obviously, we want to find better ways to make choices so
our body doesn't need to get sick to rescue us. I'm a perfect example of
this particular old story: every fall I get a cold or the flu. My old story

must be that in order to take time off from work, I really have to be sick. And sure enough, although I don't believe that message, on some level my body still operates from it.

When I get my down time every November, I never get deathly sick, just sick enough to keep me on the couch. It is fascinating how the timing is always so perfectly sandwiched into my schedule. My illness is always wedged right between teaching assignments — as if I had indeed set it up on some unconscious level. I certainly don't tell myself, "I want time off, so bring on the cold or the flu," but on some level my body has gotten that message from my mind — my personality self.

It's interesting also that we don't usually get sick before vacation, but we surely do before an exam, before an event that scares us, or when we need to do or say something that is uncomfortable. Our thoughts are powerful, and the stress that is generated certainly closes us down. And the part of our thinking that generates our stress is — you guessed it — our personality.

CHANGING OUR OLD STORY

Sometimes we intentionally choose to follow our old story, believing it to be a worthy plan. A client named Shawna was a lovely young woman with anorexia. She was aware of the seriousness of her illness, but to her, what was happening to her physically was less important than how it allowed her to call attention to her needs, which she felt had always been neglected. She was proud of her amazing discipline in not eating and felt this was a true test of her power.

However, Shawna's desire to fully understand and work with her old story gave her the energy to slowly create a new story. To do this, she chose a character to whom she could closely relate — a story with a healing ending — and pretended she was that character. As she contoured her life to the story, creating *her* new story, she found that she had the support she needed from herself (from her inner healer or spirit and her wisdom mind), and she began to change her eating habits. The key to her finding her way toward a healing path was that the new story came from her. It didn't come from someone else telling her what to do.

The decision to convert our old story into a new story can be the result of many experiences: psychotherapy, psychiatry, energy work, spiritual direction — or just because it's time and we've found the path ourself.

We need to understand what we've been saying to ourself and its impact on our body. We need to become aware of the unconscious programming that is running our life. Developing our new story takes us into healing, happiness, and sound and lasting relationships. After years of telling ourself the old story, we finally realize it is time to peel away the familiar and risk living a new dynamic story.

We may have to look hard to identify our old stories, since they are so familiar and ingrained in our ways of thinking. Old stories can often be recognized by the following thoughts: things never change; the doctors don't care; I'll never have enough money to get out of this rotten apartment; there is no one who will help me; my job is to take care of everyone else; or it is God's will to give up what I love for another. Can we identify what physical or lifestyle piece has resulted from telling our old story? Can we accept that it is our old story, a program run by our self-critic, and that we're ready to change?

Living in our old stories is like barreling down a hill in a car with no brakes. We're zooming through our days, unable to stop and enjoy the interactions that make life meaningful and pleasurable.

ASK YOURSELF

What old story am I aware of?
  What new story might I allow to grow from the old story?
  What are my believability factors for this change?
  What does my deep heart tell me about how I'm going to be successful?

AN OLD STORY AND A NEW STORY

Luellan came to see me for chronic fatigue syndrome. She told me a powerful old story that had kept her literally immobilized for years. Most recently, for a year and a half, she had found it almost impossible to even sit in a chair for more than a short time, and she had to quit her job. She said she liked her job writing copy for a local environmental magazine, but it still wasn't what she really wanted. She confided that she wanted to be a healer and work in the healing field.

I shared with her what my research and client practice has shown me about chronic fatigue: at an energy level, it provides us with a time-out in how we earn a living or make our major contribution. The body interprets our uncertainty about our career — how to find it, live up to it, explain it, or merely do it — as the reason to slow things down until the work thing is sorted out.

As Luellan and I talked, it became clear how many fears she had around claiming the role of healer, particularly in her family. She recognized that the first part of her healing journey from chronic fatigue meant claiming the role of healer. Her old story told her she had to stay out of harm's way by remaining invisible, since it hadn't been safe in her family to have an opinion or disagree with her father. Today, she is writing a new story that is growing from her inner conviction, her deep heart and wisdom mind — creating believability factors — that she can and is becoming the healer she has longed to be. Her body has begun to listen to the changing story, and she is making lasting progress in creating her new life.

I often feel that if only one person really cares about us — whether that is a professional counselor or a close friend who listens to us with sincerity — we can move to a more positive outlook and create a new story for our life. This is truly the healing journey.

As we make the Attitude Shifts in this chapter, we can realize how we've grown and how these powerful new energy thoughts will assist us in our life and will help us solve the problems and challenges everyone faces.

❧ ATTITUDE SHIFTS ❧

1. One of the most important attitude shifts I can make is to understand that I have the power to think about my life differently. I can change my reaction to the events of my life by realizing that I have the ability to reframe them. My perception of the event is more important than the event itself.

2. My personality self keeps me in a small and narrowly focused view of the world, and it is a naturally oppositional state of being.

3. I have the choice to move out of my limited view into my higher mind — my wisdom mind — which leads me to love, spirit, and true healing.

4. When I am in my wisdom mind, I can love and be kind simply because I can. The natural state of my wisdom mind doesn't calculate what I will get in return.

5. Switching to my wisdom mind is as simple as pausing and placing my hand over my heart and making the conscious choice to change the channel from my personality mind.

6. It is only from the vantage of my wisdom mind that I can have a meaningful conversation with my personality mind and decide what thoughts and reactions to keep and which ones to throw away.

7. I have a choice of which words I accept and which I reject. Only those words I accept influence my healing.

8. Learning the four stages of my emotional development helps me understand why my personality mind believes so strongly that it is protecting me. My personality mind actually has a positive role to play in allowing me to experience being an individual.

9. Switching to my wisdom mind allows me to move into my new story rather than stay in the old story, which is my personality's limited and critical, I-told-you-so view of my life.

10. My new story holds all the beautiful healing potential of my life as I want it to be — expansive and connected to Spirit.

11. It is important that I do the work to identify my old story and beliefs about myself and my abilities so that I can begin this healing journey with all the potential of my new story.

CHAPTER ELEVEN

Wisdom Mind Is Our Helper

A hero ventures forth from the world of common day
into the region of supernatural wonder:
fabulous forces are there encountered and a decisive victory is won:
the hero comes back from this mysterious adventure with the power
to bestow boons on his fellow man.

— Joseph Campbell

Our wisdom mind comes alive when we are quiet — when we use our intuitive perception to discover a different way to handle an old grudge, for example. Our wisdom mind shows us a way to make more meaningful choices and stop running away from what we think will come next. Our wisdom mind is the jumping-off place to our deep heart, our soul. The great spiritual teachers tell us that eventually our longing to be completely in the unconditional loving space of Spirit will lead us to practice staying steady in our wisdom mind more often.

A client of mine once shared an experience that is a wonderful example of how our normal thinking generates our miseries, feelings of unworthiness, and inadequacy, while our wisdom mind prompts a different, more meaningful response.

Jasmine was a bright thirty-year-old who seemed to have her life totally together. She told me how she had started a small computer business with a friend, and together they had hoped to create a successful business. Then Jasmine and her friend had a falling out. The friend left, joined others, and eventually became a widely recognized business expert. In the meantime, Jasmine struggled to find her footing; she always seemed to come up short in the eyes of the world and thus in her own estimation.

One day, she was feeling especially dejected as she carried heavy grocery bags into the house. As usual, she was struggling with feelings of jealousy, envy, and self-pity. Suddenly, she said, with a bolt of Divine insight she recognized what she was doing to herself. She knew she had to cease fighting her friend's success and instead enjoy it with her.

Since Jasmine and her friend weren't speaking, she was at first confounded on how to enjoy her friend's success. Then she heard a voice inside say that since there is no true separation — that all is truly one — she could imagine walking up on the stage with her friend to accept an important award. She could enjoy her friend's joy and success because energetically it was also her success.

Jasmine told me the idea felt like rubbing her hand against the grain of a piece of wood where all the splinters jabbed painfully into her. She realized that she felt so pitiful because she was listening to her self-critic, which kept telling her that she would never have the same success as her friend. But she also now heard a new voice that said this assessment was false and that the way to success was to surround herself with it — in all shapes and forms — rather than cut herself off from the abundance of the Universe.

Jasmine couldn't escape the pain of her resistance, but she recognized a wiser and truer understanding that could release her from the false competition and comparisons she had set up in her mind. She could instead see herself through the eyes of a true winner — through the eyes and the thoughts of her wisdom mind.

It is a difficult thing to make peace with our mind. We believe that if we have just a little more of whatever we crave — food, money, power, love — we'll be completely satisfied. J. Krishnamurti — an Indian scholar and teacher well known for his spiritual teachings — used to tell his students, "The end of the road is the same as the beginning." This means that our wanting something different than what we have will be the same at the end of our life as it is right now, unless we learn to make friends with our mind — both our self-critic and our wisdom mind.

ACTIVITY

Listen for Your Second Opinion

A wonderful way to feel the difference in your body between your self-critic and your wisdom mind is to practice this second-opinion exercise.

1. Call to mind a question about your health or your life. (For example, *How can I stay safe from disease?*)
2. Place the palm of one hand on either side of your face, along your cheek. This perspective reflects your normal thinking personality self. As you ask yourself this question, notice the normal dialogue that takes place and what actions it directs you to take.
3. As you listen to your personality's dialogue, slide your hand down and rest it over your throat. This is the location energetically where we find our own authentic words, and it is also where we parrot those of others who we believe know better about us than we do. Sense the feelings that come with your personality's discussion about creating a means to solving your problem.
4. Now slide your hand down so it is centered over your heart chakra and ask your question again. As you ask your Spirit or inner healer for guidance, you'll sense a quieter, more peaceful sense of *knowing rather than just thinking*. How do you experience this response as being different than the one you received from your personality self?

As you sense the words of your personality with your hand next to your cheek, you'll hear a familiar dialogue of what to do and how to fix the situation. When you rest your hand against your throat — reflecting how your body receives this energy of your personality's words — you'll find a distinct tightening, anxiety, or sense of emergency because the directives are an impossible jumble of what you must do, find, create, or become in order to solve your problem. You may be left feeling exhausted and at a loss about what to do.

As you rest your hand over your deep heart — the center of your chest — you'll connect with your guidance and your inner knowing, and your wisdom mind will be put to work to help you. You may sense a word or phrase or simply an inner reassurance providing comfort and the message to slow down, relax, and open to the possibilities around you.

PICTURING THE PROCESS

Here is a picture to help us understand the relationships among our deep heart and its guidance, our creative right brain, and our left brain, where we experience making a choice between the personality self and the wisdom mind.

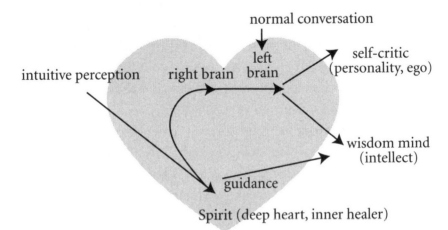

As you follow the direction of the arrows in the diagram you will discover three important insights. First, Spirit is the entire environment of our reality. Second, intuitive perception is the way we ask our deep heart or spirit for information. This information is called guidance, and it automatically triggers our wisdom mind to generate self-knowing and inner confidence. This inner knowing continues as long as our words and thoughts stay centered in our wisdom mind. Third, normal conversation enters our processing of thoughts at the left brain, and then we have a choice whether the thoughts go into our self-critic or our wisdom mind.

ACKNOWLEDGING RESISTANCE

The first time I heard about spiritual energy, I thought the idea was pretty "out there." Actually, times have changed, and this is no longer such a strange concept. Most people now recognize our body-mind connection, and in this book I'm expanding that to encompass our body-mind-spirit connection, which is all-important in healing and in living.

Still, we may react negatively to new concepts, and when we are struggling with a problem — be it cancer, heart disease, arthritis, diabetes, our marriage, our lack of a partner, our debts — we may also be sensitive and resistant to anyone suggesting what we should do.

This is understandable, but we need to acknowledge and understand our reaction. When we respond in these ways, it is our self-critic who is leaping up and putting a defensive wall around us. This defensive wall is not meant to protect us but to keep us from changing. Our self-critic often becomes defensive in two ways: one is to take all the blame, to tell us that we are a true failure who cannot hope to be saved by whatever is being offered. The other is to take none of the blame and to dismiss what's being said as useless or irrelevant. Our self-critic is at its finest when it is building up our defensive postures, and it becomes stronger the more we give in to it.

If there is any point worth remembering in this part, it is that we should watch out for these messages and turn them over to our wisdom mind, which will provide the appropriate response.

Most often, the wisdom mind's response is somewhere in between the self-critic's defensive stances of all or nothing. We certainly have the power to heal and change ourself and our troubles, but we also usually bear some responsibility for the situation we are in. Taking responsibility requires the same pathway to our wisdom mind. When someone says something to us that we really need to hear even though it's hard, our connection to Spirit comes in to help us in this way, too. We want to run away — our self-critic will tell us to not pay attention — but acknowledging our part of an argument, a divorce, or an illness may well be what can help us turn the corner, so it needs to be listened to. As we move another's accusations or quiet reminders to our wisdom mind and see what we believe to be true in them, we are able to say *I'm sorry, I understand my part of this,* or *I realize that I've hurt you.*

People often say, *It takes a big person to admit being wrong.* Actually, it takes a person in touch with her wisdom mind, who can move away from self-criticism into the wise counselor, to do the right thing, say the right thing, and think the right thing.

When we bring our defensive reactions to our wisdom mind, it allows us to make choices in our perception and attitudes. Change is rarely easy, but a little at a time gets us there. Turning our life in a new direction is similar to the way a powerful little tugboat guides an ocean liner into harbor. How can such a small boat move such a large one? The answer is that the tug is very powerful, and it exerts consistent pressure on the ocean liner in just the right spots to accomplish the task. The translation for us is that *a single powerful idea, taken to heart and applied steadily, will change our life and bring us into our own safe harbor.*

❧ ATTITUDE SHIFTS ❧

1. If I stay in my personality mind and define myself by external things and don't learn the balance of listening to my wisdom mind, I will end my life still wanting the same things and feeling unfulfilled.

2. I can learn to feel and hear the difference between my self-critical personality mind and my wisdom mind.

3. Spirit is the entire environment of my reality.

4. I accept that any single powerful idea applied to my thinking every day will change the direction of my life toward well-being and healing.

PART THREE

Reality Check — We Are More Than Our Genes

Some of us are very aware of the way that our moods affect our bodies —
how anxiety tenses the muscles, how depression leads to fatigue, how joy creates energy, and how gratitude and love open the heart.

— Joan Borysenko

CHAPTER TWELVE

Our Spiritual DNA

I have heard enough warrior stories of heroic daring.
Tell me how you crumble when you hit the wall,
the place you cannot go beyond by the strength of your own will.
What carries you to the other side of that wall,
to the fragile beauty of your own humanness?

— Oriah Mountain Dreamer

We have a higher standard of living and more healthcare options in the West than in many places in the world. Certainly, there are many who still live in poverty, but for the most part we have access to adequate food, shelter, and work to maintain good health. When illness does strike, we have many choices for wellness. However, none of this truly matters if we don't take responsibility for our own health and heart first. Knowledge is the key. When we get sick, as the holy man Sai Baba suggests, it is our mind that we need to send to the hospital, not our body. We need to educate ourself to make the most of the healthcare options we have, and we need to understand how our personal thoughts and feelings might be impacting our health at all levels.

When we are stopped in our tracks with an unexpected diagnosis or other life experience, we are called to take more seriously the impact of our perhaps overworked and overstressed life to make room for healing.

Healing means learning about the various treatment options so that we make appropriate choices and direct those who want to help us in the ways that are the most useful for us. We need to be fully engaged in every question, such as whether to pursue chemotherapy, radiation, and/or surgery when fighting cancer; whether to place a stent in a blood vessel if we have heart disease; or what kind of treatment is right for depression and panic attacks. We need to explore to what extent or in what combination to visit a massage therapist, an acupuncturist, or another healer. Healing requires our renewed participation in order to rekindle kindness and passion from within toward what matters most to us.

It is actually empowering to realize that we are in charge, to a large degree, of what happens in our body. This means, however, that we need to honestly assess and evaluate ourself — our habits and addictions. Often, the first step is to undo our assumptions that external remedies hold the exclusive key to our healing. Once we appreciate that life's healing journey involves what we eat, how we live, and what we think and feel, we can begin to weave a healing practice.

No matter where we are in this process, we'll be most successful if we take it slowly, carefully exploring all the elements of our lifestyle and making new decisions based on how we feel inside. Without beating ourself up, we need to view our life as a lovely portrait of our best self. Everything that doesn't belong in this picture as part of our health and well-being, we can slowly find the courage to face and shift. We have the time, the patience, and the tenacity to find our best course for healing and for living.

HOW MUCH OF ILLNESS IS PREDETERMINED?

It is common to want to search for the source of an emotional or physical illness in our family history. Are we predetermined to get certain problems? If our mother had a nervous breakdown or mental illness, are we automatically headed down the same road? If our mother had any of the reproductive cancers or heart disease, does that mean that we're destined for the same fate? These are big questions.

Similar to the age-old debate over personality, this question really asks whether nature or nurture is more important when it comes to illness. Does our physical heredity dictate our health? Do we develop certain sicknesses because they are linked to our physical DNA? Or, do environmental influences have a greater impact on our health, such as pollution, diet, and exercise, as well as our thoughts, feelings, and beliefs? If it's a combination, then to what degree?

In my work over the years I've found that lifestyle elements — including thoughts, feelings, choices, fears, stress, and insecurity over change — all contribute more to the onset of disease than just having a gene that is earmarked as producing a certain illness.

From studying the various flows of energy in a person's body I've learned that the way these flows are interrupted and why tend to be the triggering culprits in stimulating the onset of disease; in addition, these energy flows show us how to better promote healing. Of course, viruses and bacteria exist and cause specific illnesses. But why do viruses and bacteria affect only some people who are exposed to them and not others? What I've found is that our inner environment plays a major role in when, or if, such agents take root and make us sick.

Research and the experience of medical professionals confirm this. For example, one of my students, Dr. Robert Lang, a well-known endocrinologist, shared some of his research one day in class. He described the case of identical twins who had been separated at birth and who each developed entirely different illnesses. The twins had the exact same genes, but one twin never got sick with the same conditions that affected the other twin.

Clearly, environmental factors, not heredity, made the difference with these twins. In his book *Biology of Belief*, Dr. Bruce Lipton describes research that shows that the environmental factors that affect our health include thoughts and feelings, as well as other, more obvious external factors like diet. As a cell biologist, Dr. Lipton has researched the issue of genes for years, and he has found that genes, for the most part, do not determine whether we get cancer or heart disease, or anything else for that matter. Our genes hold the potential, but they are not self-determining. In other words, genes do not turn themselves on and off.

Dr. Lipton writes, "DNA blueprints passed down at birth through genes are not set in concrete. Genes are not destiny. Environmental influences, including nutrition, stress and emotions, can modify those genes without changing their basic blueprint. And as few as 5 percent of cancers are related to genetic predisposition, and the rest are a combination of these other factors."

Additionally, scientists can study both the contribution of genes and the contribution of nurture, or environment, through what is called epigenetics. Epigenetics is a new science that means, literally, control over genetics, by modifying factors such as nutrition, stress, and emotions.

In the August 2003 issue of *Molecular and Cellular Biology*, in an article entitled "Diet Trumps Genes," Duke University researchers reported on a study of mice that had a genetically abnormal gene that produces yellow coats and obesity. In the study, after being given an enriched diet of folic acid, vitamin B_{12}, betaine, and choline, the mice produced offspring that were born normal, with brown coats and normal weight.

It's exciting to see scientific proof that it isn't our genes but what turns them on and off that is the key to both getting sick and healing. This is indeed the focus of *Spirit Heals*, identifying the ways we feel, think, and perceive ourself and our world, and how those things affect the ways our genes turn on and off. Do we see the glass half full or half empty?

Additionally, of course, we need to pay heed to other environmental factors, such as pollutants, poor nutrition, lack of sleep, and so on. There are many negative environmental factors that can impact our life and weaken our resistance. I suspect that today disease seems so rampant because, generally speaking, we are more stressed than ever before, and many of us have less stamina.

We are using our head and thinking more while producing less with our hands and our heart. Because of the enormous pressures to handle our life, our body is weaker and less resistant to the viruses and bacteria around us. Why is this? One of the reasons is that we've lost ourself in believing the myth that if we focus only on external antidotes for our care, we are managing our health well.

For example, we believe that if we scrub the bathroom with disinfectant, our children will be safer, but actually we're finding that when we eliminate germs, our children build up no natural immunity. We believe that if we provide every imaginable material opportunity for our children and grandchildren, they will be happier than we have been. And yet giving everything to our children keeps them from trusting that they can find their own way. We sometimes cripple them with our best intentions. If we step up our vitamin and supplement consumption, we think we're handling our health. However, more than one report suggests that many of the vitamins we take move through our systems untouched and unabsorbed.

It is time to return to basics and take responsibility for the inner healing that enhances our physical healing. We benefit the most when our spiritual determination guides our thoughts and actions — in other words, when our personality self heeds our wise inner Self. In this way we impact our body and our life from the power within us — from our spiritual DNA.

OUR SPIRITUAL DNA

In the early days of my spiritual work, I spent many years trying to make sense of my inner teachings and instructions on the energetics of spiritual healing — spirit-directed healing. These teachings always focused on Divine Love as the true energy of healing, and while I believed in the power of Divine Love, I wasn't sure this power was manageable for us unenlightened human beings. I searched for a way to explain how love could and did heal our thoughts and feelings and also our physical body.

I wondered why someone who was negative and difficult could suddenly have a flash of gladness, delight, and compassion. What was it that broke through the normal self-consuming worry? How, for example, could a grumpy old man, bitter about what life had handed him, smile with genuine delight as a small child looked up and offered him a lick of his ice cream cone? Why would a gunman, frustrated at life, take a hostage and, instead of murdering his victim, respond to her love by repenting and turning himself in to authorities?

It occurred to me that, akin to our physical genes, we must have spiritual genes that are part of our Divine heritage. Once ignited, these spiritual genes can change the direction we are heading, whether that's toward divorce, bankruptcy, or disease. When we see this momentary shift that allows us to light up in happiness — this temporary illumination — we call it having a change of heart.

In fact, I have come to believe that we do possess spiritual genes, our very own extensive spiritual DNA, which connects all our feelings and emotions to our physical self and our lifestyle choices. Our spiritual DNA is part of our lasting spiritual heritage because we are already part of the One God or Presence.

Our spiritual DNA is awakened through the power of love. *Spiritual healing means opening the channels of Divine Love within us in order to experience our own change of heart.*

SPIRITUAL DNA GIVES US THE ABILITY TO LOVE

Spiritual DNA acts most directly on our thoughts, feelings, and attitudes, which in turn act on our body. I have come to believe that our inner energy of love, once released, is able to reestablish physical health by overriding, and in some cases eliminating, negative emotional patterns.

Over the years, I named these *spiritual gene sets* and found where they fit in the human energy field, correlating them to specific attitudes and emotional behaviors and which specific physical systems they affect. I call this the Stillpoint Model of Integrative Life Healing, and it is the basis of what I teach.

I feel that these spiritual gene sets are the reason we can become more caring, sharing, loving, and approving in spite of our normal negative and self-defeating thought patterns. Even the gradual evolutionary development of our brain doesn't account for our ability and desire to love. Although we've gradually added layers to our brain — which have taken us from the reptilian brain (focused only on survival and procreation) to the cortex and the neocortex (allowing us to differentiate and respond to emotions expressed in facial expression and body language) — this still doesn't account for the X-factor of loving.

I believe that through spiritual development, we learn to expand our brain still further as we connect to Spirit and our deep heart. In this way we bypass our ingrained emotional reactions and instead bring forth a different set of kinder and more compassionate reactions toward ourself and others. I believe that this new understanding of spiritual gene sets helps us better grasp the concept of Divine Love and the ways we can use this energy to turn on greater caring and compassion for ourself, so we can do the same for others.

As we turn on our caring, we aren't aware that we're accomplishing something that is perhaps our next true evolutionary wave. After the neocortex, might we develop a firm bridge to loving that will become the supercortex? We'll be hard-wired to love — fascinating to think about.

Spiritual gene sets are the awakening voice of Spirit within us. When we can access them directly, healing is more readily available to us.

❧ ATTITUDE SHIFTS ❧

1. Beyond my genetics, the combination of my thoughts, feelings, and lifestyle choices have enormous impact on how well I am.

2. I have spiritual DNA that is a gift from Divinity, and I can access it for my healing journey.

3. I awaken my spiritual DNA through the power of love.

4. Using the Stillpoint Model of Integrative Life Healing, I can identify my spiritual DNA, and by understanding what it is and how it works, I can turn on greater caring and compassion.

CHAPTER THIRTEEN

Our Seven Spiritual Gene Sets

The ego is not only the unobserved mind,
the voice in the head which pretends to be you,
but also the unobserved emotions that are the body's reaction
to what the voice in the head is saying.

— Eckhart Tolle

*J*ust as physical DNA can be turned on and off by attitudes, beliefs, nutrition, and environment, the same is true of our spiritual DNA — it too can be turned on and off. Our spiritual DNA is activated when we are living in accordance with our true Self — such as when we are attentive to our choices; when we strive to find ways of compromising, seeking solutions to problems that used to send us over the moon; and when we hold back anger and rage until it calms — and we calm — and find a wiser way to proceed.

When we think well of ourself and others, we enhance various genes that deal with particular emotional responses. When we listen, for example, to another person's opinion and genuinely look for compromise, we are strengthening the gene set of Joy & Inner Peace, which activates our authentic voice. If we are passed over for a job promotion,

but continue to trust our own creativity and stay steady, we're benefit-
ing from the spiritual gene set of Inner Power & Presence. This gene set
helps us make peace with our need to overly control people and circumstances and to feel competitive with everyone and everything that
seems to be getting ahead of us.

As we stay in our inner knowing, we are rewarded with greater trust
in ourself and belief in the truth that life is a process that involves both
the fair and the unfair, the good and the not-so-good. How we interpret
it — we're not much at all, or life happens and I'm still here — determines our happiness and our health. It's our choice moment by moment.

All the ways we treat others have implications, from how we care
about the needs of our dog to how we interact with our neighbor. We
are either building energy or losing it, either enhancing our energy
through loving or doing the opposite. Our actions stem from either
our fear or our love, our inner critic or our inner healer. Spiritual gene
sets are the way that we can understand being made in God's image.

I think being made in the image of the Great Mystery means that
we have the capacity to choose love, which could take the form of
something as simple but as difficult as resisting the urge to jump on the
bandwagon of negativity when others criticize a colleague at work.
Every time we choose love, we move incrementally toward greater emotional, mental, and physical health. Each thought and action has con-
sequences for our joy and our sadness. We want to practice feeling our
joy more than our sadness, or otherwise, the sadness slowly creeps over
us and diminishes the quality of our life.

The rest of this chapter describes the seven gene sets that are one
part of the Stillpoint Model of Integrative Life Healing. The gene sets
have also been organized as a chart (see pages 106–7), which also includes the physical systems that are involved in these attitudes and beliefs. Because our gene sets are linked to our way of thinking and feeling,
which affects our physical body, I've identified the appropriate energy
center or chakra for each. Many people are familiar with chakras, which
are the small energy centers that rest in the energy field and are approximately aligned with our spine. These energy centers hold and sort

the energy of our beliefs, attitudes, emotions, and thoughts. Everything we think moves through these small rotating energy vortexes, influencing our behavior and our health. The chart identifies the location of each energy center or chakra in relation to the body.

OUR SEVEN SPIRITUAL GENE SETS

Wisdom

7th Chakra

Wisdom is activated through unity.

Treat all forms of life as our brothers and sisters.

Wisdom is the spiritual gene that helps us make choices that involve the best for ourself and others. Rather than considering only our own needs, wisdom comes from our inner knowing that we are all connected at the level of our heart and its Divine energy. We ask to be mentored by the Universe so we may learn to care for all life as if it were personal to us.

AFFIRMATION: I will always look for the good and highest potential in every person and situation.

Vision

6th Chakra

Vision is activated through perception.

Sense and listen to Spirit's voice,
through which we will find comfort and support.

Vision is the spiritual gene that asks us to acknowledge the fire of our inner knowing, which allows us to discover and acknowledge our own guidance and the vision for our life. Rather than looking for unconditional love and support only from our family or friends, we need to look for it in our own deep heart, which will never desert us. Realize

OUR SEVEN SPIRITUAL GENE SETS

Chakra	Region of the Body	Gene Set	Spiritual Gene Set Attributes	System(s) and Corresponding Function(s) of the Body	Affirmation
7th	Forehead and crown of head	Wisdom (Safety & Authority); activated through Unity	**Treat all forms of life as our brothers and sisters:** Wisdom is the spiritual gene that helps us make choices that involve the best for ourself and others. Rather than considering only our own needs, wisdom comes from our inner knowing that we are all connected at the level of our heart and its Divine energy. We ask to be mentored by the Universe so we may learn to care for all life as if it were personal to us.	Nervous System: Receives and conveys impulses to other cells in the body.	*I will always look for the good and highest potential in every person and situation.*
6th	Head, particularly the area around the eyes, ears, and sinuses	Vision; activated through Perception	**Sense and listen to Spirit's voice, through which we will find comfort and support:** Vision is the spiritual gene that asks us to acknowledge the fire of our inner knowing, which allows us to discover and acknowledge our own guidance and the vision for our life. Rather than looking for unconditional love and support only from our family or friends, we need to look for it in our own deep heart, which will never desert us. Realize that Presence is within each of us and guiding our life. As we surrender our ego will, or our personality self, to our Divine will, or our true Self, we receive the gift of Grace. Through daily guidance we are better able to realize our fullest potential for life.	Endocrine System: Contributes specific substances to the body fluids, which affect the healthy activity of cells, organs, and tissues. Special organs of vision and hearing.	*I see Divine Guidance coming to me daily in many forms.*
5th	Nose, mouth, and throat area	Joy & Inner Peace; activated through Intention	**Pay attention that our words and actions reflect our true attitudes, beliefs, and feelings:** Joy & Inner Peace is the gene set that asks us to hold the intention of our authentic self and to use this energy as encouragement for us to speak the truth, aligning our words with our actions and thoughts. We are guided to find our authentic voice when we remain congruent — with our beliefs, feelings, thoughts, words, and actions in alignment. We strive to focus our intention and give our attention to those endeavors that foster love and compassion in the world. We listen within before speaking.	Respiratory System: Provides oxygen and eliminates excess carbon dioxide.	*I use words and actions that always help and never hurt.*
4th	Chest, including heart, lungs, and breasts; also arms, hands, and fingers	Love & Compassion; activated through Passion	**Use our time to focus on the essential parts of our life that evoke a genuine passion for what and whom we love:** Love & Compassion is the gene set that asks us to experience love, kindness, compassion, and freedom from our woundedness. Every moment of every day involves the energy of our heart, since it is focused on bringing our love and compassion into the world. Our passion is born of compassion and enables us to nourish our body and our emotions — to help us love our partner, family, and friends more fully — and to enable us to love those far away who also need our attention.	Circulatory System: Distributes bodily fluids to all the cells, maintaining the tissue fluid that bathes the cells continually. Immune System: Defends the body against disease.	*I put my heart and passion for living into all that I do.*

3rd	Solar plexus and abdomen, including liver, stomach, pancreas, gall bladder, upper section of large intestine, small intestine, and kidneys	**Trust Spirit and then we'll be better able to trust our own abilities: Inner Power & Presence** is the gene set that asks us to trust that to be successful we must contribute our unique gifts and abilities to make a difference with our life. In order to develop our natural creativity so that we can contribute our best effort to the world, we learn to believe in our true Self, for it is here that we are filled with the empowerment and self-confidence to persevere where necessary and relax control where appropriate.	**Digestive System:** Receives, digests, and absorbs food and liquids. Eliminates wastes not excreted through skin or kidneys. **Muscular System:** Causes movement by contracting. Maintains static skeletal and postural support.	*I perform my work with integrity and excellence, knowing that new doors of opportunity will continually open to me.*
	Inner Power & Presence; activated through Trust			
2nd	Pelvis, including bladder, uterus, and specific male and female reproductive organs	**Stay centered in the Now rather than living in the past or the future: Intimacy & Community** is the gene set that invites us into balance, which is steadiness within ourself in order to create enduring spiritual community with others. To be comfortable with the nature of life, which is change, we are asked to observe the natural world in which all seasons pass only to return again. All life is cyclical and always returning to rebirth and renewal. We're learning to feel whole and intimate with our Spirit so we can model new cooperative relationships in the world.	**Excretory System:** Eliminates the waste products resulting from cell activity and digestion. **Reproductive System:** Brings new life into existence.	*I live in ways that enhance love in the world, thus bringing harmony to all.*
	Intimacy & Community; activated through Balance			
1st	Lower part of the back, sacrum, and coccyx; also legs and feet	**Serve others with an open heart with whatever means we have at hand, and life's richness of experiences and opportunities will flow to and through us:** Abundance is the gene set that asks us to manifest prosperity, health, and well-being in order to have ample to share, and in return we need to receive the grace and gratitude that flows to us from others' hearts. We create movement in energy of abundance by staying connected to doing our best rather than focusing on outcomes. We leave the outcome to Spirit.	**Skeletal System:** Supports, protects, and helps the body move. **Membranes:** Protects organs and supplies lubrication for organs as they move over each other. **Tissues of the body:** Supports other tissues of the body. Creates boundaries between various body parts, allowing for movement and the transmission of impulses.	*I give joyful service to others as the greatest gift I can give myself.*
	Abundance; activated through Manifestation			

that Presence is within each of us and guiding our life. As we surrender our ego will, or our personality self, to our Divine will, or our true Self, we receive the gift of Grace. Through daily guidance we are better able to realize our fullest potential for life.

AFFIRMATION: I see Divine Guidance coming to me daily in many forms.

Joy & Inner Peace
5th Chakra

Joy & Inner Peace is activated through intention.

Pay attention that our words and actions reflect our true attitudes, beliefs, and feelings.

Joy & Inner Peace is the gene set that asks us to hold the intention of our authentic self and to use this energy as encouragement for us to speak the truth, aligning our words with our actions and thoughts. We are guided to find our authentic voice when we remain congruent — with our beliefs, feelings, thoughts, words, and actions in alignment. We strive to focus our intention and give our attention to those endeavors that foster love and compassion in the world. We listen within before speaking.

AFFIRMATION: I use words and actions that always help and never hurt.

Love & Compassion
4th Chakra

Love & Compassion is activated through passion.

Use our time to focus on the essential parts of our life that evoke a genuine passion for what and whom we love.

Love & Compassion is the gene set that asks us to experience love, kindness, compassion, and freedom from our woundedness. Every moment of every day involves the energy of our heart, since it is focused on bringing our love and compassion into the world. Our passion is born of compassion and enables us to nourish our body and our emotions

— to help us love our partner, family, and friends more fully — and to enable us to love those far away who also need our attention.

AFFIRMATION: I put my heart and passion for living into all that I do.

Inner Power & Presence

3rd Chakra

Inner Power & Presence is activated through trust.

Trust Spirit and then we'll be better able to trust our own abilities.

Inner Power & Presence is the gene set that asks us to trust that to be successful we must contribute our unique gifts and abilities to make a difference with our life. In order to develop our natural creativity so that we can contribute our best effort to the world, we learn to believe in our true Self, for it is here that we are filled with the empowerment and self-confidence to persevere where necessary and relax control where appropriate.

AFFIRMATION: I perform my work with integrity and excellence, knowing that new doors of opportunity will continually open to me.

Intimacy & Community

2nd Chakra

Intimacy & Community is activated through balance.

Stay centered in the Now rather than living in the past or the future.

Intimacy & Community is the gene set that invites us into balance, which is steadiness within ourself in order to create enduring spiritual community with others. To be comfortable with the nature of life, which is change, we are asked to observe the natural world in which all seasons pass only to return again. All life is cyclical and always returning to rebirth and renewal. We're learning to feel whole and intimate with our Spirit so we can model new cooperative relationships in the world.

AFFIRMATION: I live in ways that enhance love in the world, thus bringing harmony to all.

Abundance

1st Chakra

Abundance is activated through manifestation.

*Serve others with an open heart with whatever means we have
at hand, and life's richness of experiences and opportunities
will flow to and through us.*

Abundance is the gene set that asks us to manifest prosperity, health, and well-being in order to have ample to share, and in return we need to receive the grace and gratitude that flows to us from others' hearts. We create movement in the energy of abundance by staying connected to doing our best rather than focusing on outcomes. We leave the outcome to Spirit.

AFFIRMATION: I give joyful service to others as the greatest gift I can give myself.

❧ ATTITUDE SHIFTS ❧

1. When I live in alignment with my true Self, my spiritual DNA is activated, and I can find a wiser way to proceed on my healing journey.
2. Every moment, my choices either enhance love and energy or diminish them.
3. My spiritual gene sets correlate to my seven energy centers (my seven chakras):

   7 – Wisdom
   6 – Vision
   5 – Joy & Inner Peace
   4 – Love & Compassion
   3 – Inner Power & Presence
   2 – Intimacy & Community
   1 – Abundance

CHAPTER FOURTEEN

Recasting Our Relationships with Our Mother and Father

Something unexpected has been placed in my bowl.
There must be some spirit reason I'm being asked to do this.
I may not understand what that is right now,
but I will do my best to suspend judgment.

— Sue Bender

*A*s we consider the major influences on our health and happiness, one of the most volatile and important factors is our relationships with our mother and father. Our relationships with our parents have a significant and lasting impact on our well-being and thus our opportunity to heal and change successfully. Our feelings about our mother and father and the lingering impression they have made on our life can either enhance our positive choices and trust in ourself and others, or do the opposite. Thus, any remaining unfinished business with our parents — any frustration, pain, or shame — will continually send up clouds of confusion and mental pollution, which keeps us from aligning with our powerful spiritual gene sets. Instead we struggle to find our way and believe in ourself.

Both at a conscious and subconscious level, our first sense of our-self in relationship to the world comes through our contact with Mom and Dad. If we were raised by someone other than our biological parents, or if we have several mothers or fathers through remarriage, then we have a wider set of experiences to manage. Whether our relationship with our parents was positive or negative, fabulous or catastrophic, we are deeply influenced by them. Why? Because they represent the issues of *safety and authority* that we need to come to terms with in our own lifetime.

SAFETY IS LINKED TO MOTHER ENERGY

We are driven by both biological and spiritual forces. While we have a biological relationship with our mother, we also have a spiritual one. This spiritual relationship is predicated on the issues of safety. We have a deep need to create a safe harbor for ourself and others — whether we help the person being criticized at work, take special care with the distressed child in our elementary school classroom, or stop to pick up an injured owl to take to a wildlife rescue center.

Our mother is actually the conduit through which we are meant to learn about our inner safety. We are to learn about safety by feeling safe with her. We are meant to feel loved completely and unconditionally, to know that we are special and capable of a wonderful life because we have everything we need to be successful.

Of course, this being Earth School, and because we are all on our own learning path, no one really ever feels safe with one's physical mother, if only because we know she will eventually die and leave us. So we come up short in believing ourself to be safe, and yet we stay tethered to the idea that we will achieve safety if we can just get her to see our point of view, or if we can just let go of our rage or frustration with her, or whatever binds us. This "if only" keeps us tied to our physical mother or her memory.

We need to set ourself free. How? By recognizing that our need for safety is actually a spiritual need and one that only we can give to our-self. We are called to feel safe because we are part of the One, the Cre-ator. The only way we'll ever feel steady and safe, loved unconditionally, and completely capable is to reconfigure our needs from wanting our physical mother to love and be with us to accepting that our spiritual mother — meaning the mother aspect of our own Spirit — is already with us and waiting to be invited in.

Our inner mother or Divine mother energy never leaves us because she is the best of us. She will never hurt us because all she recognizes is love. She will never betray us because she sees our union and con-nection rather than separation.

We each are at different stages in our relationship with our divine mother inside. Some of us may already have experienced this more for-giving and fully living side of us. We may already be on our way to feel-ing safe within ourself. Difficulties often produce this meaningful result — we feel stronger within ourself.

Some of us may still be pretty much unaware of our inner spiritual mother. When this is true, we may find ourself expressing this anxiety in a number of ways: exhibiting excessive bravado or lack of courage in showing up, always needing to have an opinion or never wanting to share one, remaining perpetually angry and resistant to change, or falling into every possible shifting circumstance but never having any-thing to show for our efforts.

Safety is linked to realizing that we need personal permission to successfully slide among the three aspects of our personality: the child with emotional needs, the parent who keeps schedules and metes out discipline over rules and regulations, and the adult who is flexible, con-fident, and able to express her feelings and thoughts freely.

It is important in our healing to allow ourself to wear various emo-tional hats. Rather than only being the responsible adult, sometimes we need to be the carefree happy child; at other times we need to reel ourself back in as the parent to manage our responsibilities.

However, at times we can get locked into one role or another. When

this happens, we find ourself losing confidence and unable to understand what is wrong and how to set it right. When we fall into the role
of the child, we seem to create situations in which we are always being
acted upon by someone or some life circumstance. As the child, we feel
unable to alter our circumstances; we continually feel frustrated and
angry that we're locked into the way others want or need us to be. But
whenever it's appropriate to offer our ideas, needs, and follow-through,
we hold back or hesitate, creating a vacuum, and of course someone
else always steps in to fill that vacuum.

When we find ourself locked in the parent role, we become the true
self-critic. Nothing we do is ever good enough, and we find ourself
driven by invisible ghosts toward more and more accomplishment,
greater and greater success, while also feeling less and less steady or
trusting in ourself. The parent energy pushes us overboard in our need
to find safety. We believe we need to earn the right to feel safe, and yet
what we do never seems to be enough to inspire others to recognize
our need and save us.

SEEN AND UNSEEN THROUGH MOTHER'S EYES

In the extremes, we often feel that our mothers see us in one of two
unhealthy ways: either as fulfilling everything or as satisfying almost
nothing. The former was true for me. My mother and father never really found harmony together, and so her unmet love was showered on
me in what created a truly enabling relationship.

Growing up, I found it extremely difficult to find fault with someone who loved me more than herself and whose every wish was to do
something to be involved in my life. This kind of unhealthy love, however, as many of us know, creates a true double bind. We are loved but
in a stifling way, in which we are expected to become the parent, and
then the parent becomes the child. These crossed wires caused me
many years of anguish as I tried to find my own voice and not hurt her

in the process. I vacillated between the demanding parent and the emotional child within myself.

Healing for me has involved giving myself permission to be the child sometimes, loosening my feelings of constriction and control. At the same time, I allow myself to wobble off into being the parent, although that risks pushing too hard and expecting too much of myself and others. In time, I'm also finding the adult — who embraces both the child and the parent, realizing their positives attributes while being aware of how easily their unwanted aspects can take over the house.

There are other ways we might, as children, be given or take on a "parent role" in our family. We might do so by working and supporting our family when one or both parents cannot, or by keeping secrets about dysfunction or even abuse. We might become the go-between among our parents and our siblings; we are always in the middle, negotiating the peace.

The other familiar pattern is where we feel invisible. Rather than being the sun, moon, and all the stars rolled into one for a mother who loves us over the top, we feel we're not even a small sunbeam on the living-room carpet. We feel that our thoughts, needs, and attitudes are dismissed, and the things we've done right are never quite good enough. We become afraid to risk having opinions for fear of being shot down, and we grow up always looking over our shoulder for the person who is going to see through us and find out that we're an impostor.

Both of these scenarios can bring out the child, the parent, and the adult. Realizing that we can allow ourself to move freely through these various personality roles keeps us from getting locked into only one role.

AUTHORITY IS LINKED TO FATHER ENERGY

The idea of having power or inner power rests in our masculine mind or male side. Inside, we need to be in touch with our Divine Father energy as much as we are with the Divine Mother energy. Men and women alike need to balance these two aspects of themselves, the masculine and feminine.

Having authority actually arises from the core mother energy of safety. Perhaps this is because it is the mother who gives birth, and just as our mother energy holds the baby safe in our womb, so we are intended by Spirit to hold the child, and then the adult, safe in the world. As we grow up, we must internalize our sense of safety from our mother and allow it to grow in our own deep heart. This may be why those of us whose biological mothers couldn't manage safety for themselves tend to struggle with issues of safety *and* authority.

What does it mean to have authority, and to recognize the genuine authority of compassionate power? If our living father embodied genuine heart-centered authority, then we may know this instinctively, but if we have had no direct experience, then we may also struggle to believe in ourself and to know we can risk failing. True personal authority can often be measured by our willingness to risk failure in support of a meaningful goal.

This may sound like an improbable definition of or path to success. But actually it is in the risking, the trying and finding who we are beyond preconceived limitations — our own or others — that we allow ourself to garner the greatest meaning from our existence. We fly high and sometimes we crash, it's true. But playing it safe and never venturing far from what we know, never reaching for more than what we feel certain we can achieve, makes for a boring and unfulfilled life.

We yearn for adventure and challenge. We thrive on opportunities to advance a cause or further a mission. Each of us is a great ship built for the wide-open seas; we aren't meant to be tethered in the harbor for our entire life.

Risking suggests we're not in control all the time. So we can take risks only when we trust that we have inner authority. This sense of personal authority is something we carry with us all the time, just as a turtle always carries the protection of her shell. Our protection against feelings of inadequacy — from fear that we're not making progress in our job or in our spiritual aspirations — comes from being in touch with our inner authority.

Whenever a fear of failure overwhelms us, we can put our hands over our heart and find that connection to our inner authority, our Divine Masculine power — the power of our father as part of our Spirit. Then we will again be ready to pursue our destiny and to feel completely protected.

We alone can assign value and meaning to our world. We need to no longer give others the power to play God in our life. We do know best, and slowly we find that the best guidance is from our inner stillpoint, our Spirit.

WHEN FATHERS UNDERMINE OUR SENSE OF AUTHORITY

As we take stock of our own sense of inner authority, we can ponder our relationship with our own father and what we received. Did our father act in ways that helped us trust our unique gifts and our ability to be successful in the world, or did his actions undermine that sense in ourself?

Just as there are extremes in the ways that we were mothered, there are extremes in the way we were fathered. While some fathers disappear into their own needs and exhibit no authority, others can become authoritative disciplinarians and "over the top" in exhibiting the wrong sort of authority. Ultimately, our challenge is to find the inner quality of appropriate authority in ourself and realize that it is linked to our Spirit. The quality of the Divine Father within has always been part of our Spirit.

My growing up meant compensating for a father who lacked authority. While my father was a kind and dear man, he was so shadowed by his own inner demons that he stayed beyond everyone's emotional reach. As a result my quotient for risking was very small. I was always tempted to play it safe, never reaching beyond what I felt certain I could accomplish easily and successfully. But over the years, I've found that the praise of the world isn't the best barometer of success because much of what is applauded is passing in its appeal and is meant to appease our emotional addictions, rather than awaken us to our true spiritual mission of becoming whole and remaining awake.

Our Divine Father never fails to show up when we need self-confidence. Our Divine Father is always awake, present, and available for guiding and encouraging our dreams. Our Divine Father is our own Spirit making itself known through the experience of having authority and trusting that we can use it well. Our Spirit's voice, through the Divine Father energy, encourages us to live fully and be unafraid in the pursuit of our deep heart's desire.

ACTIVITY

Take Back Your Authority and Safety

This practice helps you take back your belief in your own safety and authority by differentiating between the power you've invested in your parents and the power you now invest in yourself through Spirit.

1. Take a piece of lined paper and draw a vertical line down the center. Over the right-hand column write the name of your mother (or the person who acted as your primary mother figure). Over the left-hand column write Divine Mother.

2. In the right-hand column write as many characteristics and attributes of your biological mother as you can think of.

3. Once you have listed all of them, draw a plus or minus sign next to each characteristic according to whether you determine it to be positive or negative (or not positive enough).

4. For those characteristics that you deem to be positive, simply rewrite them in the left-hand column under Divine

Mother. If it is a negative quality, then think of what the positive would be and write that in the Divine Mother column.

5. Now place your hands over your heart, and acknowledge that you now embody the spiritual quality of safety that lives in your deep heart. It no longer matters whether your biological mother gave you this quality; you have brought what you always needed into your own deep heart. It is now forever yours.

For example, my mother was enabling. I would write *enabling* in the right-hand column and then *unconditional love* in the left-hand column for how I want my Divine Mother to love me. Make special note that all the qualities of your Divine Mother in some way add up to safety — in other words, helping you feel safe to be completely yourself.

Now do the exact same exercise for your father, making two lists of attributes. All the qualities that you place under your Divine Father are meant to give you confidence in your own authority to hold your own in the world and to realize your dreams successfully in alignment with your true purpose.

❧ ATTITUDE SHIFTS ❧

1. My mother and father, whether my relationship was good or bad, represent my feelings and beliefs about the issues of safety and authority.
2. As a woman I have a spiritual need to create a safe harbor for myself and others.
3. My mother serves as a conduit for safety, even though I may struggle with this relationship, if only because she will eventually die and leave me.
4. I can understand that my need for safety is a spiritual need, and I have the ability to provide it for myself, without my mother.

5. True safety allows me to successfully navigate among the three aspects of my personality: the emotional child, the authoritative parent, and the mature and flexible adult.

6. Feeling unsafe keeps me locked in the authoritative parent role, the role my inner critic loves best.

7. My sense of inner authority, which comes from my father, is inexorably tied to my feeling of safety from my mother role model. Feeling safe is essential to making choices from inner authority.

8. When I feel safe in my inner authority, I can risk trying and failing over and over on my path to my true purpose.

9. When I have both my own inner safety and authority, I no longer give my power over to anyone else. I hold my own meaning and value.

CHAPTER FIFTEEN

Dealing with Anger

The word is not just a sound or a written symbol.
The word is a force; it is the power you have to express and communicate,
to think, and thereby to create the events in your life.
The word is the most powerful tool you have as a human; it is a tool of magic.

— Don Miguel Ruiz

*I*n solving relationship problems and sorting out our own thinking and attitudes, we inevitably come up against the best way to
face and deal with anger.

Our world suffers from a level of anger, fear, and frustration
that seems unprecedented in human history — not because it wasn't
present in past ages, but because it is now so commonplace and all-
pervasive. Today, frustrations and fears are often expressed through violence; our society thinks in violent terms, both obvious and subtle,
and attempts to solve problems with more violence. We experience violence daily, sometimes directly, and sometimes through the media:
absorbing the everyday violence in "entertainment," and hearing news
stories of government fraud, war, crimes against children and animals,

and attacks on the poor and defenseless. This behavior has reached epidemic proportions, and we can't help but be affected by it in our personal life and thoughts.

And yet, as women moving through cancer, heart disease, a broken marriage, kids in trouble, or financial worries, we also have our own experience with anger, frustration, and rage. We certainly don't believe that our anger gives us the right to pick up a gun and shoot someone — to express our anger by taking it out violently on others — yet our anger is similar in that we, too, believe our anger is completely justified, given our situation.

Our anger can express itself in many ways. Anger may feel like depression or being continually victimized by circumstances. Our anger may fly out in the sharp words we use to defend our attitudes and opinions — feelings based in our fears of what may come next, or our profound sense of isolation and separation from those we love and those who are healthy. We may react angrily to those who offer what seem to be trite and condescending suggestions about how we might heal or why we got sick in the first place.

As we recognize our own angry responses to the world and our own circumstances, we must ask, Is there a place for anger in our healing?

RECOGNIZING AND RESPONDING TO ANGER

The short answer to our question about anger is that spiritually, no, there is no place for anger in our deep heart. But emotionally — yes. Our anger can teach us much about ourself and even be a goad for tackling difficult tasks essential to our healing.

In other words, our healing path winds through our emotional reactions to life, and this process brings up our entire range of feelings. Also, while exploding over our frustrations does no good in the long term and actually depletes our energy in the short term, it may propel us through a difficult decision or circumstance.

Anger is something that most of us feel uncomfortable expressing, and yet getting cancer or suffering any other physical or emotional set-back may create a level of anger we have never experienced before. Anger is a powerful emotion that can be expressed openly in obvious ways and also in quiet and subtle ways, through what we think and the words we choose.

If we find ourself exploding with anger, at ourself or others, we need to become aware of what we are doing and why it is happening. We may recognize that our feelings may be short-lived, yet if the circumstances that led to the emotion don't change, we are likely to experience the same anger, over and over. We need to anticipate that we will have moments of overwhelming anger, and we must strategize ways to express and release that anger without pouring it on those who are in our life. We can ask a friend to just listen to us and not offer any suggestions; we can learn from inspiring books and mentors about new ways of dealing with major crises. We can put our hands over our heart and ask for guidance, healing, and direction. We can read about anger and the way to simply sit with it until it dissipates, as Thich Nhat Hanh, the well-known Cambodian monk, shares in his many books and teachings.

Although our bursts of anger are understandable, they can also create deep pain in those who are trying their best to help in their own way. Tell the people around you what you are feeling; let them know you are aware that your buttons are getting pressed a lot of the time. Reassure them that your anger doesn't mean you no longer love them, but it's an expression of the struggle you're facing.

I learned a great deal about the effect of anger on caring loved ones during a talk with a group of breast cancer survivors and their spouses. After my talk, one of the husbands came up to me and asked me if he could share something with me. Of course, I said. He said, "My wife had breast cancer twice, and I tried to be there for her in every way possible. But nothing was or is good enough — everything is always about her. I retired thinking that I would have some wonderful time to explore what I love, but that isn't what has happened. I've developed heart trouble, and I'm quite sure I'll die before her simply from a broken heart."

Simply being aware of what we need as well as the feelings and needs of those who are close to us, and acknowledging both, goes a long way. It helps our entire extended family and community of friends to understand our needs and that our anger is a result of the stress we feel as we identify what hurts and find our path into healing.

Ultimately, as we look around and see the people we love, and become more aware of who we really are — which is more than the diagnosis of breast cancer and more than this physical body — we can sometimes find a sliver of wisdom that allows us to respond genuinely in ways that are no longer filled with anger, whether at another person, at life, or at ourself. Life is life, and growth, which means healing, is always a possibility.

There is no single answer for when anger is appropriate for our healing and our life — but the more aware we become of our desired way of walking in the world, the easier it is to define that for ourself.

CARING FOR OUR DEEP HEART

It's helpful to realize that all human beings have strong emotional reactions to everyday life — the difference is that we want to handle these frustrations in ways that do no harm, to others or our own deep heart.

Figuring out how to handle frustration is a process that begins with caring for ourself so that others can also care for us. As we realize this in our life, others may learn from our example how to care for themselves in healthier ways, and thus awareness is enhanced, love grows, and anger and violence decrease. This isn't an easy, fast, or obvious path to reducing violent tendencies within ourself or our culture. But it's worthwhile to take the long view: when we learn how to care for and heal ourself, we do more than heal a single person — we spread healing to the world at large. This is particularly important when it comes to dealing with and transforming anger.

ASK YOURSELF

What fuels my anger today?
How have I handled my anger in the past?
What was the fallout from the way I handled or expressed my anger in the past?
How am I handling my anger today?
What is the fallout or reaction today when I'm angry?

We can continue to use what we learn with the people in our life. We can watch our reactions, and rather than getting angry — again — we can find another way as we place our hand over our heart. We will continue to find new ways to express our fear, anxiety, worry, concern, upset, and frustration so it doesn't get lumped into an angry outburst or simmer angrily inside us for years. As we find the words we need to say to the people we need to say them to, we enter a new stage of dynamic and meaningful interactive relationship, one that teaches others new ways of coping with their anger. And even if we can't say the words in person, in our deep heart we can say them to the other, and from that deep heart place, they can receive it.

❦ ATTITUDE SHIFTS ❦

1. I must look at and take responsibility for the role anger plays in my healing journey.
2. Anger may have a short-term role in helping me handle parts of this journey that are difficult, but in the long term it is harmful.
3. Unloading my anger on myself or those around me is not the way to handle my feelings. I can learn how to manage my anger by understanding its source as fear.

CHAPTER SIXTEEN

The Power of Being a Woman

Go ahead, be brave, say it anyway: "I am a writer."
Over time, the image in your mind and the reality will become one,
if you continue to practice.

— Natalie Goldberg

When we look back at how we felt just before being diagnosed with a disease or an imbalance, we often recognize that we weren't quite up to snuff; something was pulling us down. We may remember not feeling quite right, feeling unduly preoccupied, or feeling overwhelmed from trying to meet too many people's needs. After the fact of illness or when we recognize our genuine unhappiness with our life, women sometimes tell me that they now realize they had been numbed out, operating on autopilot, and were out of touch with their own honest feelings. We are complex beings with many doorways; some lead us into imbalance and some out of it. What we need to remember is the connection between our own emotions and the impact they have on our physical body.

We also often fail to recognize that seemingly unrelated worsening physical conditions indicate the body's misalignment energetically. What begin as upsetting and annoying symptoms need to be taken seriously because each represents a change in the energy flows within us. When these misalignments are identified and understood early on, they tend to clear up more quickly.

Sometimes worsening physical symptoms, however, represent significant energy shifts that are meant to be healing and spiritually enlightening. For the most part we aren't aware of these necessary energy shifts — into womanhood, and into full womanhood — until we look into what isn't working right in our body or our life. Rather than the worsening of physical symptoms representing only bodily breakdown, it can also mean breakthrough, the opportunity for change and deep healing emotionally and spiritually.

One of the major energy shifts that is natural and essential for all women — but can feel anything but — is the movement into menopause, with all its accompanying physical changes.

Let's explore the movement from being biologically at our peak and able to conceive children to the journey toward and into menopause, which has a decidedly different calling. Also, we may have prematurely come to menopause as a result of our treatment for cancer, which makes this discussion doubly important.

MENSTRUATION — A CALL TO A DIFFERENT KIND OF UNION

There is nothing so wonderful for a young girl as having the first signs of her very first period. It truly marks the beginning of her childbearing years and her full biological maturity. The capacity to conceive a child and birth it into the world is like no other. I will also say, however, that the process of having a child, while wonderful, isn't essential to being a mother. Being a mother is what we do after the baby is born.

As I have adopted a daughter and also conceived a son the home-grown way, I know for certain that love springs forth when you hold a child in your arms; it really doesn't matter how the child got there. All the same hormones are released when you love a child as when you give birth to one, and with a little patience, our body cooperates even to allowing us to nurse an adopted baby. The body is amazing in its response to loving.

But along with the joy and delight of having wanted children, we find that menstruation can also become a challenge for many girls and women. Many women have PMS, or premenstrual syndrome, which is a group of symptoms linked to a woman's menstrual cycle. Symptoms usually occur a week or two before the onset of menses and go away after blood begins to flow. Symptoms can include a range of things: acne, breast swelling and tenderness, feeling tired, having trouble sleeping, upset stomach, bloating, constipation or diarrhea, headache or backache, appetite changes or food cravings, joint or muscle pain, trouble concentrating or remembering, tension, irritability, mood swings or crying spells, and anxiety or depression. What a list for a natural process. What has happened that we have all these symptoms for a normal way of replenishing our uterus to receive potentially fertilized eggs?

To understand PMS we need to first explore menstruation and what it really means. In ancient times it was noticed that a woman's monthly flow was the only time (along with childbirth) that blood was shed without wounding, and thus it was regarded as special. The word *ritual* actually comes from *rtu*, which is Sanskrit for "menses," and the blood from the womb, which nourished the unborn child, was believed to have mana or the breath of life.

The word *menstruation* comes from the Greek *menus*, meaning both "moon" and "power," and *men*, meaning "month." And so a woman's *moontime* was seen as her most creative and spiritually attuned time of the entire month.

At her time of the month, it was believed that she had the power to do what perhaps wasn't open to her at other times. She had the inclination and the ability to listen deeply inside and ask for guidance for herself and her clan. It was honored as a time of renewal and replenishment both for her and for the community.

Each month as blood flows, a woman creates new life — if not in the creation of a new child, then certainly within her own life and in harmony with Mother Earth.

THE RISE OF PMS

Speaking strictly physically, the symptoms of PMS occur as a result of the precipitous drop in the hormones estrogen and progesterone after ovulation because no fertilization took place in the uterus. PMS ceases when we stop menstruating, at menopause. Not all women experience a problem, but certainly some do, even severely. Hormones are simply chemical messengers: they first alert our uterus that a baby may be coming and then abruptly say, *Oh sorry — no deal — go back to the way you were.*

At an energy level, this feels like being invited to a union that never takes place. This necessary union doesn't mean we were supposed to get pregnant, as in the union at the physical level between the sperm and the ovum to make a fetus. It does mean that what could have included union with the spirit of a new child now needs to be acknowledged as union with our own spiritual nature.

Our union at our special time of the month — *moontime* — is between our mind and our heart to create a more complete and whole sense of ourself. Each menstrual cycle we are asked to deepen our understanding of the woman we are spiritually and what we are doing with our life. We are asked to grow our inner knowing and expand our guidance, just as we perceive the moon growing from sliver to fullness. As we enter moontime, we awaken our spiritual gene set of the second chakra, which is Intimacy & Community. We wake up our deeper listening and valuing of all life, and we become a useful and powerful instrument for positive change. We are no longer afraid of or timid about showing up for the life we believe is essential for all beings and creatures.

PMS results from a deficit of spiritual energy, which results, in this case, from a lack of attention to our moontime, or union with Spirit. Menstruating is a profound and mystical aspect of being a woman — it isn't just another bodily function.

We resist time apart from our everyday activities as much from habit as anything else. It is easier to be thinking all the time than to be silent for even a short period. It also isn't easy to remove ourself from the normal fray of life. And so our ways of observing moontime have to change.

Our roles of breadwinner, partner, parent, and child of aging parents pretty much fill our life, but we now realize that we've been neglecting a critical component — namely, going within. Instead, we can make time for ourself, at least in small doses; our family will understand because they want and need us to be around and to be happy and healthy. While we can't separate from our partners at our moontime and move into a special lodge as Native American women did, for example, we *can* take some extra time for ourself.

Here's a novel thought: At our moontime, we can ask our partner to pick up some of the house chores, giving us a little extra time for ourself. In this way our partner gets to express his or her own creative way of being with the children or managing home affairs, which benefits everyone. Picking up some of the chores for a few days can be a special way of strengthening a partnership for both people.

MENOPAUSE AND BEYOND

Moving into menopause and our full womanhood is a time to honor all children and our Mother Earth, which is home to all. As menstruating women, we create union both physically, through getting pregnant, and spiritually, by using our moontime for spiritual replenishment and guidance. As we move into menopause, we come to understand that we are no longer responsible for just ourself and our personal children but rather for the world's children and the resources of Mother Earth.

Unfortunately, menopause is usually acknowledged only as one more sign of our physical aging, and so as women we're ashamed of it. Our fanatical desire to look and act unnaturally young suggests we don't value the life we've already lived or the wisdom we've collected.

We can say that we have to look young in order to keep our jobs and our partners loyal. But I might ask all of us — myself included — where, then, does change come from in viewing women's lives and contributions? Who originates the change that regards a woman's life as precious and beautiful precisely because she grows in wisdom as she grows in years? The first step is to believe we are growing in wisdom and a more lasting kind of beauty because we are practicing inward time during our moontime, whether or not we're actively menstruating.

While it's true that after our mensus ceases, we are no longer bleeding, our cycle nonetheless continues physically and energetically. We have our moontime as mood swings and changes in our physical body alert us that we are moving toward our special time of the month — our intuitive and inner power time of the month. Our cycling into truer acceptance of ourself even though we're not actually menstruating is like a person who has a leg amputated but still feels the phantom pain. In our case, we feel the phantom flow, and rather than pain, we feel the light.

This phantom flow as light is meant to carry us through the physical changes into our real work, which is to participate more fully in ways that fit our inner yearnings and desires to make the world a better place. We have become the guardians of the world's children, natural resources, and spiritual light. We are being called to answer a different vision, one that includes more than our immediate biological family — either the one we grew up in or the one that we gave birth to. Our mission has changed from bringing a few lives successfully into the world to bringing many lives into their spiritual destinies — the fullness of their awakened spiritual knowing. By participating in our life as if we mattered, we begin to see that others also matter — even those people we don't like very much or are afraid of.

During this time in our life, we may feel like we're hitting speed bumps the size of boulders, whereas before we raced down the road. As we move toward menopause, we may find that we no longer are close to the same friends. We may find that our partnership moves to more understanding and lasting love — or to the opposite. Even our careers may shift as we release ourself to do the work of our heart.

In this stage of becoming our fullest expression of womanhood, we continue to live our ordinary life even as we develop our own personal vision — to stand free of past intimidation and fear, either that we have nothing to say or that no one will listen. We begin to realize and perhaps verbalize a sincere desire to serve the world — by serving those near us or by traveling to other countries to assist in different ways.

It is only as we enter the cycle of moontime, spreading our inner light by honoring our times of union with Spirit, that we engage what can become our spiritually active path.

ACTING ON WISDOM

While we are menstruating, we are waking up the power of our moon-time. And as we move into the flow of light (rather than of blood alone), we know we must act on this wisdom.

A recent conversation with a client, Johanna, showed me the power of this inner shift when our moontime serves to push us into action to manifest our path of loving service.

In her fifties, Johanna has had a long history of physical problems, from stroke to debilitating back problems and surgeries. The list of her physical ailments is so extensive that it would be tempting to imagine she would long ago have thrown in the towel. But not so — she remains emotionally loving and available. She recently told me that she announced to her husband and son that after the beginning of the new year she was going to learn sign language — a long-held dream — because she knew that in some way she was meant to use this to help others.

The intensity of her knowing and the passion for opening a new door into service revealed the passion she was sensing from her own moontime awakening. There is a time in our affairs when we are ready, willing, and able to spread light in the world. And the power of this inner awakening is what makes for healing at all levels. *Our heart must be happy for our mind to be at peace.*

ASK YOURSELF

What can I do to give myself a little time at my moontime, whether I'm actually having a physical period?

What dream, vision, or passion is making its way to the surface, which I recognize as guidance?

What women do I admire who are showing me that it is safe and essential for me to find my own path of action — of loving service?

What special music, books, paints, or other creative materials will I bring with me into my moontime?

As we consider our health and the ways that we are now more aware of the power and preciousness of our womanhood, we'll find our feelings about our illnesses and monthly struggles changing. Our softer words regarding our body and spirit will open us to greater creativity, which will show up in many ways throughout our various endeavors.

Slowly we can fold into our deep heart our knowing of our true power as a woman. And perhaps we can also heal our heart at the core level — the level where we have all felt the pain of a world in which full spiritual womanhood has not yet been recognized. But — here we are and times are changing.

❦ ATTITUDE SHIFTS ❦

1. I must take the time to connect my emotions with the impact they have on my physical body, so I can sense my energetic misalignments and deal with them.
2. Sometimes there is a gift in physical misalignments: breakdown can sometimes be breakthrough.
3. Being a woman puts me in a unique and powerful biological position as I move through my life. Each stage has beauty and potential.
4. My menstruation is a profound and mystical aspect of my womanhood. It is more than just a biological function; its rhythm provides me with a deep and creative connection with Divinity and my own spirit.
5. Menopause allows me to shift from my ability to bear and care for children to understanding that I have a responsibility to all children and Mother Earth as well.
6. Even when my physical bleedings stops, energetically I am still on the same cycle, and that energy propels me to use my gifts in the broader world.
7. Menopause energetically calls me to stand fully in my own power and contribution. This is another time that I must stand in the center of my own life.

CHAPTER SEVENTEEN

The Power of Being
an Everyday Mystic

I give thanks that I now receive the righteous desires of my heart.
Mountains are removed, valleys exalted and every crooked place made straight.
I am in the Kingdom of Fulfillment.

— Florence Scovel Shinn

As we consider our life as a woman, we come inevitably to the idea that we are being called to take our everyday spiritual yearnings more seriously. I call this being an "everyday mystic."

Being an everyday mystic suggests that we each have a genuine relationship with Spirit, one that has nothing to do with any established religion or any formalized spiritual role. We are born knowing about God or Divine Intelligence because we come from the spiritual realm and will return to it after this life. Our journey while in physical form is to become an authentic human being. Being an authentic human being means that we understand what we perceive and know intuitively, yet also realize that the greatest of mysteries are known in a language that is somewhere between poetry and parable.

The *knowing* that guides us toward Spirit isn't available for intellectual study. Rather our intellect is the property of that which gave us
life, and it is this Source of Love that continues to express love through
the creative potential we call life.

This puts us in a bit of a bind, since we love our thinking processes.
If our thinking about God and Spirit can't take us to an absolute level
of understanding, then how can we expand our mystical leanings into
a working understanding and a useful vocabulary? We can begin by
considering our progress as authentic human beings.

BECOMING AN AUTHENTIC HUMAN BEING

What does becoming an "authentic human being" mean? We can ask ourself: Are we generally compassionate and aware of what is going on
around us? Are we appreciative of life in all its myriad forms, from the
smile on a child's face to the bugs that eat our flowers? Do we engage in
activities that support and sustain life, whether they involve people, creatures, nature, or just maintaining ourself in a good way? Our answers are
significant and may well give us pause. What I'm suggesting is that being
an authentic human being has to do with ordinary life and extraordinary
perceptions. The degree to which we can value and appreciate the gifts of
life is the degree to which we are an authentic human being.

Are we someone who wants to understand the spiritual energy at
play in our life? Are we concerned more with what we can't see than
with what we can see? Are we aware of the presence and loving power
of what we can't clearly grasp, but which we trust is available to us in
ordinary and extraordinary ways? In other words, are we in the world
but realize that we're only visiting and that our real home is where the
stars meet the infinite spheres of light and music?

Do we need to move to an ashram to be spiritual and have mystical leanings, or can we live a good and happy life in the everyday world?
Oh, that we were lucky enough to move to an ashram and focus only
on our spiritual life. Unfortunately, or fortunately, we are called today,

as everyday mystics, to live in the world — and that is so much more difficult. The people we know who are peaceful and happy and who seem *present* are those with mystical leanings, and that is what calls to us. We choose to be near people who know Spirit in their own ways and seek to mirror that knowing to us so that we, too, may know.

Every day, people with mystical leanings live their lives realizing that how they live is their message, and it doesn't matter who recognizes it or honors it as long as they do. We sense in those with well-developed mystical leanings a knowing that is unpretentious but genuine. Perhaps this is how the Creator intended for us to learn — by example, following the lead of those who are a step or two ahead of us as well as those who are light-years away. Still, we know we are on the path.

EACH OF US CAN CONNECT TO SPIRIT

In our healing journey through change, illness or despondency, it is important to realize that we each are completely and naturally connected to Spirit. Our recognition of this fact and our desire to further develop this relationship is what constitutes the depth and quality of our spiritual inquiry. Because spiritual energy is the power of love manifested in our body, which is what we ultimately call on for our healing, it behooves us to put our hands over our heart and wonder about our mystical nature and the way we are irrevocably linked to Divinity.

Miriam of Magdala — Mary Magdalene — described Jesus the Christ in *The Gospel of Mary Magdalene* as saying, "Those who have ears, let them hear."

ASK YOURSELF

Do I have inner ears to hear the quiet whispers of Spirit?
   In what ways am I an everyday mystic, and what would it mean if I realized that I truly am an awakened woman who is on the spiritual path?

Who might I tell?
What is my reaction?

Recognizing ourself as an everyday mystic may feel like a leap, and perhaps the title sounds too grand or too spiritual. But what if we truly are an everyday mystic? What if we hold this knowing in our heart and try it on for size, basking in the possibility that our loving heart is the only requirement we really need to qualify? No one can see — why not believe?

It is easier to fall into blaming others for what is wrong than to seek to right those wrongs, so to begin, we can resist the urge, or the encouragement of others, to blame our discomfort on the world around us: on the global crisis, the inadequate education of our children, the unfairness with which we're treated at work, the lack of responsibility in our government. As an everyday mystic we are guided to face our own and humanity's quintessential fear — which is feeling separate from a God of Love.

On the one hand, we all experience fear, terror, animosity, anxiety, and a need for retaliation, while on the other, we can lay claim to an inner certainty about the beauty and the meaning of life. At times, the challenges of our life seem to close us down, and at other times, our joy and understanding seem boundless. When these two opposing energies come together, we often find inner doorways that open to new understandings. We discover a merging of two paths that have previously been separated by our uncertainty. We may have often felt like one of the early Christians wandering through the underground catacombs and asking, *Who has a light, and why aren't they shining it where I can find my way?*

BECOMING AN EVERYDAY MYSTIC

God considers us in a mystical way whenever we put Love at the top of our list. I certainly wouldn't have thought of myself as an everyday mystic until I had one of those mind-shifting and heart-opening experiences that, symbolically, told me that loving was indeed enough.

It was early morning, and I was sitting in bed struggling with my purpose. Oh, I knew what the work was, or seemed to be — but what was my soul's purpose? Was I doing what God had intended? I felt uncertain.

Old fears had crept in over the previous months as I found myself losing interest in teaching workshops, and I wondered what Spirit had in mind next. Was there more? I found a personal inner truth that seemed impassable — I didn't want to continually create materials, using here-today and gone-tomorrow concepts, that were just sugarcoating around the real thing. I wanted to teach what had lasting meaning — *that love is all there is.*

As I poured my heart out to God, a book I had been reading on Sai Baba fell off the back of the headboard and landed squarely in my lap. There on the cover was a picture of Sai Baba. He wore an orange robe and his extraordinary head of hair looked like a giant Afro. But his eyes, they completely captured me.

I decided that Sai Baba was the one to ask, and so I sobbed my way through an explanation of my troubled heart. The second I finished my extended prayer, the telephone rang. At first I wasn't going to pick it up because I was having this important conversation with God, and I didn't want to be interrupted with a mundane phone call. But fearing that one of the children perhaps needed help, I reluctantly padded over to the bedroom phone and picked it up.

It was my mother, who lives in the next town. She told me in a rather hushed tone that she had been sitting in her favorite chair rather quietly when suddenly she heard inside that she was to call me and tell me, "God knows — God knows." She asked, "Does that mean anything to you?"

My mother is not normally given to such thoughts, and at first I couldn't even respond to her — I couldn't comprehend such a connection, either its immediacy or that it was connecting to God.

But slowly I did realize that Sai Baba was in fact acknowledging my heartfelt plea. I hung up and leaned back in the chair. As my eyes traveled up the wall toward the ceiling, there on the white wall was the perfect image of a human figure. It was lit with gold. In the center of the chest, in the area of the deep heart, a brilliant fuchsia light radiated out. The image was a good size and stayed for what seemed a long time.

Eventually the image faded, and still I sat there. I heard the message in my own heart — *Yes, it is enough to love, for love is all there is.*

Indeed, we are all everyday mystics, whether or not we have obvious experiences that confirm that our loving matters. Perhaps, if reading this scenario touches your heart, then you have your own answer about who you are.

ACTIVITY

Open and Close the Day with a Prayer of Blessing

 The beginning and ending of each day holds a special energy. When you first open your eyes in the morning, you benefit from putting your hands over your heart and setting the intention to open to the blessings of the day. An equally important time is at night, when you've turned off the light; you again place your hands over your heart and receive in gratitude the blessings that came to you that day.

1. With your first conscious thought, place one or both hands over your heart center and express the thought that you are opening to the blessings of the day.

2. As you prepare to go to sleep, place one or both hands over your heart center and call to memory the blessings of the day. Any experience that makes you smile qualifies. As you ask to recall these special simple blessings, pay attention to those that come easily and reexperience them in greater detail. Remember, this is a time for acknowledging only the positive, simple blessings that feed your body, mind, and soul.

These times of reaching out to receive blessings, and acknowledging in gratitude the experiences that have fed you, allow you to move along through your day in grace like riding a gentle wave. Although there are storms aboveground in the form of everyday struggles and challenges, in the grounding of your being, you receive the goodness that is registered in your heart, thereby reducing mood swings and decreasing stress levels.

As you remember to use this practice, your energy relaxes and flows more easily, and many daily experiences that usually go unnoticed become suddenly visible. These simple blessings sound a bell of happiness in your deep heart, making it easier to find things that please you rather than displease you. These are events like the baby throwing her spoon on the floor and then smiling that special smile, so that you don't mind picking it up for the millionth time; your friend's six-week-old golden retriever puppy nuzzling your hand when you stopped for a quick cup of coffee; or the few moments lingering in the sunshine before walking back into your office.

It's difficult not to smile at these simple blessings, which are gifts intended for those who walk through life with their lights on — those who are awake and aware emotionally and spiritually.

Yet the smiles, well-wishes, and unexpected goodness that come to you are often overlooked in the search for the "big events" that you believe will turn the course of your life in more positive directions. Actually it is the repeated acknowledgment of the simple blessings that turn the tide in your healing and in the quality of happiness you experience.

As you wake up to the process of opening your heart and you go to sleep reaping the benefits of having opened your heart — you might ask yourself, *How am I more sustained by this practice? Will it really make a difference?* Of course, it will. You are the heir to the grace and happiness that you never realized you could collect.

Imagine what can change in your life as you focus on and receive the simple blessings that your life overflows with.

🪷 ATTITUDE SHIFTS 🪷

1. I can create a workable vocabulary for my mystical connection to Divinity.
2. Growing into an authentic human being means living an ordinary life with extraordinary perceptions.
3. My life is my message, and it's enough that I recognize its value.
4. As I travel my healing journey, I am assured that I am constantly and irrevocably connected to Divinity.
5. My loving heart is the only requirement to meet Spirit.
6. I can receive the Grace of my connection to Divinity in small consistent ways if I open the day with the intention to receive all its blessings and close the day with gratitude.

PART FOUR

A Conversation about New Beginnings

Those who wish to change things may face disappointment, loss, or even ridicule. If you are ahead of your time, people laugh as often as they applaud, and being there first is usually lonely. But our protection cannot come between us and our purpose. Right protection is something within us rather than something between us and the world, more about finding a place of refuge and strength than finding a hiding place.

— Rachel Naomi Remen, MD

CHAPTER EIGHTEEN

Our Reproductive System and Its Subtle Energy Wisdom

To find real emotional security, we have to
develop our inner lives to the fullest, not in a narrow, self-indulgent way,
but in the sense of developing faith in the sustaining value
of our own experiences.

— Nancy Lonsdorf, MD, Veronica Butler, MD,
and Melanie Brown, PhD

*W*hen we become aware of a need for closure, healing, and reconnection — whether with a friend, our partner, our work, our body, or God — we enter a learning time. I like to think of this time, which can be a moment or years, as filled with teachable moments. A teachable moment is one in which we discover something we've not known before. A teachable moment comes when we become available to new influences, information, greater inspiration, or direct healing from Divine Love.

As we enter into a discussion on our reproductive system — the energetic flows and wisdom that support our ovaries, uterus, vagina, and breasts — we need to think in terms of subtle energy. Subtle energy refers to the energy movement within us that we cannot see with our physical eyes but that we appreciate because we experience the results. We see and sense health and the lack of health, for example. We know when our head or heart aches and when we feel clear and aligned with our true Self. Subtle energy is the essential architecture that supports our physical organs and systems.

In order to sense what is happening at a subtle energy level, we need to stop physical activity, get quiet emotionally and mentally, relax our need to find an immediate solution or outcome, and just sit with ourself. In this way our intuition deepens to *intuitive perception,* or the ability to perceive what lives at the subtle energy level rather than only at the physically manifested level. For example, we might feel deeply tired, and after getting quiet for a little, we recognize our need for an hour without interruption. And so we clear our schedule for that hour.

When we sit quietly and without our normal agitation, even if we still have lots of disruptive thoughts going on, the immense power of our intuition and its next, more refined level — intuitive perception — can guide us toward the rebalancing agents we need. These are teach-

able moments, when we're open to a different way of approaching our illness or difficulties. This all happens at the subtle energy level.

Having plenty of physical energy is not to be confused with the movement of subtle energy. We can easily override our awareness of subtle energy imbalances with bursts of energy or adrenaline, which keep us moving in our single-minded focus on our goals and the outcomes of our efforts. When we are physically busy, we have our eye on what we want to happen tomorrow and how we will get there, rather than on the process we're in right now and how we feel about what is going on in the moment.

THE THREE LEVELS OF HEALING

To understand the flows of energy that support our health, we need to be aware of the three levels of healing: physical, emotional, and spiritual. Physical healing comes from our lifelong commitment to well-being and our awareness of all the body's processes and our lifestyle and activities. We heal emotionally by changing the ways we react to others and ourself: when we change our perspectives, we shift our attitudes and beliefs, which in turn affects our behaviors. In other words, our actions align with our refreshed way of perceiving the world around us. We heal spiritually by finding our place within the Great Mystery — or God — within us. This can be as simple as a prayer, a smile, or an alignment with what is good and lasting — that is, Love.

Every organ and system in our body interacts in a complex and mysterious way. True healing must take place on all levels — on the level of the physical function of the organs and on the levels of the energetic functions of mind and spirit. When we interrupt one natural flow of energy, another is often able to compensate, keeping us from realizing the degree of imbalance that may actually be present. Eventually, as we age, the natural flows have more to contend with, and so more care is required.

These three sets of subtle energies are distinct to the degree that we can sense them individually, but they are not separate when it comes to our health. Imagine walking into a grocery store and picking up a head of broccoli, a gallon of milk, a box of dried noodles, and a package of shrimp. These are separate items, but once we combine them to make a casserole, their energies merge into a single dish. You can still distinguish the broccoli from the shrimp, but they have come together. Further, the freshness and health of each item is essential to the quality of the casserole. When the individual energy flows of our body are likewise compromised, the total state of our health is jeopardized.

When we have a diagnosis of any of the reproductive cancers (breast, ovarian, uterine, or vaginal), or any other major imbalance, we benefit from taking a much closer look at the flows of energy that directly affect our reproductive system and what we can do to restore balance and health. Our entire reproductive system is most generally concerned with helping us build on our past. It holds the energy of the teacher, the builder, the creator, the pioneer, and the healer. In this chapter, we will look at the individual energy flows that are aligned with each organ in the reproductive system, but overall, issues with our reproductive system ask us to rethink and reframe our past in order to generate a powerful future and to be in touch with and live from that passion right now.

WHAT OUR FEMALE ORGANS DO PHYSICALLY AND ENERGETICALLY

Let's consider the energy flows that feed our female reproductive system in order to better care for ourself. Realize that just because we've had a mastectomy or a hysterectomy, or for that matter any surgery, the body energetically still perceives all the original organs in place in a healthy way. This means that our body holds a perfect representation of our most perfect and whole self. It is this most perfect representation that helps us return to health as we eliminate all the emotional confusion and negative thoughts that block this message of health from reaching our actual physical tissues.

We can better understand the needs of various organs if we reflect first on their physical function. What an organ does tells us energetically what its wisdom message is for us. For example, our ovaries hold and release ova, which when fertilized develop into the fetus held in our uterus. So, from an energetic point of view, our ovaries hold our dreams and the hopes and desires of what we can eventually give life to.

 As we read the descriptions below, consider the emotional needs our body is expressing when it is in balance and out of balance.

A Woman's Cycle

The female reproductive organs lie protected within the pelvic cavity, which can expand to accommodate a growing fetus. At birth, the ovaries harbor their lifetime complement of some six hundred thousand immature eggs. By puberty, many of these have disappeared; before menopause, about four hundred will develop into mature ova. Typically, one or two mature during a menstrual cycle.

Each month during a woman's reproductive years, an ovary is stimulated to mature a follicle, which then discharges a mature egg. The egg enters the fallopian tube, where, if circumstances are right, fertilization takes place. Within twenty-four to thirty hours, the merged cell divides, and over the next four days, it continues to divide as it travels to the uterus. In six to seven days, the embryo implants itself in the uterus lining, the endometrium, and continues to divide and grow.

The Ovaries

Each ovary is one of a pair of female gonads found on each side of the lower abdomen, beside the uterus. At ovulation, an egg is extruded from a follicle on the surface of the ovary under the stimulation of certain hormones.

Subtle Energy Wisdom of the Ovaries

Ovaries act as the holder of our dreams, aspirations, and passions for our life and those we love.

The Uterus

The uterus, or womb, is a pear-size female reproductive organ that nourishes the fetus until birth. The uterus is a hollow, thick-walled organ about the size of a fist. It is composed of the uterine body and the cervix. The muscular wall of the uterus is called the myometrium, and the inner lining is the endometrium. The fallopian tubes serve to deliver the ova to the uterus.

Subtle Energy Wisdom of the Uterus

Just as the uterus holds a growing baby, it holds the space or helps hold us in an appropriately supportive environment so that our dreams can develop and our passion can be nourished.

The Vagina

The vagina is located directly below the urethral opening and is often referred to as the birth canal. It is an elastic muscular tube connecting the cervix of the uterus with the outside world. It serves as the receptacle for the penis during sexual intercourse.

Subtle Energy Wisdom of the Vagina

The vagina reflects our emotional stability and the self-belief in our dreams that allows us to successfully deliver them into the world.

The Breasts

A woman has two breasts that are configured to produce milk to feed a child. For the most part, a woman's breasts consist of fat and connective tissue. There are also other less conspicuous parts, such as lobes, bulbs, arteries, and lymph nodes.

Subtle Energy Wisdom of the Breasts

The breasts provide the continued feeding and support of our dreams and passions. They allow us to follow our dreams and our passion to find the ways to make our unique contributions count.

Our Subtle Energy Wisdom

These subtle energy wisdom statements help us understand how our body thinks, which in turn allows us to stay healthy and to better facilitate our healing. It is important to restate here that no one consciously tries to get sick. Yet things happen and we do get sick, as well as just sick and tired and in need of rejuvenating and rebalancing.

If we're healing from a disease, it isn't enough for us to stay current on the latest scientific information on medications. We have to pay equal attention to the significant but less obvious impact of our emotions and our spirit. Our subtle energy flows are altered over the course of everyday living. As we pay attention to our thoughts, beliefs, actions, and lifestyle, we gradually bring about different and more harmonious flows of energy in our body.

Body, mind, and spirit healing involves working with the body's natural wisdom to facilitate positive change. We need to support this natural wisdom rather than interfere with it or unknowingly block it. We are partners with our body. Our body brings its own predispositions for how well it functions, and we bring our mental and emotional abilities to positively support our body's efforts. Both sides need to be strong. And our lifestyle needs to support what our mind tells us is important for our health.

Let's explore how our physical system actually embodies these subtle energy wisdom statements, and let's begin by appreciating what our dreams and passions really are.

OUR PASSION AND OUR DREAMS

Our destiny in some very real sense originates and is recognized through the energy flow that moves from ovary to uterus to vagina and then to and through our breasts. Our dreams are really our passion for doing what we love most. We often have an inner picture or sense of what we want to become when we grow up. This passion begins as a dream, not a business plan. A young girl, for example, may tell her mom that she wants to be a famous dancer and to dance all over the world to make people happy. She may not, in fact, decide to become a dancer as an adult, but the young girl describes her dream in the vocabulary and life experiences that she has available to her, and it holds the seeds of her real passion. As she grows, the shape and expression of her dreams may change, but they will continue to hold and grow the same abiding passion, which she and others need to take seriously.

Strangely enough, all of the various ways we express our passion turn out to be similar, to have something in common. We know what we love — we just get talked out of it or convinced that we are unable to bring it about. But we usually keep checking inside to see if "now"

is the time we can do something with this great idea that keeps showing up.

Returning to an awareness of and belief in our passion is the most
significant thing we can do to get our reproductive system on track.
What this means will vary for each of us. We don't need to leave our
family and go backpacking across the Andes, although that might be a
goal for some of us. Small steps begin the process and produce success.

It is so interesting that we all want to know what our purpose is in
life, but we get that confused with what job or career we want. We
should really be asking ourself, *What is my passion, and how am I prepared to advance it?* Our passion, then, is the essence of this new life
energy that keeps popping up each month, just as an ovum keeps popping out each month. Our passion may well take shape as our career,
or maybe not. Our passion is not about paying the bills but about helping us feel happy and fulfilled. Even if we begin small, we have begun
living our passion. The power is in the beginning, and then keeping
that energy alive and allowing it to grow.

Our passions aren't something we can replace or defer, like deciding to take a vacation next year instead of this year. Our passions lead
us and inspire us to contribute to the quality of our life and our family's lives; they allow us to grow personally and to deepen spiritually.
The question is whether our particular dreams, as an expression of our
passion, are essential to our life — and no one else can tell us this. Only
we can know from the feeling we have in our heart as we put our
dreams off or have changing circumstances eliminate them as possibilities.

Our dream may be to teach physics or pottery, and the first step
may be to enroll in college or graduate school to develop the right
training. If this isn't possible, we can consult our passion for a new
plan: Should we train as a teacher more slowly or in a different field, or
find another avenue into the field that excites us? Our dream may be
to open a healing center to help men and women in their healing journeys; this may be beyond our current expertise or financial resources,

but we can take small first steps by consulting with friends or volunteering at an existing center. Our dream may be to study ancient cultures; small steps of reading and learning can lead to taking a leave of absence from work to study in Greece.

Our dreams make us better, happier, and fill our life with greater meaning. Our dreams validate our reason for living. Only we know what dreams we need to pursue, no matter what, and which can be shifted to accommodate our circumstances. Whatever their final shape, our dreams are the outward manifestation of our need to express our passion for life, our spontaneity, and to build on what we've learned and believe in.

Because of a diagnosis, a disheartening experience, or just waking up to ourself in a new way, we can feel in our heart and our gut that the time has come to reconnect with our passion and resurrect our dreams — to see how they've changed and in what ways we can envision pursuing them in our life today.

ALISSA, SUBTLE ENERGY, AND PASSION

To gain an understanding of how our passions and our subtle energies interact, particularly regarding our reproductive system, I'd like to tell the story of Alissa, who came to see me because of a cyst in her right breast. The cyst was benign, but Alissa wanted to understand why she had gotten it in the first place and what she could do to keep from getting others. A forty-three-year-old woman with two teenage children and a good partnership, Alissa worked at a well-paying job in real estate and was generally a positive and happy person. I did an energy evaluation on her, and here are the results that relate to her breast cyst.

Ovarian Energy

Alissa had already had one ovary removed because of a large cyst that had become painful and difficult. Energetically, there seemed to be some hesitation in the flow here, as if she was okay as long as she stayed within certain familiar parameters, but there was no permission to consider other possibilities.

Alissa confirmed that she was very tied to her family, but she had been thinking of pursuing something more interesting and exciting with her life than real estate, which she had worked in for ten years. The job provided security, but it wasn't nourishing her anymore. She felt that she would be rocking the boat, however, to suggest to her partner that she wanted to consider pursuing her true desire, music.

Uterine Energy

Alissa's uterus seemed stretched — not from having children, but emotionally, as if she felt stretched to accomplish more than she was interested in doing. Also, in this stretched environment, there was only conditional approval of her dreams. Her wishes had to conform to the needs of others in order to be supported. She wanted to pull back from her work and take some time to consider her music and what she might do with it, but she confirmed that she felt guilty thinking about her own needs instead of what the family needed.

Vaginal Energy

Alissa's energy felt used up, as if the mucosal lining of the vagina was tired of producing positive outer feelings when inside she wanted more for herself. She mentioned that she had lost interest in sex with her partner and that life seemed pretty much the same, day in and day out.

Breast Energy

Alissa's breasts seemed dry and worn out. She was doing all the things that she thought were the right thing to do for others, but she was turning a deaf ear to the voice of her enthusiastic passion, which wanted to be nourished. The energetic flow that nourishes the breasts is actually at the end of the line, so to speak, in the sequence of energy that arises in the ovaries, moves through the uterus and vagina, and finally arrives as a flow in the breasts. Alissa also felt herself at the end of the line, needing to recognize her own passion and discover what might be waiting for her if she could nourish her own dreams.

The Solution for Alissa

The way to restore health to the flow of breast energy for Alissa was to allow her passion for her music to surface without feeling guilty about it. Growths and tumors, whether benign or cancerous, are the result of passions that are seeking a voice but instead are denied or sublimated. When what we need to explore emotionally in our life is closed down and pushed under, it ends up growing where we don't want it in our body.

I encouraged Alissa to talk about her music and to explore what small steps she might take to enjoy it while still managing her family. She didn't need to think in black-and-white terms: family versus music. She could work on both at the same time. Alissa was afraid her partner would be mad if she suggested a change, and I suggested that this was an important conversation to have because she needed to find the courage within herself to share what was truly important to her.

Breast health is based on long-term approval and nourishment of our passions and dreams, whether or not they conform to another's expectations or needs, and whether or not they seem logical, reasonable, or make money. We don't need to cut and run from our responsibilities, but neither should we cut and run from our passion. Our passion isn't showing up to make our life difficult. Rather, our passion seeks to bring us back to our inner knowing and the contributions we intended to make.

I was glad that Alissa had sought feedback about her breast cyst, especially since she had a history of an ovarian cyst. Repeated cysts tell us that we have an interruption of the flow among our organs of reproduction, and we need to do something to restore it. By taking positive action to try to prevent cysts, hopefully, one can avoid a malignant one. So it is important to take note of problems and realize we're being called to listen more attentively to our passions.

ACTIVITY

Follow the Bread Crumbs to Your Success

How do you take your passion and develop the small steps necessary for you to realize your dreams? You wonder, for example, where to get the money you need, how to create the opportunity or the time, or who will help you.

No matter what your question or dream is, you can realize it by taking one small step at a time. Listen to your inner knowing and write down your first step. This is bread crumb #1. Now *assuming the success* of this first step — in other words, you've accomplished it and don't need to repeat it — what is the next step for realizing your passion? Write this step down as bread crumb #2. And *assuming the success* of this step, write down your third action, and this becomes bread crumb #3.

Work in increments of three bread crumbs. Once these are finished, create the next logical question and do three more bread crumbs. This practice has amazing results, because as soon as you imagine yourself to be successful with the first bread crumb, you draw to yourself the next level of success that propels you toward your goal.

The key is to visualize success before writing the next bread crumb. By contrast, what we usually do when making a list of action steps is to make a circular movement around our goal. We never actually move forward. We move sideways or simply spin on the doorstep waiting for something to happen. Rather, if we allow the energy of our passion to generate success, even just in our mind, we create steps that build, improve, and progress on each other.

Here's an example from one of my students. She was a painter with a lot of older paintings she wanted to sell; she needed the money and wanted to clear the energy of the old work to make more room for her new pieces. She wrote: "How can I sell my old paintings?"

Here was her preliminary list of steps:

BREAD CRUMB #1: Create a flyer and post it in places where people might be interested.

BREAD CRUMB #2: Post the information on a friend's website.

BREAD CRUMB #3: Tell her friends and ask them to pass along the information.

All three bread crumbs dealt with various ways to approach the problem; each was a possible place to start. She was still walking around the question with nothing accomplished.

I asked her to build on the success of her first bread crumb and imagine how she would feel having accomplished the first task of creating the flyer. She thought a moment and said, "I've never thought about how I'd feel having actually done that successfully. I'd feel really good and know that I had alerted lots of people to my artwork." She continued, "I'd feel much more confident." I asked her to reframe the final two breadcrumbs, assuming success at each level.

BREAD CRUMB #2: Go back to those original locations and post a notice showing pictures of my work and mentioning those that had already been sold.

BREAD CRUMB #3: Hold an auction of my paintings, since I've sold some and people are now aware of my work and I'm getting mentioned in local newspapers and magazines.

She could feel the energy of her excitement and her delight in success and felt that already she was more positioned for success. By envisioning her success before it actually arrived, by feeling it and acknowledging it, she was ready to bring it to her.

Create Your Own Bread Crumbs

Begin by writing your most pressing question of how to grow your passion or present dream. Then write three bread crumbs, which represent the steps you're taking in pursuit of your dream.

BREAD CRUMB #1: Write your first small step to realizing your dream.

BREAD CRUMB #2: *Assuming the success* of this first step, experience how that feels and plan what you'll do next.

BREAD CRUMB #3: *Assuming the success* of this second step, experience how that feels and plan what you'll do next.

This simple but powerful practice will move you directly into your
passion with joy and excitement.

❧ ATTITUDE SHIFTS ❧

1. I have a subtle energy system that I can perceive by using
    my intuitive perception.
2. Teachable moments on my healing journey come when I
    am open to my intuitive perception to sense the learning
    from my subtle energy, which allows me to see a new and
    different way to proceed.
3. Each of my female organs interacts with the others in the
    subtle flow of energy, and understanding their energetic
    messages helps me make better life healing choices.
4. I need to support rather than interfere with my body's nat-
    ural wisdom.
5. My destiny and my dreams originate in the energy flow of
    my female organs.
6. I can take small and important steps every day to keep my
    passion alive, and as long as I do that my dreams will live.
7. Anytime I don't live my dreams, I am creating a potential
    sense of loss, and that hinders my healing.

CHAPTER NINETEEN

Loss, Grief, and Grace — The Path to Healing

My mother's communication illuminated to me life's delicate balance
and the necessity to draw close to the "soil,"
to focus on what is vital and important.
That life is a successive pattern of seasons and changes
and in order to truly relish its magic
one must keep in mind that there is a time and a place for all things.

— Justin Matott

*L*ove and the ability to feed and nourish what we love are the essential components for a healthy life. When loss, acute or chronic, curtails our ability to nourish what we love, we inadvertently erode our passion and the dreams they generate. Losing what we love can push us further and further out of balance, which leads eventually to disruptions that can show up as various kinds of problems, most specifically women's reproductive issues.

Loss interrupts the essential energy of love that flows from our heart to our female organs that germinate the dreams that sustain us. Loss reverberates through our body's entire energy system, especially our circulatory and reproductive systems. In other words, our heart and our womanhood are especially hard hit with the loss of love.

Statistically, heart disease is an even larger threat than breast cancer. Breast cancer takes approximately forty-three thousand women each year, while heart disease claims an estimated five hundred thousand and is on the rise. In fact, heart and female energy go hand-in-hand because our heart generates the love that feeds our passion, which in turn gives us the desire to nourish and cherish our truest yearnings.

The more chronic or acute the state of loss, the more we struggle to believe that we can still live as a complete woman, with something of our own design to feed, nourish, and cherish. No matter what our sense of loss, we benefit when we take a long hard look at what we want, who we are, and how we desire to spend our time, energy, and money.

Think of a flower bulb, which has such tremendous energy to open to spring, the new season of life. It can push through concrete, around boulders, and even break clay pots in its passion for opening to life. We can afford to be no less passionate about our own opening to new life. Aren't we ready to begin again with the renewed energy of spring — of spirit?

As we allow new dreams and new energy to nourish us, we move through loss and find ourself in the grieving stage of our healing journey. Grieving is positive in this case because it allows us to use the energy of old losses to germinate new beginnings and new conversations with ourself.

As we talk and write about our losses, we actually grieve them and heal them through our tender attention to what has hurt us. By listening to ourself with greater self-honesty, we realize that while we have inner and outer work to do, so does every human being.

The challenge of imbalance isn't ours alone, it is humanity's struggle. Being out of balance is our perennial condition, and many today actively seek their return route to inner peace, spiritual knowing, and health. Certainly no one plans for an illness to be a vehicle of regaining a clearer perspective of life direction, yet it can serve us in this way, becoming our return route to a healthy and quality life.

THE OLD NURTURES THE NEW THROUGH GRACE

The loss of cherished love and hope is similar to a giant redwood tree falling in the forest. The tree represents dreams that got away as well as love that we always wanted or once had and lost. But the fallen tree, once on the ground, nourishes new growth, which springs from under its bark. What has come before is meant to be fodder for the new. There is no need to throw away our old experiences — good and bad — because they provide the nutrients for today's opportunities. The fallen tree, our old dreams, now nourish our new dreams, as we turn our attention to moving through the grieving stage. We can think of this grieving stage as *the stage of germination of the new, as we use the nourishment from our fallen dreams to welcome Grace.*

Grace is the experience of loving ourselves no matter how love was shown to us, whether faulty, judgmental, and abusive or kind, forgiving, and supporting. Grace doesn't come to us in those moments of gentle awareness and comfort, as if we've done something to have God love us more than others. Grace comes to us when we open our heart and ask for it because we need it. God is forgiveness, creative support, and opening to love from within.

Grace is the energy of love that flows continually from God, Divine Intelligence, Spirit. Our willingness and ability to receive it is what makes the difference. As we sit with ourself, whether in good times or bad, we can put our hands over our heart and feel a quiet, strong reassurance that no matter what comes to us in the future, in this moment we are loved. More than being loved just today, we are part of the Love that flows in and around the entire Universe — we were born from Love.

Grace is actually the healing energy of Spirit that helps our body listen to a steady, reassuring inner message, one that helps us settle our fears and struggles and turn them into food for our spiritual journey. When we put our hands over our heart center and realize that we are sending ourself love and recognize the impact it has inside us — that's

Grace. The healing response in our body is Grace in action, Divine Love in action, helping us on our journey of spiritual empowerment and healing.

ASK YOURSELF

What are my dreams, aspirations, and hopes for my life?

Do I give myself, or feel around me, a supportive environment in which to develop my dreams?

Am I confident that emotionally I'm prepared to birth my dreams into the world in a safe and appropriate way?

In what ways am I now feeding, nourishing, and cherishing the dreams I've given birth to?

SUSAN'S STORY

Here's an example of a woman who, although she didn't develop breast cancer, was headed down that path emotionally.

Susan was a middle-age woman who had taught primary school for ten years. She was divorced and lived across the street from her mother. Her mother had had a mastectomy for breast cancer when she was the age Susan was when she came to see me.

Susan had a difficult relationship with her mother. Her mother was extremely emotionally dependent on her, and yet this dependence translated itself into criticism of Susan. It seemed that nothing Susan could do either proved her love to her mother's satisfaction or allowed her to break free and feel supported in developing her own interests and her own life.

In the energy evaluation that I did for Susan, I intuitively saw an important image that was clearly evident in her pelvic energy center — the second chakra, which deals with reproductive energy and holds our power as a woman. The breasts are also part of this reproductive energy.

In this image Susan was standing behind her mother, fearfully peeking out, unwilling to risk stepping out in front. Interestingly, at first, Susan proclaimed that she had a perfect relationship with her mother. But seeing the image helped me guide Susan to understand the full range of feelings she had about her relationship with her mother. As we continued to talk, she shared all the ways she felt her life and her dreams had been eclipsed and she hadn't been able to feed her dreams or sense of self-confidence.

In addition, Susan had become just as dependent on receiving her mother's criticism as her mother had become on giving it. Because of her mother's criticism, Susan could blame her mother for never having given her the chance to develop her own life and views, and she had a perfect reason not to risk trying anything new. It certainly wasn't healthy — but it surely was safe.

We may tell ourself that we're nothing like our mother, and yet we may exhibit similar patterns in the ways we face problems, deal with people, and understand and nurture ourself, which we picked up from her. Our parent may have been critical and unapproachable, and while we may be different on the outside, we may be the same way with ourself on the inside. We may keep from giving to ourself what we most yearn to experience: an intimate relationship with a partner, a successful career, permission to have our own life free of guilt or shame, and a deepening experience of our spirituality — the meaning of our life.

Neediness in our mother or father tends to show up as neediness in us — it just looks different. Initially, we may not recognize the similarity of our emotional reactions because they may occur in a different context. We may have an entirely different lifestyle from our parents, for example, yet unconsciously we carry the same emotional patterns we lived with growing up. In this light, our efforts to wake up are essential; otherwise we are driven by what is invalidating. We are framed by self-criticism, lack of trust in our vision, and fear of living out our passion.

If we worry that because of heredity we are headed for cancer, heart disease, or some other major imbalance, we are wise to pay attention to what we may, consciously and unconsciously, have carried over from our parents and accepted as our own. In Susan's case, she recognized that her fear of stepping out was how her mother had always reacted to life, and that Susan had bought the same picture for her own life.

Whether our relationships with our mother and father have been loving and positive or completely miserable, within them may be the keys for why we may struggle to believe in ourself and from which we must set ourself free.

ASK YOURSELF

Which of my parents has had the greatest impact on my life, either by being present or absent?

How am I obviously like that parent or subtly like that parent?

What reactions might I now pay greater attention to so I can change any underlying destructive emotional patterns?

DORIAN'S STORY

Here is another story that makes the point of how important it is to listen to our inner knowing.

After I had given a talk at a major cancer facility, I received an email from a woman named Dorian who said she'd been part of the program at the facility. Dorian had stage IV ovarian cancer and was just completing her chemotherapy and radiation protocol. She wrote several pages of accusations that I was shocked and saddened to read.

Among other things, she was furious with me and anyone who dared to suggest that feelings and attitudes were in any way connected to her cancer. She thought this *spirit stuff* was all bunk. After sitting with her email, I decided to write back. I asked her why she was so furious, and I explained again what I had said in my talk. We went back and forth all afternoon in what became a strange dialogue that slowly moved to a place of healing and insight for both of us.

What she eventually explained was that she had first felt something was wrong several years before being diagnosed with ovarian cancer. The medical doctor she went to thought it was a digestive upset and did various tests. Nothing showed up. She felt something was wrong, but there seemed nothing to do — she didn't seek any other opinions.

Then Dorian read a women's healing book by a best-selling author. She decided to take it seriously and began in earnest to explore her emotions and her spirituality. She thought, *Well, these symptoms must all be in my head, and so if I concentrate on being a better and more loving person, nothing bad will happen to me.* Again she went to her doctor and had tests, and again nothing showed up.

Eventually, when doctors diagnosed her with stage IV cancer, she was furious. Hadn't she gotten checked out and done the right things — and most of all, how come this wonderful book on healing hadn't included the vague and mysterious symptoms that can be associated with ovarian cancer? She wrote to tell the author her story and ask that the early warning signals for ovarian cancer be included in the author's work. She received a form letter in return — which told her to refer to the original book. At this point she lost it. She had looked to two different authorities and neither one had come through for her — and now she felt it was too late. No wonder she was devastated.

Dorian's story represents one of our worst nightmares — yet many women report similar stories of breast lumps that weren't detected in their early stages or other conditions that were diagnosed incorrectly. To honor Dorian, and to share her gift to other women — which is a clearer understanding of the symptoms of ovarian cancer — I will provide those symptoms here. By themselves, they do not necessarily indicate ovarian cancer, but they may; if they touch us with an inner knowing, we should check them out further until their true meaning is clear. The symptoms of ovarian cancer may include abdominal swelling or bloating; abdominal or pelvic pain or pressure, such as feeling full; gastrointestinal symptoms, such as gas, indigestion, nausea, or changes in bowel movements; vaginal bleeding or discharge; urinary problems; fatigue and/or fever; pain during intercourse; back pain; and difficulty breathing.

Sometimes we don't find out what is wrong with us until we have major healing to do. But it is never over until it's over. I've seen stage IV cancer healed; as long as we have life, there is always good healing that can happen. Dorian has not corresponded with me since that day, but I hope that she turned the corner in her healing. She and I had a most unlikely meeting of the mind and heart. It was a gift neither one of us will forget.

WE CAN REGAIN WHAT IS LOST

We all have times when we feel out of control and despondent. Ultimately we can find opportunities to shift from loss and grief into opening to an even better and more confident life. When we're in balance, we feel self-assured and able to manage what comes to us. The way we regain what is lost is to return to our deep heart and its passion for living. When we dip back into the well of our greatest strength, we may find a readiness to once again write beautiful fresh lines on the page, creating a new chapter in our life journey.

We need to handle our feelings not by suppressing them but by directing them away from dire predictions and toward healing through Grace. What we grieve allows us to shed tears of worry, trouble, and struggle — and sometimes of emotions that may have built up over many years. Crying and laughing and the wild ride of emotions in between are good for our body and good for our soul. We are resilient in a way that is beyond normal logic. We must never forget all the love that we have going for us — and of course, it is most readily available to us through Spirit as Grace.

It is important to identify what is happening to us as an imbalance in our energy. Recognizing this fact lets us breathe a little easier no matter what has come down on us. We sense we can return to balance — that our energy can be shifted. Energy is enhanced by allowing ourself to move through and past the losses that have hurt us.

So we dry our tears, straighten the vest of our business suit or our chic evening gown, and get on with living a good life.

❧ ATTITUDE SHIFTS ❧

1. Loss creates imbalance in my energy flow, and imbalances can eventually show up as disease. Identifying my losses is the first step on my healing journey.
2. The second step on my healing journey is to fully grieve my losses. Visualizing this process allows me to go forward and build new dreams.
3. The third step is Grace. Grace comes when I allow the new to grow from the experiences of my past with an open heart. Grace is the direct healing energy of love.
4. The healing response of my body is actually Grace in action.

CHAPTER TWENTY

Putting Our Spirit in the Center of Our Healing

God gives us songs in the night.
— Job 35:10

As women, we are born with a natural predisposition toward inner knowing. We have a built-in intuition that gives us a sense of what others need, even when they haven't said so in words. When children, parents, spouses, and friends need support and comfort, we know what appropriate actions to take. We shine as leaders and circle builders, naturally tending toward a new model of partnering and shared community.

All too often we keep our intuition focused on the needs of others rather than on our own. We tend to think *we're invincible*, and in our mind *we must be invincible* because so many depend on us. We're used to managing everything and everybody, and we rarely consider taking time to have a good cry or to sit for a few hours exploring what is important to us, what is happening, how we feel, and whether we are living in a healthy, balanced rhythm.

Instead, we tend to put off our own physical and spiritual needs, telling ourself that we'll get to mulling over yesterday's problems and tomorrow's concerns later. We postpone an in-depth self-exploration because there just isn't time or perhaps motivation. And anyway, who wants to open Pandora's box? If we aren't broken, why stop the world to fix our life?

Then, when we are faced with the need for major healing, we want to do it in the quickest way possible. We don't consider changing our jam-packed life; we focus on patching ourself up as fast as possible so that our life — and the needs of others — won't be interrupted too long. It can seem very unrealistic and impractical — at first — to imagine actually taking valuable time from our busy days to go to various practitioners on a regular basis.

Taking care of our body, mind, and spirit isn't something our culture teaches us to do. Rather, we simply keep going until we get sick, fix ourself as swiftly as possible, and then keep going in the same ways until we get sick again. Instead, we need to join the increasing number of women who are asking, *What do I need to do to prevent illness and improve the quality of my life?* We need to put ourself — our needs and desires — in the center of our life, and we need to develop a range of ongoing practices that support our happiness and health on all levels of our being. We certainly need to do this when we are faced with major healing, but we should also do this before we get sick — to hopefully prevent ever needing major healing.

AN INTEGRATED MODEL OF HEALING

Healing doesn't require us to choose one system or option to the exclusion of others. Just the opposite. The best healing integrates a variety of practices and approaches. Healing begins with our intuition, in which we initially sense our imbalances, and through which we find guidance in choosing the best options for us. As we find a diagnosis for specific problems or a plan for sorting out anxieties and emotional imbalances, we should take the approach of doing the least invasive things first, and then move up the ladder to drugs and surgeries as they become necessary. Outside of addressing a specific health issue, we need to care for our health and our emotional and spiritual selves at all times, incorporating regular daily or weekly practices into our routine.

Noninvasive therapies and treatments need to form the bread and butter of our healing regime. These are the things that keep us in balance and in touch with our inner rhythms, that allow us time to focus on and consider ourself. These practices come in many forms, from meditation and massage to acupuncture, colon therapy, energy building therapies, and energetically based chiropractic. In general, we should use our wonderful Western medicine when we need it for the direct, immediate, and lifesaving techniques that it provides.

In other words, to generate the best and most long-lasting results for healing and preventing illness, we need to create an integrated model of healing, one that focuses on body, mind, *and* spirit. This is a different way of thinking about our health for many women.

In Chinese medicine, which is closely aligned with the healing model that I've developed over the past two decades, the flows of energy are considered all-important. When these healthy flows of energy are interrupted, the body can and does compensate, but it needs support emotionally and spiritually to regain energy and support the body during difficult treatments, or just to maintain itself over the course of our busy life. As women, we know intuitively when something is not right. Perhaps we know what is wrong and realize how to proceed, or perhaps we need someone to help us identify the source of the imbalance.

While we may wish to take a pill and be finished with it, this may not re-create energetic balance. A quick fix rarely lasts unless accompanied by other changes. Likewise, surgery, chemotherapy, radiation, and other major interventions are very hard on the body and need to be supported with other energetic practices. These invasive procedures can be lifesaving, but we need to help our body regain its energy flows during and after they have been disrupted.

In addition, medicines have their own side effects and they can be abused; in the United States, medicinal complications account for over a hundred thousand unnecessary deaths each year. Medications are part of the equation of healing, but other factors are extremely important: lifestyle choices, nutrition, thoughts and feelings, and spiritual practices.

Healing, therefore, involves a wider sweep of ways and means to support our body's energy balance, to help us deal with our fears, pain, and losses, and deepen support from Spirit. This final component is the most difficult to find.

FINDING SPIRITUAL GUIDANCE

Just as there are many paths to healing, there are many ways to find spiritual guidance. Returning to or becoming more deeply involved in an organized religion is not the only way. In fact, many of us may have found that — apart from the spiritual direction offered by individual ministers, priests, or rabbis — organized religion has not traditionally entrusted us as individuals to find God through our own direct connection. We may have lost our trust in ourself and in the offerings of organized religion.

We live in changing times, however. Meaningful spiritual guidance can be found in a wide range of settings and traditions, led by well-respected spiritual teachers and mental health professionals of all kinds. More important than the particular type of spiritual guidance we receive, however, is that it should validate and enhancing our personal path to God. This is what our integrated model of healing calls for. Our path is the one that allows us to tap directly into sacred inner space through our prayers, meditations, personal inquiry, and inspirational writing and reading.

I do believe, however, that having a spiritual teacher is essential to our spiritual growth. We need to find a path and follow it sincerely and with dedication, and spiritual guides are invaluable in helping us to do this. It is too easy to dabble, to sample here and there and have so many practices and conflicting teachings that we don't know what to do — so we end up doing little or nothing. We read but don't develop a sustaining practice.

In fact, all true spiritual teachings say basically the same thing.

- Connect with Divine presence — Spirit within — and let it guide you.
- Get out of your own way and remove your ego from directing your life and pushing you to chase the things of this world that will only pass away.
- Live your most meaningful life by caring about others as much as you care about yourself.
- Dedicate your life and your work to a God of Love, which is the heartbeat of all Life everywhere through the Universe.

When searching for an appropriate spiritual teacher, we should inquire into any approach to spiritual healing and spiritual development that interests us. Second, we should sample the work and teachings — by attending a workshop or two, going on a retreat with the teacher, or simply sitting with her or his teachings for a time. When we are convinced in our heart that we have found the right path for us right now — not necessarily forever, but for the foreseeable future — we should stick to it and not be swayed.

Staying on the spiritual path we've chosen can be difficult. There is always a new idea, a new system, a new teacher. But we make progress only when we stay with a teacher and her or his approach for a period of time. There are many worthy spiritual teachers to choose from, and yet choosing one and developing a relationship is essential. We need the comfort of ongoing guidance and direction offered by someone we trust, someone who comes to know us and the particular spiritual route we are traveling, perhaps because they have traveled it, too. A spiritual teacher can help hold us in the experience of Divine Love — Spirit — which allows us to generate our own inner energy and find our way clearly to our own deep heart. Our teacher can also guide us through the personality pitfalls that fill any spiritual path.

Slowly the power and presence of Spirit within permeates at the cellular level, and we then expand — so that our circuits are capable of running significant flows of energy. Rather than just managing to stay healthy physically, we choose now to increase the flows of energy directly from Divine Intelligence to become a true instrument of world peace and support.

In *Spirit Heals*, I hope to help us do more than heal our body. I'm really interested in helping to enhance our spiritual energy so that we can use our healing as a jumping-off place to true spiritual advancement. Wherever we are on the path is just where we should be. There are no mistakes. No matter where we currently are, we're perfectly positioned to be successful in our spiritual journey. *When the time is right, our teacher will appear.*

DECIDING TO CHANGE

Ultimately, it is empowering to realize that we are in charge, to a large degree, of what happens in our body and in our life. This means, however, that we must take responsibility for monitoring our habits — such as our diet and ways of thought and being — and proactively changing those that become addictive or unhealthy.

Healing requires us to participate in questioning old attitudes and assumptions and replacing them with new attitudes that rekindle our kindness and passion and keep us pointed toward what matters most to us. We must monitor even our "good intentions" — such as our desire to serve and support others — since these can also camouflage telltale signs that we're not quite as relaxed and whole inside as we once were. Certain illnesses develop over many years as the result of multiple factors, which eventually reveal themselves in physical imbalances or symptoms. This happens when we slowly lose our intuitive sense of our healthy inner rhythm and get acclimated to one that is slowly winding down — just like a clock that someone forgets to rewind.

Can we learn to recognize when we are out of balance before something goes wrong? Typically, we only question ourself when something serious happens. For small signs, we tell ourself, *Better to not pay attention and maybe it will go away.* This is why yearly mammograms and monthly breast self-exams, and having our cholesterol and blood pressure regularly monitored, are all essential prevention measures.

Of course, being diagnosed with a serious problem is always a call to take charge and change. It can also be a source of relief and focus; for some women, having a diagnosis finally puts an end to denial or clarifies symptoms that until then had been unexplained and defied healing efforts. It is helpful, for example, to finally know we have Lyme's disease or multiple sclerosis; knowing this, we can formulate an effective healing plan.

Sometimes we get a diagnosis when we've had no warning signals. Suddenly, we have a pain, a lump, irregular bleeding, or a pink slip from work. We weren't expecting it. We feel the wind knocked out of us. When this happens, we need to stop, calm our emotions, and do nothing but settle into ourself.

No matter how we've arrive at the decision to change — whether because of a diagnosis or simply an unbidden awareness that change is necessary — we need to right our own ship and proceed to give to ourself in the ways that feel perfect at the time.

Once the decision to take action is made, there is no wrong way to proceed — as we're weighing our options, we may sense that we need to ask more questions, that we need a little more time, that we need to find out more from our surgeon or get a second opinion. Our healing may come from an unexpected place: perhaps another, better job is hiding behind the one we just got eliminated from, or a timely call to human resources can give us a heads-up on the way to transfer our insurance or health benefits.

Our healing also arrives at our own pace. The timing is ours. We know what we need and when we need it, so we should move at our own speed. We are in the driver's seat.

ACTIVITY

Imagining Your Inner Rhythm

Shut your eyes and imagine a stream of water flowing around and over stones and tree limbs. This stream of water is like the stream of energy flowing through you. When this inner stream flows smoothly with minimal obstruction, then you feel in rhythm or in harmony — in the flow. You are healthy in body, mind, and spirit. When you experience emotional, spiritual, or mental obstructions in the stream of your living energy, you don't feel in the flow and you have to use extra effort and energy to keep things moving.

1. Take your journal and a pen and give yourself at least ten minutes in a supportive environment where you can relax without interruption. Light a candle, put on some soft music, and sit in your sacred healing space, your meditation room, your warm comfortable bed, or on the couch — wherever you feel comfortable.

2. Put your hand over your heart and ask your spirit inside to help you sense the flow of your body's energy at the time of your diagnosis. Imagine going back to that time of your life and sensing without judgment what was happening, what you were doing, and what was on your mind.

3. Now ask what the inner rhythm of your body is showing you right now after healing has begun, whether through medical treatments or any other path. Note the ways you are calmer, more aware of your feelings, more sensitive to what overloads your circuits.

4. Write down these differences in your inner rhythm. At first blush you may think perhaps there are no differences. But

there are bound to be, so stay with the practice until you identify how you have, in fact, begun to bring healing energy to your body and are more sensitive to the inner world of energy. Find the improvement — what has made the difference?

SETTING THE INTENTION TO MOVE TO THE CENTER OF OUR LIFE

Sometimes we may feel we have no options, but we feel this because *we haven't created the intention that will open the door to new choices.*

The most powerful way to create that intention is to step to the center of our life. This is a beautiful and useful exercise in which we take charge of our life and ask others to support us as we walk into the center of a circle. Imagine that on the periphery of the circle are all of our loved ones: doctors, healers, and energy workers; ministers, rabbis, and priests; spiritual directors; and our support network of friends. All those we trust to support and help us form a circle, and we alone stand in the center.

Imagining that picture, how do we feel? Do we feel tentative because we think others would think we were puffing ourself up as too important? Do we shrink back because we think our partner or friends would call us selfish and too concerned with ourself — too egotistical? Do we fear standing in the center because we think God might mistake our inner authority for willfulness or false pride? Do we fall away from standing proudly in the center of our life because we worry we're not smart or knowledgeable enough? Are we concerned that our opinions would anger our partner, children, or doctors?

What hinders us from taking charge of our healing emotionally, physically, and spiritually? Each of us may have different reasons, but we need to discover anything that might have us looking over our shoulder, so to speak, as we take greater charge of our healing and our life. We need to put ourself in the center, and if something is in the way of restoring and recharging the energy flows in our body, we need to identify and remove them for continued healing.

Healing requires us to believe in ourself and our inner knowing, which allows us to choose more effectively who and what can support our efforts. We don't need to walk alone in our life, but others can't and shouldn't make our decisions for us. It is too easy then to blame others. We must not be afraid to speak up about our beliefs. We are within our rights to allow our brightness to shine fully into every aspect of our life.

ASK YOURSELF

As I begin to enhance my vitality and the flow of healthy energy, I can read each suggestion and notice how my body feels, what my thoughts and feelings are, and how my spirit is responding.

SUGGESTION #1: Taking care of myself means giving my own needs as much consideration as I do the needs of others.

QUESTION: How can I remain more mindful of my needs and listen to, rather than cover up, my inner voice, which alerts me to what I need to say and do?

SUGGESTION #2: Reducing my stress means enlisting the help and support of others as I get more realistic about what is possible for me to accomplish in a day and in a week. I need to take into account two aspects of reprioritizing my daily tasks: how many linear events I can comfortably factor into my day, and how much emotional recovery and processing time I need in between.

QUESTION: Who can help reduce my work load, and will I allow them to? When I consider my daily task list, what needs to change? Why?

SUGGESTION #3: Making room each day for spontaneity, fun, and laughter is essential because I consider my healing and my desire to have a good life a priority. I may think it should be automatic to be relaxed about my life, but it isn't. Being more spontaneous is actually one of the most potent healing remedies that renews my body and my spirit.

QUESTION: What makes me laugh? What is my response when someone asks me to do something fun that breaks the normal routine of my life? What would happen if I said "yes" to fun more often than I said "no"?

SUGGESTION #4: Finding time each day to be grateful for love is a key to my healing. I can honor the love that is already in my heart and the love that I share with others (whether or not I believe it is returned in the same measure) by accepting that I am loved by many whose lives I've touched unknowingly and who bless me now.

QUESTION: Is it easy for me to love others? Who loves me the most right now, and how does my knowing that they love me truly feed my heart?

SUGGESTION #5: Discovering something to love in the work that is mine now is important to regaining my health and joy. While I may sometimes yearn to be somewhere else, doing something else, I have responsibilities and obligations that I care about and can accept gratefully.

QUESTION: Given my responsibilities and the work or way of contributing to family or community that I've chosen, what can I find to love in what is available to me today?

SUGGESTION #6: Living in awareness of my human connection to all life makes me mindful of the needs and desires of others that are the same as my own.

QUESTION: How many times a day do I feel appreciative of the living environment that supports my needs and the many thousands of unseen faces who make my life easier, more interesting, creative, and enjoyable?

❧ ATTITUDE SHIFTS ❧

1. As a woman I have a built-in inner knowing. The challenge is to focus it on myself in addition to everyone else.
2. I can change the attitude that "I'll fix my health when I get sick" to "I'll do what I need to do now to prevent illness."
3. When I sense something wrong, I need to check into it, finding its source and taking charge.
4. Finding a spiritual teacher or guide is enormously helpful in keeping me focused and moving forward on my spiritual path to healing.
5. I can find my spiritual teacher or teachings, just like I did my healing plan: review my options, sample the ones that appeal to me most, decide on one, and make a commitment.
6. Just as with my healing plan, I need to stick with my spiritual path even (and especially) when it gets difficult.
7. I have to make the commitment to pay attention to myself, since as a woman it can also be my natural inclination to put everyone else's needs before my own. Doing that means I can miss important signals.
8. I can now step into the center of my own life, asking others to gather around me in a loving and supportive way.

CHAPTER TWENTY-ONE

The Positive Energy
of Every Situation

No plant grew higher than my head.
For a while, I heard only miles of wind against the Ghost;
but after the ringing in my ears stopped, I heard myself breathing,
then a bird note, an answering call, another kind of birdsong, and another;
mockingbird, mourning dove, an enigma.
I heard the high zizz of flies the color of gray flannel
and the deep buzz of a blue bumblebee. I made a list of nothing in particular.

— William Least Heat-Moon

Life isn't fair, and bad things do happen to good people; it's true. However, we can decide how we will *receive and perceive* what happens to us. Our healing isn't based on what happens to us as much as on how we interpret these experiences and the actions that then flow from our perceptions.

Our physical healing is also impacted by other subtle spiritual energy factors, such as influences from past lives that make up God's bigger plans for us, which we'll never entirely understand. I like the thought of God smiling as we make all our plans, which of course always get disrupted by our Earth School, but somehow we eventually come to recognize that we are not alone as we fumble along in the dark trying to figure out our life and our healing.

Our healing is a balancing act of many factors. We must move through the process of loss, grief, and grace; we must understand and put to use the wisdom messages of the body; and we must learn that Spirit will fill in much of the healing that we're not even aware we need.

What is it that Spirit helps us with? Trust. A big piece of our healing equation involves *trust* that there is a benevolent cosmic plan for our life. We heal from the inside out, from our spiritual connection to Love, which clears the emotional clutter and residue in our mind and body, allowing our authentic spiritual nature to directly impact our physical health.

Creating a positive environment then becomes essential as we seek to change our mental, emotional, and spiritual perspective on our life — on our failures, our successes, and our healing. Yet it is an interesting and terribly challenging affair to receive the positive energy from difficult relationships and circumstances, those in which we don't believe that we've been wished well or, more to the point, those in which we've felt ignored or intentionally slammed.

CREATING LEMONADE OUT OF LEMONS

We all have difficult and demanding people in our life. So how can we stay positive when others become negative?

The answer is not to believe others are negative or angry because of us. We are not the source of their pain and fury, even if they want us to believe we are. Every person needs to seek their own answers about how to feel better as well as seek guidance in connecting with the source of grace and forgiveness within their own deep heart.

Once we step out of the shared emotional equation, we're free to receive the best useful information offered in the interaction. We can take responsibility for what belongs to us, and we can receive any good intentions that we sense under otherwise not-so-nice words or actions.

We are free to create whatever we choose from every encounter. If our perspective is positive and we are focusing on our own intention for the conversation from our deep heart, unexpectedly good things can happen for us and others.

We can choose to be happy, not because we have nothing to feel sad about, but because we realize that sadness comes of its own accord when we can't control our life and other people's reactions. We have to deal with what we have in front of us. Yet there are two sides to every coin: happiness and sadness. When we choose a kind and positive perspective and *give up the need to be right or have the last word*, it is amazing what can happen for us and others.

FINDING TRANSFORMATION IN ILLNESS

Dealing with difficult people is one thing, but is it possible to find the positive gift within a serious illness? It is, and this is one of the major challenges of our healing journey — to see and appreciate our "wake-up call" to a better life.

As the following personal story makes clear, one of the ways to create support for our positive thoughts is to create a special place all our own and to use it as our healing space. This is the space where we go to find peace of mind and inner confidence, to pray or think, to write in our journal or talk to God.

Nancy's Story

My name is Nancy, and I was adopted at birth. I grew up feeling and looking different from other family members. I felt confused, lost, and alone a lot and *imperfect, why else would I be given away?* I thought someday I'll have a family of my own and I won't make any mistakes, so no one will give me away again, and I'll feel safe. As a result, I have used my family life as the vehicle through which to feel whole and happy. This meant that my husband, daughter, and son had to be feeling okay and well for me to be feeling safe or okay. This was impossible!

I was focused on taking care of and pleasing others. I didn't consider my own needs — I didn't even know what they were. This was a shaky foundation on which to build my feelings of happiness and safety.

The breast cancer journey is forcing me into the center of my own life rather than vicariously living through family members. I hope to get in touch with my own emotions. I have always been afraid to express my anger, fearing rejection, but in order to be more authentic, I have to risk it.

Not being home to myself may have contributed to my illness. Until recently I didn't believe I was supposed to be here. I've run away from intimate contact with myself — once again fearing the shadowy dark side that may have contributed to my being given away — not rational, I know.

This continual lack of groundedness and lack of acceptance of all parts of me has certainly contributed to my struggles. This floaty feeling has extended to the creation of my sacred healing place. I've created it, but it's in the room with the bills and other yucky stuff — self-sabotage so I won't look inward with peace?

I look forward to positive change and healing!

CREATING OUR SACRED HEALING SPACE

By creating a sacred healing space, we are answering an authentic and universal call to connect with the holy; tending this connection is important to our happiness and our healing. Our space needs to be meaningful, beautiful, and reflective of our way of finding inspiration and feeling graced. In it, we might place pictures of loved ones, such as children, friends, lovers, and spirit guides, or images of angels, gurus, spiritual teachers, or sacred symbols. We might want stones, crystals, candles, incense, or a single flower — all of the above or none of the above.

The physical representation of what we consider sacred isn't as important as the feelings that these objects generate within our deep heart. It makes no difference whether our healing space occupies an entire room or a closet, the top of a bedroom dresser or a small place on our kitchen windowsill. It can be several places. It may be a single special picture of a loved parent, a friend's birthday card, or an anniversary remembrance; these can be the beginning of a special space, which we can add to as we choose.

For some, the decision to create a space in itself may be a challenge if we believe we will have to explain or defend ourself to those we live with. If this is our situation and we want to avoid conflict, then we can be discreet, putting a rose and a picture of our favorite angel on the top of our dresser and making that our space. The power isn't in the number of objects or the size of the space. It derives from the meaning we give it — as long as it draws us inside, away from the worries of the world, opening a secret garden gate to our own inner world.

The other important part of creating a sacred space is to use it, regularly and consistently. Having a routine is important for helping us show up for what we believe can help us. We can decide to take five or ten minutes in the morning, at a point when we can create a break in the action; we can put down what we're doing, close our eyes, breathe, and put our hands over our heart. I think of time in our healing space as heart-to-heart time with God, time to stop doing and to remember the magic of just being. Slowing down, we can feel our body relax. We can then feel our worrying and planning mind slowing down a little, and finally we can surrender to the beauty of what we believe in.

ACTIVITY

Prayers and Our Sacred Space

Making time for quiet meditation and prayers is an ancient practice. We need to pray and make contact with a Source of Love to which we can tell our troubles, receive guidance, and feel blessed. We are happier women and feel less burdened when we give ourself quiet time every day. If our daughter, for example, requested that we not bother her for fifteen minutes while she was quiet, we would go to every effort to honor that request. We can, in turn, ask our family to honor our request because everyone knows how much responsibility rests with Mom.

1. Decide where your sacred space will be. Clear whatever needs to be cleared to make room for the objects and items you want to put in your healing space. See how these things feel when combined. For example, you may honor your grandmother, but when you put her picture in your space, it may not feel right. This is your space.

2. Put something new into your space on a regular basis. Make it beautiful. Change it with the seasons or when a package arrives with a glorious new ribbon — put the ribbon around one of the pictures and add new energy to your space.

3. Use your space every day, whether for an hour or a few minutes. As you show up, you are really showing up for yourself. You're taking a breather and touching your deep heart — to grow, heal, love, and care for yourself and others.

4. Give this gift to yourself.

❧ ATTITUDE SHIFTS ❧

1. How I interpret my experiences impacts my healing.

2. Trust is a major factor in my healing with Spirit. When I trust that Spirit is here to support me, I can begin to heal from the inside out.

3. I must create a positive environment for my healing and my life.

4. I can create whatever I choose from each encounter I have with people. The choice is mine to be positive or negative.

5. I will create a sacred healing space that gives me an actual physical place (no matter how small) to go to daily to stay connected to Spirit.

PART FIVE

The Original Love Triangle

I cannot dance, Lord, unless you lead me.
If you want me to leap with abandon,
You must intone the song.
Then I shall leap into love,
From love into knowledge,
From knowledge into enjoyment,
And from enjoyment beyond all human sensations.
There I want to remain, yet want also to circle higher still.

— Mechthild of Magdeburg

CHAPTER TWENTY-TWO

Our Heart Is Our Life Partner

*I have come to understand that the key to genuine satisfaction
lies in the inner world, the world of stories and memories.
It comes not from any outer achievement but from the richness of
experiencing life and sharing the inner experience of life with others.*

— Rachel Naomi Remen, MD

*T*he heart is our life partner. Our heart and our brain are in permanent alliance — doing a dance, each with its own responsibilities and gifts. The brain holds, activates, and implements the wishes of the body and mind. The heart supervises the brain and adds the essential touches of love and compassion. Where the brain would only seek to get the job done, the heart wants the job done in style.

Let's think first about our physical heart. Our heart is a muscle about the size of our fist. It has four chambers and four valves. Its job is to circulate the blood in our body, receiving the blood that is oxygen-poor, passing it through the lungs, and then returning it to the body oxygen-rich. The heart beats continuously and is such a quiet partner that unless something is wrong — we notice a pain or a missed beat, for example — we remain unaware of its unceasing contribution to our well-being. Ultimately, of course, the heart muscle wears out in spite of its valiant efforts because physical life is meant to end.

In the fetus, the heart begins as a tube and then slowly develops the upper chambers of the heart (atria), which separate into two; then the lower two chambers of the heart (ventriculi) separate. In a seven-year-old, the heart beats about ninety times a minute; by the time we turn eighteen, the heart stabilizes at an average of seventy to eighty beats per minute. The heart delivers oxygen and nutrients to three hundred trillion cells. Each day, on average, the heart beats one hundred thousand times and pumps about two thousand gallons of blood. If we live seventy years, our heart will beat more than two and a half billion times, pumping approximately one million barrels of blood.

Our heart at a physical level is the miraculous and enduring pump that circulates our blood and keeps us alive. At an energetic level, our heart is an emotional and spiritual pump that circulates love to and from our many relationships with others. It also bonds us with Presence — the essence of Creation that is within us and all around us.

As we study the heart and how to help it heal or stay healthy, we are discovering that the heart wants and needs love, sharing, community, and appreciation for its efforts. As these essential ingredients are offered, marked changes in healing our heart occur.

Dr. Dean Ornish, a clinical professor of medicine at the University of California in San Francisco, is well known for his landmark research into reversing heart disease without drugs or surgery. He was also one of the first well-known physicians who talked about the importance of love in healing. He says, in his Heart Healthy Lifestyle Program, "Awareness is the first step in healing. We all know that diet, exercise and smoking are important factors in health and well-being, but many people are not aware how important love and relationships are. When we understand that the time we spend with our friends and family is essential to our health, then we can view these as important to our survival, not just luxuries."

As we heal our heart — which doesn't mean just eliminating

disease, but alleviating dis-ease — we need to look more closely at the energy of love. Love is certainly an emotion, but deepened it becomes our means of trusting ourself, our healing, and our life journey. Love deepened into compassion allows us to become a useful instrument of positive change in God's hands.

OUR HEART HOLDS OUR TRUE INTENTIONS

Just as our body holds a physical space for our heart in the center of our chest, likewise energetically our heart holds a space in our center to grow into greater love and confidence in making life better. At the energetic level, our heart guides us to love using three primary intentions or directives: to love ourself, to love another without giving ourself away, and to love other people and creatures.

The first intention allows us to love. Following it means slowing down and easing our resistance to what is in our life. As we stop resisting we enhance the true flow of inner grace and love, which awakens us to a steadier and more peaceful way of facing our life.

The second and third intentions direct our love outward, and most of us have experienced these types of nourishing love: falling in love, caring for our children and family, following a meaningful career, and enjoying friendships. All three intentions get expressed through the course of everyday life — through our love of sports, poetry, music, the outdoors, chocolate, roses, and so much more.

Love isn't a product of our thinking mind but of our knowing mind — the inner healer. When we are in a loving mood, all things go better in our life, and this is true no matter what our circumstances look like. Especially when we encounter difficulties, our knowing mind urges us to trust in love and its continual flow into our heart, mind, and life. Love is expressed not only with flowers and boxes of candy: it shines whenever we make it through another round of difficult treatments, whenever we manage a breakup without giving up, whenever we lose people who were mainstays in our life without completely falling apart, whenever we fail at some endeavor but trust there will be another chance, whenever we cope with mind-numbing depression or anxiety without losing the light of hope.

LOVE FUELS OUR LIFE

Our heart flourishes on fuel — love — that is pure and full-strength. Allowing love to fill our heart is like putting high octane fuel in our car's gas tank. However, we need to pay attention to the quality of the fuel as well as to having the proper mix. Symbolically, love that is the wrong mix or of poor quality can cause sputtering in our heart — an irregular heartbeat — or it can clog up the heart — a heart attack — or it can foster a loss of belonging over where to find love — a stroke.

Often we drive our life on a minimal amount of love. We pursue one or two of the heart's intentions, but not all three. Many times, for our life to run properly, we need to love ourself better. It isn't enough to love others and count ourself out of the equation of worthiness. Conversely, our life will misfire if we see only ourself as important, and we discount the needs or feelings of others. Further, loving ourself and those close to us should lead us to help grow and realize love in the wider world. As we express love in all these ways, believing in our own value and making ourself useful in this world, we can truly experience a level of love within our deep heart that is real, potent, and complete. In this way, we avoid traps of neediness and fear that may tempt us to throw ourself into relationships out of a desire to feel loved or to find wholeness through someone else.

In addition, just as the quality of gasoline helps our car's motor perform better, we need a steady diet of high-quality love to help our heart work better. Any time that love — whether for ourself, others, or God — feels inauthentic or misaligned, it weakens our energy field. It's like trying to run our car on watered-down gas. This happens when we say we believe one thing but act out of integrity with that belief — such as when we express our love for someone when we see them, but as soon as that person leaves the room we're quick to point out their faults to others. When our thoughts, feelings, words, and actions are not aligned, we lose the very power of loving intent that we need for our health and our life. However, when we are in alignment, we have a strong sense of our inner knowing, which is our genuine connection with Presence, a God of Love within our heart.

❧ ATTITUDE SHIFTS ❧

1. My heart is my "life" partner.
2. My heart needs and wants to love.
3. Energetically my heart holds the space for me to grow in love and deepen my confidence that I can make life better.
4. Energetically my heart has three primary directives: to love myself, to love my partner and family, and to love all others.
5. The purer and more consistent my love is, the better my heart works.
6. The more my thoughts, feelings, words, and actions are in alignment, the stronger my inner knowing and connection with Spirit.

CHAPTER TWENTY-THREE

Knowing When to Give

Some keep the Sabbath going to church.
I keep it staying at home,
With a bobolink for a chorister,
And an orchard for a dome.

— Emily Dickinson

oving others, putting ourself in service to others, is the way we return to our own heart to know what love really is. This is how we
enhance love within ourself and our world. Our awareness of the needs
of others, along with our intention to help them, effectively ramps up
the energy of love available to us. It lets us carry more love and of a
higher and more refined quality.

The desire to give comes from Spirit. It is essential to become aware
of the needs of others in order that we can better understand the community of life around us and to find the ways to live and work co-
operatively with others. What we put out is what we find returned to
us. We learn to be inclusive rather than exclusive.

There are basically two kinds of giving. The first is sharing with the people we love or those who touch our heart because of their need. The second kind of giving is offering what we've learned, created, or discovered through our life journey to the wider world, to those we don't know yet. We do this in the belief that our writing, teaching, talking, and sharing will be useful to other people on a similar journey.

The books and seminars we find most helpful aren't random encounters. Someone shares how they have walked through their own fire and come out the other side, and what they have discovered or found to be true applies to us.

Here are two stories, one from a client and one of my own, that exemplify how giving love fosters unexpectedly wonderful and sometimes deeply healing outcomes.

MARJORIE: HELPING OTHER WOMEN

Marjorie is a perfect example of a woman whose desire to help by sharing what she had been through in her healing attracted the circumstances that allowed her to give back.

Marjorie was in her early forties, and she had two teenage boys and a caring husband. A year previously she had completed surgery, chemotherapy, and radiation for breast cancer, and she had now returned to being more fully with her family and also working part-time with her husband in running the family business.

I had seen an interview in the local paper of her healing story, in which she talked openly about the way she had approached her healing — choosing to undergo surgery, chemotherapy, and radiation as well as pursuing other essential forms of healing, such as acupuncture, massage, nutritional counseling, and homeopathy. Stillpoint was planning to offer a free program in the area for women healing from breast cancer, and I met Marjorie for lunch to ask her advice on how to alert the local community.

Marjorie was warm and bright, and as she talked, it was clear that she had a great deal to offer. She said, though, that she didn't think she really had anything to share; nevertheless, she had been willing to be interviewed for the paper because she thought it might help other women. Her willingness came from a quiet inner intention to help. She didn't know how things would work out, but she was showing up where opportunities presented themselves. She described other ways she had since shared her story, which had materialized through no effort on her part, and how good it made her feel to think that her story was in some way helping other women.

She was, in other words, expanding her identity; already a mother, partner, and business helper, she now was a teacher and supporter of other women's healing journeys. This quiet way of stepping up to help is often the way our life work arrives. It comes from our spirit's intention to love, and as we respond, positive outcomes arrive unexpectedly. In other words, we need to *take the first step in order that the Universe can take the second.*

LETTING LOVE GUIDE OUR SERVICE

Our healing moves us forward in our life and our work. As we are ready to move out into the world again, we want to stay tuned to the lessons we've learned about energy. The expanded energy of love heals us and provides the sometimes missing factor that will make our efforts, whether in business or relationships, successful. Our healing provides the energy and sometimes the goal.

Just as with Marjorie, our healing itself may fill us with a passionate desire, one we want to share with the world. We may not know how to proceed, and we may imagine that expanding our heart-centered work will require Herculean efforts and lots of money. Actually, we can expand our work most successfully by staying attuned to the energy of love. That is, *what is born in love can only expand through love.*

Since our way of helping is born from love, the only way we can develop and grow our project is to maintain the same intention and energy of love. We are responsible for holding the intention of what we love in a sacred way. We need to maintain a clear path energetically from our original intention to the desired outcome. The more kinks and turns in our thinking, the less energy is finally delivered to others — whether they are customers, clients, or friends.

We need to keep the lines of energy as straight as possible from our heart to our recipient's heart. Then, when we're ready to share, the opportunity will present itself. In other words, we need to watch for the Universe to say Now! and be ready to respond — to return the phone call, take the class, or show up through our effort. Our desire to better the lives of others sets this in motion.

We also need to be flexible. The Universe can be playful, and we need to be ready to join its game. Here is how: *stay connected to the effort and not the outcome.* This means our request must come without strings attached; we cannot direct God on how or when we will participate. We must simply show up, ready to participate — guided by Spirit — and not be attached to the shape of the end result.

This is, of course, very difficult. We are often very attached to a particular outcome, whether for our healing, our relationships, our career, or our kids. Perhaps we get caught up in "winning," believing there is only one winner and everyone else is a loser. Perhaps we feel if we come in "second," our accomplishment doesn't count. But participating is the real gift. Few Olympic athletes win, for example, but most describe the thrill of participating, of being given the chance to do one's best.

We need to approach our healing the same way — we must stay in the process of healing and let tomorrow take care of itself. We need to keep our eye on the moment, since this is where all the action happens. When we feel inclined to share our story or extend a helping hand, then the energy of our intention will bring about an opening for participation.

In addition to offering our service to the wider world, we also should focus our service on those close to us and whom we love dearly.

MELANIE'S HEALING —
WHEN LOVE FILLS US COMPLETELY

Decades ago, when I was just beginning to wade into the water of spiritual experience, I had a most astonishing occurrence. In retrospect I know that this healing was merely a glimmer of what is possible when we trust the loving process within us. This inner presence of Spirit allows us to open to the power of love available from God and to become a channel, a conduit, of that love.

My five-year-old daughter, Melanie, was spiking a very high fever; this had happened once before and caused her veins to collapse, creating a serious health crisis, and I was afraid that it was happening again. I sat on the floor, holding her in my arms and trying to comfort her, while I waited for the pediatrician to call. Inside I heard a voice say, *See your daughter filled with Love.* I didn't know what that meant, so I did nothing. Again I heard — *See your daughter filled with Love.* And so I imagined a golden light filling her body from her head to her feet. When we're frightened about someone we love, we often suspend disbelief and open to help even when it comes from an unlikely and invisible source.

I held her for several moments until the phone rang. I left her to answer the call, and when I returned several moments later, Melanie was bouncing on the bed completely well. I could not believe my eyes. This wasn't possible — one minute she was deathly sick, and the next minute she was fine. How had my clumsy attempt at visualization healed her?

The gift of loving flows into us with great strength when someone we love is in serious trouble. We forget our own inhibitions and fears and silently ask the Universe, God, Spirit to assist. We open the doors to healing in our mind and our soul — and allow for healing to happen. Perhaps healing happens in this way sometimes because, on an unspoken level, we accept that Divinity loves us even more completely than we love our own.

SPIRIT LOVES US

I'm reminded of how much Spirit loves us in a story that I heard from a Sai Baba devotee. Having traveled to Puttaparthi, India, to witness Sri Sathya Sai Baba's amazing healing love, I'm aware of the ease with which powerfully focused love produces physical, emotional, and spiritual healing.

The story is of a woman who had traveled from Poland to see Sai Baba because her son was about to undergo serious heart surgery and was not expected to live. She spoke little English, but thinking that Baba spoke only English, she struggled to learn several words to convey to Sai Baba in person her fervent prayer for her son's healing if she found the opportunity.

Thousands of people were seated in the temple on the day that she was present, and she had miraculously found her way into the front row. (There are no accidents in the seating arrangements at the ashram, as anyone who has ever been there can attest).

During Sai Baba's darshan — the walking past of a holy person — he stopped in front of her. She blurted out, "My son is in trouble. I'm afraid for him. Help him please." And Sai Baba looked into her pleading face with an expression of penetrating love and kindness — a look that I've been privileged to feel myself — and he said to her in a soft voice, "My son, my son." In other words, the woman's son was his son, too, and he was already aware of the man's need for healing and was engaged in helping in the appropriate ways.

All is known at the higher levels of consciousness, so Sai Baba already knew of her son's need, whether through her prayers or just because Love knows what is needed. Remember, there is no spiritual separation among any of us — we are one interwoven and interconnected Universe.

This is an important story because we tend to think that being healed means having our symptoms immediately cured. And sometimes it does, as in Melanie's case. But many other times the healing that is needed may take other forms first. We may need healing emotionally or spiritually before a lessening of symptoms can occur. And sometimes the point isn't to take away the symptoms, but to free the spirit to awaken more completely.

I've found that a healing always occurs on the appropriate level when we earnestly pray for healing. God — in all forms, through Sai Baba, Jesus, or Allah — is always on the case whether or not we're calling attention to a need. It certainly makes us feel better, however, to bring our needs to God's attention.

An additional way to consider healing that happens in direct response to love is that Divine Love — meaning unconditional loving — actually raises the vibratory level of the energy moving through us, thereby enhancing our own body's responses as well as any treatments we're taking. The intention of unconditional love offered to ourself or another focuses the most powerful energy of the Universe. Imagine a forty-watt bulb shining in a warehouse — pretty dim. That is the usual flow of chi throughout our body. It just keeps us alive. Now imagine a laser light focused directly on the intention for healing — it amplifies the energy so that out-of-the-ordinary shifts happen.

ACTIVITY
Feeling the Power of Love

Throughout *Spirit Heals*, I often ask you to put your hands over your heart. This gesture is a powerful means of connecting with the energy of love from Spirit and giving it to yourself. Here is another way to experience the focused power of love right now:

1. Rub your hands together and then separate them about an inch.
2. You'll feel the normal chi or prana energy between your hands. The energy feels thick, warm, or fuzzy in the palms of your hands.
3. Now rub your hands together and open them slightly again. Only this time, in the open space between your hands,

picture in your mind's eye someone you love with all your
heart.

4. Paying attention to the tiniest sensations, you'll discover
   your hands are ever so subtly being pushed apart.

5. Now rub your hands together and place them directly on
   your chest over your heart center.

6. You are now giving yourself the same heightened energy
   of love for healing.

LOVE IS ENDLESS, WE ARE NOT

Our heart needs to love in order to stay healthy, and we can imagine it
was the Creator's plan that we balance our giving and receiving of love
 by understanding the energy pattern of our heart center. From an energy perspective, we are always urged to give because it fills out our
heart space. Each time we give, we grow in our capacity to love. And the
more we use our love, the more love we generate and the quicker our
recovery time when we are depleted.

However, we need to realize that, unlike Divine Love, we can de-
plete ourself. We have limits. We can overextend and exhaust ourself in
our giving and find ourself feeling resentful of or victimized by the demands of others. We can tire ourself physically and even exacerbate a
 chronic condition that we're trying to heal. We definitely feel the energy
drain *when we give knowing we're giving energy we don't have.* Our energy isn't unlimited any more than our money is.

While it is true that we have unlimited access to the energy of love,
we are limited in how much we are able to hold at any one time — like
a bucket that can hold only so much water. Even if we try to access
more love, we can't hold it — the energy flows over the sides. If we
want to be able to hold more love, we need to become a larger bucket.
 We expand our capacity to love through daily connection to Spirit and
using and giving the love we have appropriately.

Thus, while it is essential that we give, it is just as essential to give in a balanced way that maintains our heart energy. We should watch out for falling into the trap of trying to do everything our personality self tells us we should do.

For instance, I talk to my ninety-three-year-old mother every day, and I visit her as often as I can. She always immediately forgets that I've called, and so I'm continually reminding her of all that my husband and I do for her each day. It gets wearing, and it also makes me feel as if I'm supposed to give more and more, but giving more doesn't register.

Recently, I hadn't seen her in two weeks because I'd been traveling, and once I got back I promised to go see her on a particular day. However, when that day came, a winter storm of freezing rain was forecast, and I was working feverishly on writing this book. I didn't want to suspend my work; nor did I want to be on the road later in the day when the storm arrived. What to do?

My situation was no different from anyone's — we often must balance competing needs and desires. So I took a moment to turn off my self-critic (which was telling me I had to go see my mother even if I ended up in a ditch) and listened to my wisdom mind, which is guided by my deep heart. As I inquired inside, I realized that I didn't have the energy or the will to make the trip to see my mother that day. I held out the intention that another way would appear. Just then, my husband appeared and asked if he could help — and he set off to visit my mom before the storm hit, while I kept working.

This story illustrates another important lesson. Our intention to find a solution can open the door for others to participate. We benefit from remembering to *let other people help*.

LETTING OTHER PEOPLE HELP

Recognizing that we have limits means that there will be times when we need help from others. While some people always lean on others to help, most of us err in the opposite direction — we try to do it all. In fact, allowing others to help balances their heart energy. Remember, it isn't just we who are prompted to give, but others also are prompted to give love to others — whom can they give it to? They can give to us with the same delight that we would have in giving to them.

As long as we hold the intention that *I can do this by myself*, then the Universe respects that and leaves us to it. As soon as we request help, the intention goes out that help is needed, and it comes in all kinds of unlikely ways. We all have stories of how someone who we're convinced is an angel — actually or figuratively — finds us when we most need it and comes to our aid.

Yes, by respecting our limits and saying no we may sometimes disappoint people who are depending on us. We may be seen as the bad guy — can we live with that? Do we have the courage to say no? When we do need to say no, we can put our hand over our heart and send out the intention for help to arrive — and it will.

OUR INHERITED AND ACQUIRED GIFTS

We each have inherited gifts and acquired gifts, both of which come together in our life as abilities and desires to serve others — I call this the urge to help — and become a healer and a mentor.

Being a healer and mentor doesn't mean we necessarily become actual healers — in the sense of putting our hands on someone, although we might — but rather that we realize we are connected to the Divine Source, and through our intention to hold a loving place within us we can be a conduit for positive healing and change in whatever way we choose. We might bring balance and love to our workplace through the way we go about our daily job. We might increase the loving energy at our children's day care through our everyday conversations and normal routines. Our intention to hold love is what gives our actions power.

What I call our inherited gifts are our capacities for loving that we bring into this life. As we become more aware of our capacity for loving, we become more willing and prepared to use those gifts. We inherit the gifts of love, compassion, caring, and genuine friendship. We come into this life with an aptitude for loving — we desire and pursue love. We find it quite natural and satisfying to care about others, to interact and form lasting relationships. We seek out ways to make a statement with our life and to improve conditions around us.

What I call our acquired gifts are the ways that we learn to love, which we develop through diligence and effort. Our acquired gifts of loving are those that don't come easily to us, such as learning to value ourself as truly worthy or recognizing that our usefulness isn't only in doing for others. Learning how to love often takes us through the difficult terrain of love affairs and marriages that don't work or that become quiet stalemates. We learn what makes for a good friendship no matter who is at fault for a problem; we also develop our ability to let go of resentments and take hold of the life that is offered.

Learning to love is difficult for all of us. None of us comes to this life completely prepared to love unconditionally. We all begin by loving very conditionally. I'll do this for you as long as you do this for me. The Source of Love within our deep heart, however, is the way we learn how to love differently.

Because our heart is home to our ability to love, using both our inherited gifts and acquired gifts, each of us must learn the lessons of loving because it is the only way to make our life work. We learn how to tap the energy of love and focus it toward greater happiness in our life, greater intimacy and caring in our relationships, and less fear and anger. Love is the true healing energy that is continuously available to us. Just as our physical heart beats to circulate blood, our energetic heart beats to circulate our intention to love from greater wholeness and empowerment.

☙ ATTITUDE SHIFTS ❧

1. By identifying my intention to help others I increase my healing power.

2. I can give by sharing with people I love the specific things they need or by sharing what I've learned with the wider world.

3. Being open to sharing my gift of love without being attached to the specifics of how allows the Universe to open the way.

4. What I give birth to in love expands in love.

5. I need to stay focused in the effort and not be tied to the outcome.

6. My healing journey may not lead exactly where I had hoped, but I can settle into my deep heart and focus on the Universe providing what I need.

7. Connection to Divine Love actually raises the quality of energy flowing through my body and enhances my healing.

8. My heart needs to love in order to stay healthy.

9. I can give only when I am full of love myself. I can't give what I don't have.

10. I can increase my capacity to love and be loved by keeping my daily connection to Divinity vital and using the love I receive wisely.

11. I need to let others help me. It benefits us both.

12. I was born with the capacity to love. It is my inherited gift. My acquired gifts are the ways I choose to share that love.

13. My energetic heart beats to circulate my intention to love, just as my physical heart beats to circulate life-giving blood.

CHAPTER TWENTY-FOUR

Tend and Befriend —
A Woman's Response to Stress

With a single note the nightingale
makes me notice the rose
falling into that place
where everything is music.

— Rumi

In addition to holding a healing intention of love, we help our heart by becoming aware of how we react to stress. Loss and stress affect our heart health, the health of our reproductive system, and, of course, all the body's systems because we are one interrelated whole.

For many years, it's been believed that the universal human response to stress was *fight or flight*. Faced with a wooly mammoth, we instinctively either pull out a spear and attack or run for the nearest cave — fast. However, while this stress response is accurate for men, it turns out that women actually respond very differently: studies show we *tend and befriend*.

In a landmark University of California study in 2000, six researchers, who coined the term *tend and befriend*, proposed that while women are biochemically alerted to stress from within their own bodies, their response is different from that of men. Rather than fighting or running away as their first line of defense, they tend to make allies and interface with others within social groups in order to minimize stressful conditions. The researchers found that women under stress release a hormone called oxytocin — which can be thought of as the tend-and-befriend hormone because it has a calming effect. By contrast, while men under stress produce oxytocin, this is overridden by testosterone, and so the calming effects of oxytocin are lost.

Men, it seems, are biologically programmed to defend, attack, or flee when threatened. Woman are biologically programmed very differently. Perhaps because women are the ones who carry the child inside, nurse babies, and care for small ones, they aren't programmed to attack or run. When an enemy threatens, a woman's response is to tend the community and to befriend and transform the danger. Her greatest strength comes from making peace where she stands, finding ways to solve the conflict while protecting those in her charge. In the face of danger, a woman doesn't fight or flee and risk abandoning her children or other community companions; instead she seeks to bridge differences and solve problems differently.

These words — *tend and befriend* — are transformative for our psyche. They hold the keys to our understanding of women's heart disease. Our desire to tend and befriend explains why we stay in terrible partnerships, rationalize unviable jobs, and hang in when others tell us to fly away. When we are stressed, we respond to a deep biological and perhaps spiritual need to gather others around us and find our way toward a solution.

When the bonds of relationship are broken, the impact can be catastrophic for a woman. Her relationships with her family, friends, and work colleagues — all those who make up her community — are essential to her heart health. In healing our heart we must take an inventory of our circle of loving support and find where there are cracks or empty spaces. We need to fill those holes and repair those relationships or seek those connections that produce the love and continuity that we need. Our reaction to stress is to circle the wagons, and if we can't do this, we can't relax.

When I first read the words *tend and befriend* I was shocked by the profound impact they had on my heart. I knew with everything in me that this concept was true. It explained so much of my own behaviors and the behaviors of female clients and friends.

We've heard so much about being a victim — let's finally realize that, *if we've been the victim, it was because of our deeply rooted biological need to tend and befriend.* That said, a biological tendency is no excuse for sacrificing our real value and for staying in situations that no longer serve us — even if leaving is hard.

THE POWER OF BEING A NONTHREAT

Author Carol Lee Flinders in *Enduring Lives* describes a perfect example of the tend-and-befriend response elegantly displayed by Jane Goodall, known for her groundbreaking work with the chimpanzees in Gombe, Africa. As Goodall went for her daily walk in the dense African forest, the wild chimps, assuming she was a threat, began throwing things, uttering high screeches, and mounting charges — clearly threatening her. The chimps were strong and could have easily torn Goodall to shreds. Rather than either *fighting* — which would have been ill advised — or *fleeing*, she hunkered down. She crouched low, nibbled on grass, and kept her eyes on the ground, demonstrating that she wasn't a threat. Eventually the troop moved on. She became a nonthreat.

When we aren't a threat to others, they share their most intimate thoughts and feelings with us. We see their true selves more clearly and are better able to understand or at least witness what is troubling and making difficulties for their deep heart and its loving intentions.

Women, or those having a predominantly feminine mind-set, are closer by nature to participation in relationship — emotionally and spiritually — yet this closeness to nature and to the earth has led to the harassment (and worse) of women by those who are not in touch with their feminine mind and find it threatening.

Women by their biology can sense where healing is needed and often know what to do or how to bring new energy to an old wound. We recognize that the hope for the future comes from us standing together in our power and beauty as women and conscious men to shift the world's perspective toward a truer picture of equality and shared respect.

WHAT BREAKS A MAN'S HEART

Let's look for a moment at heart disease in men, to help us understand the contrast with women. As with women, when a man's heart hurts emotionally or spiritually, it sets up serious stress factors that tax his physical heart. But what leads to this?

Men seek to be valued, respected, and nourished for their very willingness to go out into the jungle of life and protect their cherished ones. They need to find meaning in their work as protector and to receive concrete, immediate rewards for their services to those they love. Men need to have close and intimate ties to those they have chosen to protect.

When men feel abandoned by their mates, unfulfilled emotionally and sexually, overlooked or disregarded in their work, it leaves them vulnerable to heart imbalances. Since the drive to protect and care for their loved ones is so often funneled through men's jobs and work, the people men work with can be as much factors in their sense of happiness as their family.

However, many men find it hard to satisfy their needs in the workplace. Many consider the work they do as only a means to earning money, or perhaps a conduit for gaining greater respect and position in their chosen arena. The work itself often offers no lasting meaning. In corporations, layers of middle management, red tape, and bureaucracy often distance men from drawing satisfaction from the end result of their efforts. Many say they are rarely recognized for their efforts or get any direct positive feedback for their time and energy.

Just as the tend-and-befriend response speaks to a woman's biology, so a man's fight-or-flight impulse kicks in when stress arises, when his heart and passion are not engaged. Men may seem remote, unwilling to express what they feel, think, or fear. But women are not fooled. We have a clear sense of what makes them tick; we just want men to own their uncertainties and express their feelings. We may wait a while for this.

When men become anxious or their needs are not met, they may become even more competitive, more difficult, standing up and shouting at the enemy. Men, or those with a dominant masculine mind-set, can be easily taken off track if they don't understand the direct way they are contributing to those they care about.

Consider reproduction: for nine months a woman carries and nurtures the fetus in the womb, while a man contributes sperm during intercourse and then stands back to support, protect, and await the birth of the new one. Women produce the new child, or original concept, as part of their biology, while men help conceive and then await the birth as protector, until they join in guiding the new child — or new idea — into the world with genuine authority.

HIDE AND SEEK: THE DANCE OF COUPLES

In the land of couples, one person is always leaning more intently into the relationship than the other at any one time. This is the reality of hide-and-seek, and we are better off not taking it personally — although of course we do. The ties or bonds that we desire as women and men appear to be different, but actually we all want intimacy, whether physical, emotional, or spiritual.

For example, women, or those with a strong feminine mind-set, tend to want more emotional and spiritual bonding, and so they lean forward toward their partner at times when they hope this deepened sharing and conversation may be forthcoming. By contrast men, or those with a more dominant masculine mind-set, tend to lean into the relationship at times when they are hoping for friendship and physical closeness. We benefit from remembering our basic biology: a woman needs to feel loved to make love, while a man needs to make love to feel loved. Love is what we all want, but we go about indicating that very differently.

We can improve our relationships by recognizing and understanding this energetic shift from seeking to hiding and back again. When we're seeking, we want the other person to respond, communicate, and come toward us. When we are hiding, we want to be left alone; we want to think and consider our own perspective, to mend our own fences before sharing. When we are hiding, no amount of pushing or prodding is going to unstick us from our position.

Sometimes we each need time away from the other, and at other times we need to feel closely connected. Sometimes we need to be with close friends and not have it interpreted as rejection or abandonment of our partner. Sometimes we want to be touched, and sometimes not.

Rather than continuing to push the one who is hiding, it is much better to give them deep-hearted attention. *Communication that is felt is so much more useful than communication that is only heard.* By this I mean that we should stop pushing, arguing, asserting, or denying what our partner might be doing, and instead we can move into our deep heart and really listen and respond in a loving and meaningful way. This way we can level the playing field.

Deep-heart communication, loving because we can, coming more than 50 percent of the way — this helps us understand what the other person is needing, and then we are more willing to understand the teeter-totter of relationships, how we go into hiding as the other goes into seeking, and so on. Remember, our partner is never in the same place at exactly the same moment we are until we invite him or her in. This shift is continual and fluctuates in every relationship, but it is most marked in partnerships.

Ideally, when we hide, we are really generating energy for ourself and our partner, while when we seek, we are expanding the partnership energy and increasing opportunities as a couple. In a healthy relationship, each person takes turns hiding and seeking; but have the freedom to change and expand their role as they choose. In an unhealthy relationship, one person is always seeking, and the other is always hiding.

We can really grasp how we feel about another person when we allow ourself to express this hide-and-seek dynamic in our body. Donna, a psychotherapist who is a friend of mine, offered to help my first husband and me find ways to bring closure to our twenty-two-year marriage. She suggested we each strike a pose in relationship to each other that represented how we felt toward each other and our impending separation.

It was a fascinating and creative exercise. My body moved into a posture in which I was leaning back and away (hiding), while he was leaning forward as if in anticipation of more information (seeking). Our bodies showed us the essence of what was happening and how we felt about it.

As we imagine striking a pose with our mate, we'll discover who is hiding and who is seeking right now in the relationship. This helps us understand how each person feels in the role and whether there is agreement on who is playing what role.

Hiding and seeking can be positive or negative. We hide in a healthy way when we are renewing and rediscovering our self and work, but not when we hide from intimacy and emotional connection with our partner. Seeking can be a healthy search for more in our life and in helping our partner to expand, or we can be, in unhealthy ways, pushing past boundaries and seeking satisfaction outside the partnership. This happens, for example, when we turn to friendships for our emotional and spiritual closeness rather than to our partnership. There may be good reasons for this choice, but the partnership is likely to collapse from lack of energy if the growth doesn't happen at least partly together.

It is normal and expected that both men and women need hiding and seeking energy, and that they will need to shift roles. When we are dealing with our healing, remembering this will help us understand the other person's reactions and improve our communication. However, even though we acknowledge that our biology will always be a strong factor in determining our actions, we can still make choices. There is a new energy afoot, and it is called *transformation*.

Through love, we don't need to default to acting from our biology alone. The energy of Spirit expands our natural tendencies to better meet the needs of our relationship. We can feel safe and loved enough to stretch the limits of how we learn, listen, share, give, and love.

❧ ATTITUDE SHIFTS ❧

1. How I react to stress is an important factor in my healing.
2. As a woman I deal with stress differently from men. I don't respond with *fight or flight*. I *tend and befriend*.
3. Knowing I react differently to stress helps me understand why loss of love and relationships can have such a big impact on my body and psyche.
4. I am a natural healer — this is a gift of my biology.
5. What breaks a man's heart is not finding meaning in his work or reward from those he loves.
6. If I understand in my primary partnership who is hiding and who is seeking at any given moment, I can deal more compassionately with whatever issues are present.
7. Although it is very important to understand my biology, it is equally, if not more important, to understand that through love I can transform myself and my healing.

CHAPTER TWENTY-FIVE

Self-Love — The Way Will Open

I am never upset
for the reason
I think.

— Gerald G. Jampolsky, MD

From an energy perspective, the heart center or heart chakra has three primary aspects: love for ourself (me), love for a significant other (us), and love for all others (all of us). Each of these aspects is responsive to our feelings about the way we love and are loved in return. These three aspects of our heart and circulatory energy is our original love triangle.

Energy flows down and up through the chakras and also through what are called meridians. These energy lines were mapped thousands of years ago to highlight the anatomy of the energy field. Along these lines, specific nodes or locations have been identified where imbalances can be adjusted through, for example, acupuncture needles.

Our energy field supports our physical, emotional, and spiritual bodies, and it shows where our physical body is healthy and balanced and where it is out of balance. A major center in this energy field — and the most important — is our heart center. Within our heart chakra, self-love is a major aspect of our original love triangle.

Self-love relates to the concept of *me*. There are two ways we can think of *me*. One is from our personality self, which is limiting and only concerned with making our own way in the world. The personality self is self-centered; it considers only what's in it for *me* and is continually and eternally seeing opposition. Or we can consider *me* from the expanded sense of our inner healer and spirit. Thus, *me* can relate to our small self or our larger self; we can expand the focus of *me* to our true Self, which holds our connection to the intention to love.

While our small self is as limited as our personality self and self-critic, our expanded self understands that we are connected to all life and that our behavior affects all others. We have compassion for all people and are able to realize — even in difficult times — that we are loved and that we are all spiritual beings simply having human experiences. This is our inner healer — Spirit.

We all wish for more self-love. Our sense of self-worth tends to go up and down depending on our circumstances, but we long to maintain a steady awareness of our value and positive contributions. The key is that if we look at our life through the lens of the small self, we will feel inadequate and without lasting love; if we put our hands over our heart center and choose to experience life from our own true Self, we will find the expansive self-love we seek.

The way will open is a Quaker phrase that I find meaningful because it suggests that there is a simple and unhurried way to allow life to come to us — to come into us — so we find meaning, opportunity, and enjoyment in the moment. The message is not to worry, all will be well, trust the process. Trusting that the way will open is important as we consider self-love because self-love is one of those unsolvable Zen koans. We know we need it, but we haven't a clue where to find it, how to generate it, or even what it really feels like. It is like looking at our hand, which operates under our control, but which we so take for granted that we fail to recognize it is operating on our behalf.

Self-love is not something we acquire, but something we find. We discover upon inner inspection that self-love is alive and well and simply needs to be unearthed. We find that self-love is the motive that encourages us to be "selfless": to take the time to call our aging mother each morning as she sits alone in the nursing home; to rush an armload of groceries to a friend who hasn't been able to get out of the house because of a sick child; to sit and listen graciously with a difficult friend and not react with frustration or anger; to forgo the satisfaction of blowing off the driver in front of us who is poking along thirty miles under the speed limit; and even to get up and face the day when we'd rather pull the blankets over our head and sink into despair. The motivation to show up, to open our eyes to life, comes from self-love.

True self-love, the love from our true Self and not our personality self, allows us to receive from others, completing the circle of our giving. However, when we share from the *me* self, we're looking for what comes back to us. We measure the gifts we give and those we receive to be sure we're getting enough.

True self-love is valuing ourself by our own standards and not those of others, even if we feel not another human being alive understands or values us. True self-love bears fruit by opening the way because there is lasting energy there. We often mistake our *me* self for our true Self. The love we seek in self-love is love from our true Self.

ASK YOURSELF

How do I recognize the me voice in loving exchanges?
How do I recognize the true-Self voice in loving exchanges?
When I love myself with my true Self — what does it sound and feel like? What do I respond to when I sense this truly loving voice within?

We allow the way to open through prayer, meditation, thoughtful actions, and kind and compassionate attitudes. As we give to ourself what we normally give to others, we can recognize a more restful and accepting attitude toward ourself and our various failings. We can cease the incessant circling thoughts of our mind and allow love to flow to us. As we accept that the way will happen — the way out of pain and distress; the way out of fear, anger, and worry — the way becomes available, and it is often the road not taken. This rarely traveled road is the one to our true self-love. On this road, we don't need to do more to be happy, but less. *Nonaction — the willingness to stop and allow love to be present in our life — is the way to travel this route.*

We will never reach a place where embodying self-love will be easier than it is right now. Becoming more aware of the self-love available to us right now not only enhances our healing but gives a smoothness and settledness to our life. It lets us be happy right now in spite of any issues that remain up in the air.

LACK OF SELF-LOVE APPEARS AS AN IRREGULAR HEARTBEAT

A common problem with our heart is an irregular heartbeat. A beat that is too fast or too slow indicates a blockage in our heart's electrical system, which stimulates our heart to pump. Obviously, any abnormality in our heart's regular beating should be looked at medically. From an energy perspective, the electrical signal that begins the stimulation of our heart to beat rests in the sinoatrial, or SA, node, which is in the upper right chamber of our heart. The SA node is called the heart's natural pacemaker. After being stimulated, our heart sends an impulse from the SA node to the AV (or atrioventricular) node, which rests between the upper and lower chambers of the heart, and the impulse continues to the lower chambers of the heart — causing a heartbeat.

We can equate the lack of effective electrical charge with the lack of effective and meaningful self-love. We're not talking about just feeling good but about true self-love: believing in yourself and having the ability to calm the inner self-critic and generate peace of mind — or in this case, peace of heart.

Our heart is electrically stimulated to produce a consistent heartbeat, and spiritually, it stimulates us to awaken our understanding, to trust that the way will open, to align ourself with the open spaciousness that is our true nature. This spaciousness is the feeling of being unhurried, out of emergency mode, and fully present and aware of the people and circumstances in front of us in the moment. Feeling spacious is one way to think about what it feels like to love ourself from our true Self.

STARA'S UNEASY HEART

Stara came to me for help because of a racing heartbeat, which had been getting progressively worse. She wanted to reduce these upsetting periods and better understand from an energetic perspective what was happening.

We talked about her background. Stara had been married four times, and the current partnership was problematic; she and her husband had many unsettling episodes of explosive anger on both their parts. She wasn't sure she wanted to stay in the partnership, but she couldn't bear the thought of another divorce and its effect on their young daughter. Stara worked as an acupuncturist, but she was unsatisfied here, too, feeling she was destined for a bigger mission. She struggled to find that mission and to make sufficient money to have some breathing room in her life.

I had her do a practice I call "mend your bowl, heal your life." For Stara, I asked her to envision the bowl that held her love for herself.

I asked Stara to relax and envision a bowl of any shape, size, or color that held the energy of her love in the area of her chest, and then to imagine where the bowl was cracked or broken. She immediately realized the bowl — a gorgeous red crystal vase-shaped bowl — had no bottom. All her love that was meant to nourish her heart and symbolically stabilize her heartbeat ran right through the bowl, which represented her heart chakra or center.

Even when people praised her or offered to involve her in new experiences, she held back. She was in a major push-pull situation: she longed for greater involvement and service through her work and her life, but she was afraid she would disappoint herself and others by being less than she imagined she could be.

I asked her to call up her feelings about her broken bowl and whom she blamed for it, which turned out to be her mother. She felt that her mother had failed to instill in her the confidence to stay the course when things got difficult. Instead she was shown by her mom's behavior that it was preferable to bail or fail to risk speaking up. I directed her to move into her own deep heart and imagine inviting her mother to the same inner place to join her in a soul-to-soul dialogue.

As Stara conversed with her mother in her mind's eye about why this happened, the answer Stara heard in her heart was that her mother believed she had no answers to give to her daughter and so had avoided any intimate conversation. In this vacuum, Stara had assumed that she, too, was wise to avoid emotional closeness with others.

To begin to heal, I asked Stara to reclaim something of herself from her mother that she had given away. She chose her ability to decide when it was the right time to leave or when it was safe to show up, and she settled on the words: *I reclaim my own knowing.* I then guided her to reenvision her bowl and to mend it; by filling in the bottom, she was indicating she was now able to hold her own self-love, and she had a powerful visual reminder of her healing experience.

After this very moving practice, Stara's heartbeat settled down, and the episodes became much less disruptive. She moved her office to a new location, grew her number of clients, and also began to offer additional energy work — thus expanding her visibility and making significantly more money. At last report, she and her husband were trying to work things out.

Our way will also open. Trusting in the process of spiritual growth allows our heart to open to ourself. We stop being so hard on ourself and open to others. It isn't easy being human. It isn't easy to stop chasing love and to allow love to awaken. Loving ourself lets us rest in who we are and what is happening. The rest is paperwork.

❧ ATTITUDE SHIFTS ❧

1. I can love myself in two ways, as the small personality self or the wiser true Self.
2. If I stay in my personality self, I will never experience enough love. If I connect to Spirit through my true Self, then love is unending and ever present.
3. True self-love is when I value myself whether anyone else does or not.
4. True connection to my Spirit self comes not by doing but by being.
5. Peace of heart is the state in which I can quiet my critical mind and rest fully in Divine self-love.

CHAPTER TWENTY-SIX

The Biology of Partnership

How do I love thee? Let me count the ways.
I love thee to the depth and breadth and height
My soul can reach, when feeling out of sight
For the ends of Being and ideal Grace.

— Elizabeth Barrett Browning

*H*umans may be on the top rung of the evolutionary ladder, but we must procreate to carry on our species like all other animals. Women often refer to this innate biological urge as our inner time clock, which gets louder the older we get and time starts running out for us to conceive a child.

Our biological urge to mate is as strong as our biological urge to tend and befriend. We choose someone who we believe will be a good parent to our children and who will be a steady and reliable love partner as life gets challenging. For all the talk about romance, I think most of us realize that what we want takes effort — to develop our own sense of self in order to walk side by side with our partner.

Not all women decide to partner with someone or to have a child. Many women decide that the divorce rate is too high and that they would rather channel their energy into meaningful causes or work. Or they just never find the right person. Sometimes we decide not to have children because the world is too unsafe or because there are already too many abandoned children in the world. We may decide against artificial means of getting pregnant or decide that raising a child alone is too monumental a task.

From an energy perspective, our heart doesn't care what we do — whether we are single or married, whether our partner is a man or a woman, whether we have children or not. Our heart cares only that we are in balance with the choices we've made. Our heart needs to be at peace with our decisions regarding our biology of partnership. What matters is that we're at peace with what is in our life right now.

MAKING PEACE WITH WHAT WE HAVE

In doing an energy evaluation it is interesting that what shows up under partnership in our heart center is our peace of mind — and peace of heart — over the partnership and child-rearing issues in our life. This means that even if we don't have what we want right now — perhaps our relationship is not as satisfying as we want or we are trying unsuccessfully to conceive a child — we must make peace with our situation.

But how can we do that? The answer is to shift our attention from what we need from others to what we can give to ourself; in this way we may find an answer to our dilemma. The best answer is to say *steady, steady, steady* and focus on what we love about what we have.

Often we think that we have to be in a partnership to be complete. Our ancient biology tells us this in no uncertain terms, but we have grown from those early dangerous days when two had a better chance of surviving than one. A partnership is no longer necessary for survival, and we do not need to have a partnership to have a strong relationship with ourself. Emotionally and spiritually, we redefine ourself as whole within ourself, rather than needing a partner to be complete.

We also come to peace with our current situation by accepting that love comes in different ways and different packages. We can stop pushing the river and see who around us needs love. What we have in the present is what we have. It doesn't mean it can't change, but leaning over the proverbial fence thinking the grass is always greener on the other side serves us not at all.

We definitely need to fill our heart with love for another. But that can be anyone, not simply a biological mate: it can be a child, a grandchild, or a dear friend, for example. In essence we've moved from needing to satisfy our physical biology alone by having a mate and producing children to satisfying our emotional and spiritual biology, which may or may not come in the traditional package.

Emotionally, we need to share love with someone who returns love openly and freely. This does not have to be sexual. Often we find the love we need from another person in strange and unfamiliar places. A friend of mine joined Big Brothers and Big Sisters and found a young person in desperate need of love. Together they have helped each other make the most of getting whole and realizing their dreams. My friend hopes to find a partner, and she may find one eventually, but right now her life is filled with love and she's content.

Nor is it workable to believe in the old myth that we will find one love who will be everything to us and fill every need. We have a complex, ever-evolving life. Our spiritual appetite to become more closely aligned with Divinity may also be preparing us for a partnership that we're not yet ready for.

We may be growing into our full spiritual skin, so there will be a partner or close ally in the future. We don't know. I remind myself, in situations that seem unsolvable in the present, that *if I don't know right now — perhaps I don't need to know.* Can we learn to live without definitive answers to all our questions? Can we risk staying around to see what will happen? Do we have a choice?

WE ARE WHO WE BELIEVE OURSELF TO BE

Two people may come together because they feel a need to complete themselves through the other, which is not especially healthy. However, we can grow together into a redefinition of ourself. The way we choose to define ourself can change. We may finally decide to be more than the one with cancer or heart disease, the one with no children, the one who never went to college, the one who never made a success of her career, or the one who always is poor. Often we define ourself first by our perceived limitations, but our own dear spirit can open us to an inner chamber — and from this inner sanctuary we realize that our true definition of self is broader, transcending any physical or emotional circumstances.

ASK YOURSELF

As I define my full self:
Who do I think I am?
Who do others think I am?
Who am I really?

Of course, in our day-to-day world, there are limitations all around us; we often feel limited in our ability to accomplish what is most important to us. But these external limitations are different from the conceptual limitations we put on ourself. Whether or not others are living from their own limitations, we need to set our own success markers and realize the fullness of our gifts, talents, and spiritual connection. We help transform the limitations of the world by living the best life we can.

Each day, we can remember that we are unlimited spiritually, and that spiritual energy can in many ways compensate for any physical and emotional limitations. However, in terms of our partnership, as we redefine ourself, we also change our relationship, which can be difficult. We may struggle with the other as the definition of ourself that was true when we began the relationship evolves.

We come together with another in the hope that the other person will expand our sense of self, building our confidence and self-reliance. Yet it is natural to continue growing within the day-to-day flow of our relationships. Our best approach is to allow ourself to keep growing emotionally and spiritually, keep opening up our passion, and, with love and compassion, keep helping our significant other deal with our changing horizons. We need to be willing to feel uncomfortable once in a while in our relationships to allow our relationships to grow. Growing pains aren't comfortable, but they are necessary.

LOVE AS ATTACHMENT

In the early stages of our development, beginning in the uterus, we develop a definite sense of whether we're being welcomed. One of the first realizations that comes to us about love is that love is an attachment in the human sense. We discover that love means to do what others want, when they want it, and to not complain. In our deep heart, we must recognize that this isn't the version of love we hunger for, but because we so hunger for love emotionally, we gobble up whatever is offered.

As we grow up, we may also be offered examples of love that only later do we recognize as inappropriate or even devastating experiences of abuse. I remember a middle-age man telling me about being tied to the bedpost as a young boy and whipped — while being told that it was being done out of love. It is hard to fathom how a parent could believe this was a loving act. Yet, physical violence and love are often caught in a terrible mix and then passed along to children. However, no matter what our experience of love as we grow up, our connection to Spirit is always available as our guide, and it continually seeks to show us what real love is.

As adults, we may continue to believe that love means attachment, not recognizing that this binds us in all the wrong ways. In this very human scenario, one part of the partnership or friendship feels obliged to follow and the other to lead; there is no side-by-side relationship.

Our attachments to the ways we need each other keep us from relaxing our expectations and requirements and becoming friends of choice.

LOVE AS COMPANION

Love as companion is the love that comes from walking with someone. We are trying desperately in our world and in our relationships to move away from ranking and into partnering — which means moving into a new balance between men and women and between the yin and yang within our own personality.

Where love is based on companionship, we have no compunction to hide ourself or to keep from following what we love, even when others don't see the vision we see. We're not undone by another's criticism or disapproval. We appreciate their willingness to walk a while with us, as if our footsteps are quietly measured with our breathing and we're in harmony — comforted with the company for a time. This, of course, is a very female way of approaching life, and we relate to it if we have a predominantly feminine way of looking at things. I do believe that this predominantly feminine perspective is what is needed in the world to soften long-standing battle lines and enhance people's ability to get along.

WE LEARN ABOUT LOVE FROM BIRTH

We might at first believe that as a baby we knew nothing. But we probably knew about love because we were aware, even as a fetus in utero, of what we felt.

Our early impressions as a baby and child up to the age of about six become the hard-wiring of our unconscious mind. The impressions of these years form the way we tend to operate. They include how our parents experienced life and the world and what we were told about ourself and others, about our chances for success or failure, and about our lovability or lack thereof. It's important to recollect what we can of this early hard-wiring, for these thoughts and feelings can override our loving energy and keep us from reaping the benefit of our healing and empowering efforts.

ASK YOURSELF

What are my earliest recollections from being in the uterus or during my birth?

What are my earliest recollections about the words that were used to describe me or my actions or attitudes?

What are my earliest recollections of how safe or unsafe I felt the world I was entering truly was?

To reprogram any negative hard-wiring we discover, we can begin by developing positive statements and affirmations. But to be most effective, we should bring Spirit into our affirmations and make them into belief statements.

For example, here is a possible affirmation: *All loss, illness, and poverty fall away as I step into my promised land.* To make this into a belief statement, we should add language that indicates that the power comes from Spirit through our mind and actions into the desired result. God is the doer — acting through the energy of love on our behalf. Here is the more powerful belief statement: *All loss, illness, and poverty fall away as I step into my promised land through Grace.*

Looking squarely at the way we've been programmed allows us to watch for these attitudes and beliefs — to be really vigilant when they show up — and counter them by putting our hands over our heart and overwriting them with our true loving messages, which are, in fact, belief statements.

I know from my experiences with healing, both my own and that of others, that love always heals what is not of love if we make room for it. In other words, *when we put our hands over our heart in love, a healing always occurs at the appropriate level.*

❧ ATTITUDE SHIFTS ❧

1. My biology to mate is as strong as my biology to tend and befriend, whether I decide to act on it in traditional ways or not.

2. My heart cares only that I am comfortable with my choices.

3. Despite my underlying biology to mate, I can be alone. I can have a strong relationship with myself that can be enough.

4. The more I accept that love and partnership can come to me in all sorts of guises, the happier, healthier, and more fulfilled I will be.

5. It is most important to my soul and heart that I grow beyond any limited definition of myself in my relationships and my physical health. I am unlimited spiritually, and I will become who I believe myself to be.

6. On my healing journey it is more important that I understand my needs and then hold out for my partner's understanding.

7. The sooner I understand the difference between love as attachment and love as companion, the sooner my relationships will have the depth and support that I am looking for.

8. One of the most important steps in my healing is to claim my innate worthiness to be loved.

9. I can turn affirmations into belief statements when I power them with Spirit.

CHAPTER TWENTY-SEVEN

Heart Attack — A Call to Remember Our Sacred Heart Song

After the laughter, all the muscles are relaxed, including the heart —
the pulse rate and blood pressure temporarily decline.
Physiologists have found that muscle relaxation and anxiety
cannot exist together,
and the relaxation response after a good laugh
has been measured as lasting as long as forty-five minutes.

— Bernie Siegel, MD

*P*hysically, a heart attack, or myocardial infarction, involves the death of heart muscle (myocardium). Most heart attacks result from blockage(s) in one or more of the coronary arteries, blood vessels that encircle the heart and supply oxygen and other nutrients to the heart muscle. Often, a heart attack is the first obvious symptom of heart disease, but it's usually the culmination of a lengthy process in which the coronary arteries have become clogged with fatty plaque, which is mostly cholesterol. As the arteries progressively narrow, blood flow to the heart muscle is reduced. If a vessel closes completely, the heart muscle it nourishes dies. The restricted blood flow encourages formation of a blood clot, or coronary thrombosis, which may cause the final blockage.

From an energy perspective, a heart attack may seem like a sudden

and unprovoked incident, when in fact it is only the obvious sign of a
more internal and progressive situation. Our lack of balance around
the partnership issue is basically the culprit symbolized by the coronary
arteries, which originate on the left side of the heart through the aor-
tic arch. The left side of the heart is the partnership side.

Emotions long held at bay; feelings of inadequacy, unworthiness,
or being unlovable; or the lack of a deep loving bond to others because
of one's own limitations result in excess stress to the heart and a slowing of the healthy blood flow necessary to nourish the heart. We can
think of a heart attack as one's imbalance in the energy of partnership.
In other words, in a heart attack our love supply has been diminished
or cut off — the love coming to us from ourself or others is insuffi-
cient to keep us feeling loved.

SUDDEN STRESS CAN BREAK HEARTS

Emotional stress can bring on a heart attack in someone who has coronary disease. It can also bring on a condition that looks like a heart attack in people who do not have blood clots, diseased arteries, or patches
of dead heart muscle. They have a temporary weakening of the heart
that decreases its ability to pump.

New research has documented cases of what is now being dubbed
"broken heart syndrome." Doctors at John Hopkins University reported on patients from 1999 to 2003 who experienced what I describe
above. The study — reported by the *New England Journal of Medicine*
on February 10, 2005, in an online story entitled "'Broken Heart' Syndrome Potentially Deadly But Recovery Quick" — suggests that many
people who were believed to have suffered mild heart attacks may actually have experienced a condition that only resembles a heart attack,
although it can cause death. It appears that most people recover without permanent damage. An overwhelming number of victims are
women, most in their sixties.

It is important to realize the significance of this confirmation that heart attacks, or something very similar, can be caused by emotional stress alone. As I've been sharing with you, changing our perspective to a more positive and life-affirming view — coming to terms with our life and being grateful for what we have — is the only lasting path to healing and spiritual growth. We need to find love within us to balance the inevitable losses that might precipitate this condition. We also need to find love wherever we can and let it count.

LOVING ALL — FINDING THE MEANS TO HELP OURSELF

So far, we've discussed two aspects of our original love triangle — love for ourself and love for a partner. Now we come to the third aspect of our heart trilogy, which is love for other people — for *all of us*.

Another name for this love is empathy. This is more than charity, or caring for people who are less fortunate than we are. Charity does not have any power. What has power is helping others because we realize we are all connected and our fate is tied to their fate. What happens to others ultimately happens to all of us. I'm reminded of a quote that Lynne Twist, author of *The Soul of Money*, shared from a native elder whose tribe lived in the Amazon rain forest. He said, "If you are coming to help us, go home. If you are coming to save yourself, then come ahead."

It is important for us to recognize our need to be aware of others, without the feeling that putting food in our mouths is taking it from others. It is better to be grateful for what we have and to honor and value it, and at the same time to have empathy and compassion for others that allow us to see what they need. We all have needs, and it isn't always about money. Money helps, for sure, but money without love and compassion is cold comfort. We should help others, and in so doing we bring a great deal of joy into our own life.

ASK YOURSELF

Why do I share?
How do I share?
What has been the most meaningful way I've shared this past
year?
What has opened in my own heart as a result of sharing?

 The world needs all of us who have a whole heart to understand that sharing brings balance to our own heart. Our heart needs compassion and friendship all the way around — given to ourself, to a special someone, and to others at large. We don't have to look further than our next-door neighbor, perhaps, to find a way to heal our own heart.

AWAKENING OUR GLOBAL SUN

When I was doing an intuitive energy assessment for a client about ten years ago, I unexpectedly found something quite extraordinary. I found an energy mark I had never seen before. I named it the Global Sun.

The Global Sun — or the space where it appears — is at the apex of the heart chakra, like the star on top of a Christmas tree or the reflection of the flame of the middle candle in a menorah. As I explored other clients' energy fields, I found that many people had this significant mark of Divine light. The light was sometimes brilliant and fully filling the space like a sun, and other times it was a hint or a sliver, like the early stage of the moon. The light always showed up in the place of loving, which I found extremely meaningful. It appeared in the people who expressed a desire to serve others — or more exactly, to allow their work to serve a higher purpose — which showed up through their contributions in their jobs, their families, and their personal spiritual practices.

This discovery of the Global Sun in people's energy fields is significant. It is a touch of the Divine — like the fingerprint of God on their heart telling them they will receive special guidance in this lifetime. Everyone has the outline of a Global Sun, and the more we seek Spirit in our living and our healing, the more the light fills in the space. Remarkable!

The Global Sun also suggests that, as a species, we are being helped at an evolutionary level to cross the abyss of self-interest and develop the capacity to care about others as if they were our own.

STROKES: FINDING WHERE WE BELONG

Even though a stroke doesn't directly affect the heart, it does affect our arteries, which carry our blood around the body. Physically, a stroke occurs when a portion of the brain is deprived of blood, resulting in ischemia or even tissue death. Strokes are a major cause of serious disabilities, including various degrees of paralysis, speech problems, visual disturbances, and impaired memory.

Cerebral thrombosis, the most common type of stroke, occurs when a blood clot forms in an artery supplying blood to the brain and is often preceded by *mini-strokes*. A cerebral embolism occurs when a wandering clot forms in the body, travels through the bloodstream, and lodges in the brain. A cerebral hemorrhage can be caused by the rupture of a weakened blood vessel, or aneurysm, in the brain. A subarachnoid hemorrhage is often the result of an injury in which a burst blood vessel bleeds into a space between the brain and skull rather than inside the brain itself.

From an energy perspective a stroke suggests an inability to find a place where we belong — a home where the way we love and how we want to be is appreciated. Symbolically, the clot that leads to a stroke is a sticking together or coalescence of our spirit's voice or song as it tries to fit into the world; our blood flowing through our various energy centers represents the various relationships of daily living.

When we're discouraged with our life — perhaps because of failing health, gradual loss of mobility, or the loss of a partner or close friend — we feel a generalized emotional and spiritual discomfort, as if we're free-floating and uncertain where our grounding is. We might be asking ourself: *Where do I fit? With whom do I fit? How do I fit with others? Do I need to even try to fit?* The clot takes the form of this uncertainty, this moving point of focus that is looking to find a place to lodge, to belong.

We can think of a stroke, then, as a condition in which we've lost our certainty about where and how to fit in our present or changing circumstances.

OUR BRAIN AND HEART WORK IN HARMONY

When our heart and our brain work in harmony, there is much we can solve and a great deal we can heal. The brain is as miraculous as the heart, but our focus in this book is on our heart because it is the means of awakening our power to love and to heal. The brain, the spinal cord, and their energy of thought show us the best way to direct our mental energy — toward developing our own wisdom and choosing a course in life that leads to commitment, involvement, enhanced creativity, and genuine relationships. While the thought energy coursing through our brain and our organs create the major messaging to keep our body mobilized and functioning, it is our beautiful heart that manages to infuse our cells, tissues, and organs with a will and a spirit to live.

To heal the three major heart-centered problems — irregular heartbeat, heart attacks, and stroke — we begin with self-love, move on to partnership love, and finally arrive at love for others. Together they show us the energy of our heart chakra. The energy in our heart is continually moving to bring harmony and balance. When we have a heart pain, it is good to put our hands over our heart and to name the pain rather than to suppress it. It is important to name it and allow ourself to feel it before seeking to move through it.

Pain and loss have doorways that we can find. It may feel like drinking a glass of terrible medicine, but when we have finally drained the glass, there in the bottom is the message. It is over and you're still here.

ACTIVITY

Your Sacred Heart Song

The heart actually sings a song — not a tune that you'd hear on the radio, but a cosmic rhythm played out through nature that you recognize as peaceful and soothing. This sound or series of sounds calls you home to your true Self. It generates renewed healing and inner harmony. Your body recognizes your Sacred Heart Song as the way you can best heal your heart; from an energy perspective, it harmonizes all the rhythms of your body and helps quiet confusion and worry.

This song comes from sounds like the wind rippling through aspen leaves, the trickling sound of water over rocks, the crash and retreat of the ocean's waves. This love song reminds you that you are holding an intention to heal and to love just the way you are. This particular sound is why you prefer the ocean or the mountains, why you choose certain kinds of vacations in one part of the world over another. You choose this sound (or sounds) because it feeds you at a very deep level when you're stressed out and feeling blue, when you need to make changes, find the right answer, or trust yourself. Your Sacred Heart Song is your very own love song because it is your spirit calling you home to feeling loved no matter what miseries have befallen you. It celebrates your life.

When you say, for example, *I feel heavyhearted, I am brokenhearted, I can't put my heart into it,* or *My heart is weary*, what you're saying is your Sacred Heart Song has been derailed. Your Sacred Heart Song is the antidote for a broken heart because it tells you that if you can find wholeness within yourself, then others — perhaps not yet known to you — will come along who will value you and who you are.

You create your Sacred Heart Song by combining your heart's

favored sounds from nature with several empowering words — those that tell you that you can heal, that you can love and be loved, that you have a place in your family, and that there is a special means through which you can share your loving.

By placing your hands over your heart and repeating your chosen words, you can recall the nature sounds, and as you replay in your mind your own special love song, your heart and your body will hear and respond at a cellular level, reducing stress and worry.

Repeat your Sacred Heart Song when you feel yourself resisting whatever you need to face, even if that is unwanted and unpleasant. Repeating this love song will also lessen the fear of acknowledging feelings that you may not want to feel. This healing comes to your heart because you've combined the natural world (through the sound of nature) with your mental, emotional, and spiritual intention to love well and feel the result of that loving.

Here is how to create your Sacred Heart Song:

1. Decide on your favorite natural sound, which calms and relaxes you.

2. Create a phrase that reflects how you want to love, how you want to heal and become whole and strong and aligned with your mission. For example: *I receive love to heal my heart,* or *I share love with others, and I feel them loving me in return,* or *I share love throughout my day and nourish my heart and make it whole.*

Once you've created your Sacred Heart Song, use it often and experience the difference.

You love just because you can. You love because at some deep and unknowable level, you recognize that love is the only way to find your way in a world that often seems dark and lonely. Your love song — your Sacred Heart Song — is trying to play, but like a racehorse at the starting gate, the gate must open for the horse to run the race. Just so, you must acknowledge that you are worth loving. That acknowledgment opens the floodgates of your heart, allowing you to live more fully and to heal more completely.

❧ ATTITUDE SHIFTS ❧

1. If I don't love myself enough, no one else, even my partner, can love me enough. I must love myself first.
2. I can truly help myself and others when I understand that the balance between our hearts is accomplished through sharing.
3. I have God's fingerprint on my energetic heart if I choose to accept it.
4. When my heart hurts, I can put my hands over it, connect to Spirit, and safely name and move through the pain I feel.
5. My Sacred Heart Song is a sound from nature that echoes in my deep center and brings me home to Spirit.
6. I can add words to my Sacred Heart Song, and when I sing it with my hand over my heart, it will bring me healing and comfort every single time.
7. My body reacts on a cellular level to the healing power of my Sacred Heart Song.

PART SIX

Claiming the New Season of Our Life

Hush...
Whisper earth's name in a smile, or a sigh,
Whisper earth's name... await a reply.
Whisper life's name with a breath of peace,
Whisper life's name... let hope never cease.
Whisper your name... feel the echo of your voice,
Whisper your name... the silhouette of your choice.
Whisper God's name... in truth's joy, or truth's sorrow,
Whisper God's name... in a prayer for tomorrow.

— Mattie J. T. Stepanek

CHAPTER TWENTY-EIGHT

The Best Healing Medicine

The best and most beautiful things in the world
cannot be seen or even touched.
They must be felt with the heart.

— Rumi

No matter what the individual elements of our healing program are — surgery, herbs, massage, or acupuncture, for example — we still need to remember that our healing path is rather like making a great bouillabaisse. The finished product always tastes a little different than we imagined, and so we continue to add to the mix to make it right. It is the same with our healing journey, whether it involves a life-threatening diagnosis, a chronic condition, or simply maintaining ourself in the green zone of health.

It doesn't matter what healing we need, we always find it by following these three important steps: one, survey our options — all of them. Two, sample some or all of those options. Three, make a true commitment to some or all of them for a designated period of time, and then evaluate the results and decide what to keep, what to change, and what to discontinue.

Many of us hope that our healing will involve a singular series of proven treatments, and that when we walk out that door on our final visit, we can tell ourself, that's it — we're done. But even if we finish with certain treatments that correct a specific concern, we're not finished with our healing. We need to stay aware of all that we've learned about our attitudes and reactions; we need to remain intuitively connected with our body's needs. The difficult part is staying on the healing path and continuing to be aware and question ourself: Are we doing the right thing? Are our choices leading us to get healthy and stay healthy?

THE DIFFERENCE BETWEEN HEALING AND CURING

We naturally want to hear the words *you're cured*. But in a very real sense no one can ever say that because we each are a complex, continually changing network of systems. Our diet, our reactions and emotions, our environment, our living conditions: all these factors and more change and evolve, and we change with them.

We may feel that we have healed whatever has ailed us, and we can trust this inner knowing. Often it is important to recognize that our inner knowing is telling us that we've moved out of range of an illness or fear. This can be powerful medicine. However, because the body isn't a machine, and illnesses and upsets are imbalances, we need to think about what went wrong. We must make sense of what happened, even years after the condition has cleared up.

In other words, a cure is specific and sometimes temporary, but the art of healing is ongoing. Imbalances are part of life, and so the way we live each day — paying attention as best we can — is what allows us to continue our life-healing journey through all the years of our life. We may have periods of acute imbalance and chronic imbalance as well as periods when we are well-balanced — and all we need to do is monitor our predisposition to certain kinds of stress and certain stress pathways in the body that interrupt healthy flows of energy.

We can decide right here and right now to apply the ongoing art of healing to all facets of our life: in our relationship with ourself and Spirit, with our family, friends, and partner, with our work, and with the way we intend to live and participate in the world.

Paying attention is the best way to heal ourself in all these things. It is our very best medicine.

MANAGING UNCERTAINTY

Of course, we still want guarantees, and there are none in healing. Perhaps we have "cured" our cancer, but who's to say it won't recur? This doubt and uncertainty can develop into a daily terror that our cancer will return or that we'll develop another clot and drop to our knees in the grocery store. But there is another way. The other approach is to remain steady in the realization that tomorrow isn't written, one way or the other, and that it is our today that creates our tomorrow. All we need to focus on right now is — right now.

Our best insurance is to open our mind and our heart to possibilities and be willing to explore what may help and support our healing and our life. We can soften our anxiety as we make an ally of our body, rather than regarding it as an enemy waiting to get us again. Many times when we get ill, we feel that our body has let us down. But our body probably feels the same way, asking of us: *Where have you been these past five years I've been trying to get your attention?*

Our body needs our attention when it gets sick or just slows down. Ignoring it does no more good than ignoring the strange sounds your car is making until the transmission breaks. The sooner you find out what is behind the trouble, the better.

Often we experience signs and symptoms long before conditions become serious enough to appear on an X-ray or in a biopsy or to result in the collapse of a relationship or career. We need to remain in touch with our body and its signals for attention. When our flu turns into a bronchial condition that won't clear up, when our monthly bleeding has gotten out of control, when our headaches are increasing in frequency — we must no longer ignore our feelings or intuitions or begin guessing what might be wrong. We need to find out.

Paying attention means staying tuned to our inner voice — not worrying and doing nothing or asking one expert and giving up if we're unsatisfied with the answer. When we sense that we need more guidance, we pursue more guidance and validation of our intuitions; we can also find different ways to treat our situation. As we put our hands over our heart, we'll be guided how to proceed.

As we ask questions of ourself and others and as we learn about our situation, we can inquire more intelligently of those who seek to help us. If we identify lifestyle changes we must make, we can begin to make those changes slowly, in a way that is manageable for us and our family.

As we monitor our health, as we pay attention to what we feel and think, we find it easier not to panic at the first sign of perceived trouble. We constantly replace doubt with knowing, imbalance with balance. We continue to use the practices we're learning in *Spirit Heals* to help ourself. We ask, listen, and pay attention to life's synchronicities and Spirit's voice, and follow the guidance we receive.

GIVE OURSELF TIME TO HEAL

However, as much as we need to always pay attention, after the challenge of an illness or a period of struggle or change, we can give ourself the time we need before moving on. It is rather like going over a waterfall in a kayak — we need to adjust our equipment, bail out the water that got in the boat, take hold of the paddles again, and generally get resettled before and as we check out the nature of the water downstream and decide how to proceed.

Our head and our heart may be talking to us in different ways before, during, and after a major challenge to our health or well-being. In the longer term, we may want to experiment with other approaches. Before leaping back into surgery or another round of chemotherapy, or when we want additional treatment for a residual pain or trouble as a result of those treatments, we may seek out other modalities, like acupuncture, energy work, nutritional counseling, spiritual guidance, or therapy. Integrative healing offers us a wonderful array of healing modalities, but we don't need to rush to pursue all of them. Particularly after a major challenge, we should allow ourself to rest and take stock of the most balanced way to proceed.

The way we perceive our situation allows us to honor the truth that Divine timing has interrupted our life. We can then be on the alert for the best ways for us to restore balance by cherishing our body, creating positive thoughts, and welcoming Spirit into our growth path. This longer-term path may involve forgiveness, compassion, joy, love, kindness, or perhaps finding meaning where we've found none in the past.

DIVINE TIMING AND PURPOSE

Divine timing means that all things come about according to a plan and a timetable that are completely incomprehensive and unknowable. Interruptions disrupt our life just as we think we have things pretty much under control, and our frustration at this can lead us to feel picked on. Perhaps we have just leveled out from a recent crisis, and then something new occurs. When we find we have an illness — or imbalance — it is a natural, human response to ask, *Why now?* or *Why at all?* We wonder if God is punishing us.

Whenever we find ourself questioning the Creator's purpose, we face a paradox: we want and need to believe that Divinity is as personal and intimate with us as our breath, and yet others tell us to not take it personally when bad things happen. Which is it? Is God as Divine Love personally involved with us or is God as Divine Love removed, caring about us but not involved in the immediate details of our life?

The way we want God to be with us is the way God is with us. If we only want to see Divinity in the sunset and the miracle of our glorious Earth, then it is so. If we want God to speak from our deep heart and guide every detail of our life, then it is so. If we want God or Spirit to show up when we have needs and to disappear into the background when we're happy and secure, then it is so. The answer to the question is that God is all things, and so the determining factor of God's appearance in our life depends on what we want. And what we want depends on whether we're in touch with the inner voice of Spirit or we're lost in the thinking mind of our self-critic.

Our true inner voice knows the Creator because our knowing is in touch with Spirit. It is Spirit that is the extension of God's love within our body and our mind. Our critic voice, by contrast, tries to do life on its own terms with no support from the only genuine support available to us — Spirit — and so we always come up empty-handed and desolate.

Our problems — whether breast cancer, diabetes, or divorce — are not Divine punishments, but they arise from imbalances brought about through the experiences of being human. However, our problems may be the result of Divine timing, which has interrupted our life at this moment for a reason. And what is that reason?

The reason is the possibility of initiation. When our life is temporarily interrupted by any major event, we are offered a choice: Will we see this challenge as bad luck or punishment or as an opportunity for initiation into a new life?

Will we see our imbalances — physical, emotional, and spiritual — as leading us toward greater meaning, awareness, love, and inner joy, or will we experience these periods as merely another reason to blame ourself, someone else, or the system? I'm not talking about standing up for our rights if our needs are ignored or dismissed by the medical establishment. I'm talking about how we perceive what has happened to us emotionally and spiritually. We need to take back our authority and choose what comes next instead of just acquiesce or complain.

We can't heal if we are waiting for someone else to apologize to us or for someone to make up for past mistakes. Nor will we truly heal if we ignore the imbalances in our life that led up to our illness or problem. Will we choose to see our disease or struggle as devoid of meaning — as something bad that happened to us on the way to the forum — or will we allow that Divine timing is involved in waking us up to the truth that it is time for us to refresh and renew our relationship with Spirit?

ASK YOURSELF

What am I doing with this gift of my life?

Whom and what do I value?

What will be the result of my present efforts if I could fast-forward five or ten years?

Do I like what I see when I look ahead?

Am I engaged in life in a way that feels substantive and creative?

Am I loving the people who have seasoned my life to date?

Am I grateful for the gift of my life?

How do I express that gratitude?

FINDING MEANING DOES NOT EQUAL ACCEPTANCE

Finding meaning in a challenging experience has nothing to do with enjoying suffering or accepting a life of suffering. Rather, finding meaning suggests that we overcome obstacles in our deep heart first, then in our thoughts and feelings, and finally these changes shift the disrupted rhythms of illness to the healing rhythms of health.

As we recognize Divine timing as our call to reevaluate how we've been living, what pressures we've been putting on ourself, what stories we've told ourself, we allow positive change to begin.

God didn't give us a disease or a difficult time so we would wake up. It was *time* we woke up, and the illness was simply the vehicle giving us the opportunity — portending a new day and a new way to be more in touch with our purpose and our happiness.

We have real power in our hands when we see spiritual significance and meaning in our present interruption. We can choose to call our interruption by its real name: a spiritual interruption to deepen our connection to the Source within, an event of Divine timing meant to wake us up. Calling our experience by its real name gives us power over health, and over emotional and lifestyle challenges, as well as our ability to find solace within.

ASK YOURSELF

What do I think of the idea of Divine timing?

How do my illness or life troubles suggest that a level of Divine timing may well be a factor?

What would it mean to me if I accepted Divine timing in my situation and began to think of my imbalances as connected to initiation rather than failure or bad luck?

✿ ATTITUDE SHIFTS ✿

1. Although my healing journey may change, I can always regroup by going back to the initial three steps:
    A. Survey all my options.
    B. Sample some of the options.
    C. Make a plan with a true commitment for a specific period of time and then reevaluate.

2. I can trust my inner knowing when it tells me that I've moved out of range of an illness.

3. As much as I want a guarantee that I will be cured, I am wise to stay present in the moment and remember that I create tomorrow by living fully aware today.

4. It is a mistake to ignore my body and what it is trying to tell me through my intuitive perception just because I am scared. The sooner I sense and deal with an energetic imbalance in the appropriate ways, the sooner I begin to heal.

5. It is helpful for me to know that there is a Divine plan even if it seems incomprehensible.

6. Divinity is with me in the way I want Divinity to be with me.

7. My illness or difficulty is not a punishment. Divinity is not punitive. My life has been interrupted for a reason, and that reason is so I see the possibility of initiation — the possibility of living fully in my relationship to Divinity.

8. My life healing becomes possible when I open fully to the gift of initiation and begin to live my life open to love and Spirit.

CHAPTER TWENTY-NINE

Welcoming Home Our Own Wild, Free, and Naturally Regenerative Nature

Trust is the universal law of attraction.
It's at this point that we begin to understand that
we don't have to bend, shove or manipulate the universe —
we only have to relax into our place in it.

— Gloria Karpinski

What does it mean to be free and to trust that we are capable of regenerating what we need for a good life? What does it mean to realize we can choose what we welcome in and what we take to heart — in other words, what we take into our spirit home for safekeeping and to cherish?

As we know, our body can regenerate cells and organs. We regenerate our body on a regular basis, replacing so much of ourself that we are practically new human beings. For example, approximately 98 percent of our body is totally renewed in roughly one year. We have a brand new stomach lining every four days, new skin every thirty days, a new liver in six weeks, and even the skeleton is replaced every three months.

We can also regenerate our psyche from emotional loss and find healing and wellness in shorter periods of time than we might imagine. We are able to regenerate our entire life because we are fashioned from the ultimate Source of renewal and regeneration — the creative energy of the Universe. The hard part is believing that.

It is never too late, whether we're talking about overcoming disease or renewing a hopeful attitude. What an amazing realization to accept that it is only our self-critic, our personality self, that tells us we've passed the point of no return.

OUR WILD CARD IN HEALING

We follow our personality's messages because they seem to make sense in a linear, space-time world. If things are only what they seem when we see with our physical eyes and physical senses, then we obviously may feel our outlook is hopeless. For example, from our personality's perspective, we might think if the result of surgery isn't optimum, then we just have to live with it; if our cancer has returned, then it will keep coming back; or if the person we love has left us, then no one will ever love us again.

But the Universe doesn't operate according to linear time, and healing isn't held to any standard chronology. Spirit doesn't need time to set things right to help us set things right. At the point where we begin to change and call on our own powerful spirit, an entirely fresh layer of opportunities comes to us.

Healing comes from awareness of and respect for what we face, but also from a deeper knowing that we have the true power to heal flowing within our deep heart. This *inner flow of Love is the optimum change agent — the wild card in our healing*. When we factor that agent into the healing mix, we maximize every treatment and set ourself on the path of inner healing, which inevitably brings healing to our body.

FINDING OUR WILL TO HEAL

Healing from the old messages about ourself and the world around us brings us into the sunlight of our own wild, free, and naturally regenerative nature.

It is not only us. Starfish, for example, know how to regenerate an entire limb. They can grow a new arm when the old one is damaged or cut off. What gives the starfish its amazing ability? Genetics, maybe — or perhaps it is simply the will to have an arm or the ability to reconnect with its energy body, where the arm still exists.

While we cannot yet regenerate a breast or a leg, it is important to understand that our energy body continues to see any organs we've had removed through surgery as still present. Knowing that we remain intrinsically whole is paramount in our trusting that we can regenerate our life — if not yet individual organs. The fact that the energy imprint of organs remains in our body also suggests that if there is a blocked energy line, then just having the organ removed doesn't solve the problem. It is essential to always heal body, mind, *and* spirit.

Can we heal completely when it's clear that our body is too weak to handle the medical treatments that are necessary? Myriad doctor and patient testimonies indicate that unlikely, even impossible, healings have and can take place, which means we can heal, too!

In the early 1980s, Dr. Bernie Siegel became a powerful change agent by traveling around the country talking about healing. As a respected physician and professor of surgery at Yale University Medical Center, he led group therapy sessions with what he called his "exceptional cancer patients." These were patients who were living longer and healing because they brought spirituality into their healing and accepted that their feelings played an important role in their body's recovery.

The good news is that the body is always seeking to find balance and to heal. We want to tap into this *will to heal* so we can reinvigorate the energy flows within us. The physical body checks in continually to see what the energy body is saying and feeling.

Imagine this field of energy around the physical body as the perfect matrix for our life and our healing. This energetic matrix allows our physical body to read, or reread, the important messages of function. A liver cell, for example, that has lost its way and become cancerous needs to reestablish its original healthy purpose of breaking foods apart to nourish the body. I've named this powerful healing matrix our Template of Perfection.

OUR TEMPLATE OF PERFECTION

My years of research and clinical experience have shown me that not only can we heal, but our body is miraculous in its wisdom and tenacity to keep us alive and healthy.

As I began to work with the body's powerful physical matrix, I asked myself, *Why does a change in emotions affect the body differently?* As I sought to explain how the body can change through the improvement of our attitudes and beliefs, I developed the concept of the Template of Perfection.

Imagine that we have a Template of Perfection surrounding our actual body. It is an energy body and remains close to our actual body, perhaps within an inch to six inches. Imagine that there is a continual dialogue between each cell in our physical body and the cell's counterpart in the energy body. The image of these energy cells in the Template of Perfection is perfect. The cells don't age and are not influenced by the factors that affect our physical body. They are the total possibility for our body in this lifetime, and our perfect body is always available to us.

Now imagine that there is a glass window between our actual cells and our energy cells. This glass window needs to be clear in order for the message exchanges to take place accurately. This glass gets cloudy, however, due to our conscious and unconscious negative messages. When the glass is cloudy, our energy body, the Template of Perfection, can't get through to its counterpart, our physical body. As a result, the programming of our physical body can become corrupted, and our body has a harder and harder time remaining healthy and in balance. This is what we think of as the aging process and also the path to illness.

Spiritual energy is the strongest window cleaner we can use. Because it is of not this world but the universal world, it has power to clean the window more quickly than just working day-to-day to eliminate negative emotional patterns without this supreme help.

Spirit energizes the process of cleaning the window, so our efforts to change our thinking — making attitude shifts real in our thinking — add the necessary energy to allow the clearing to happen more quickly.

In miraculous healings, for example, the window is instantly cleared. More often, healing happens over time and in direct relationship to the completeness and consistency of our efforts, both our own personal efforts and the additional energy of Spirit. When we put our hands over our heart, we invoke the power of Spirit — of Divine Love — to accelerate our healing and our awakening to our own positive potential.

This concept helps us understand why the emotional and spiritual components of healing are so essential. While many other factors of environment, diet, and ancestry may play a part, we have the best possible chance to change the outcome of our situation by putting our arms around ourself right now and valuing the courage, tenacity, and inspiration that we have already generated by ourself, and then to set out on this new leg of our journey convinced of our success.

To serve our healing, it is wise to allow rather than to dismiss what we don't fully understand. The quantum world of thinking and healing is upon us, and we can benefit from the research that is leading us to a new day in healing. We are free to regenerate our life right now — nothing is in the way: not cancer, not memories, not fears. We can take the new step to awaken our inner spiritual genetics — the power of Spirit as the heart of our healing.

This may feel like a difficult trek into unfamiliar and disconcerting territory. But it is always revealing. This journey reconfirms what we've always known inside to be true.

One helpful method for doing this is the Activity "Visualizing Your Perfect Self" (page 261). This helps us quiet our incessant mental commotion and self-judgment, and reminds us that we can and are meant to enjoy the bright side of life and the gifts we have: the lives of our children and grandchildren, our work as it grows and generates abundance, our efforts to help others, intimacy with a partner, and time spent enjoying Mother Nature's exquisite designs.

As we reflect for a few moments in meditation, we realize that no matter what things look like in this moment — whether good or bad, hopeful or hopeless — we can find meaning in observing our soul at work as it shines through in those times when things are right and we are feeling strong and courageous.

ASK YOURSELF

To find my own free and regenerating positive energy, I can answer the following questions with the first thing that comes to mind:

> *I think/feel God is . . .*
> *I think of my "wildness" as . . .*
> *When I was a child, I wanted to be . . .*
> *When I was a teenager, I longed for . . .*
> *When I grew up, I knew that I could call on . . .*
> *My greatest disappointment was/is . . .*
> *My most meaningful satisfaction comes from . . .*
> *I know I can call on my own [fill in the blank] for help and solace to . . .*
> *I'm the happiest when I . . .*
> *Others show me they love me by . . .*
> *My greatest gift to those I love is . . .*

The role I wanted to play and never did was...
The role I've gotten to play that I never imagined is...
I'm more successful than I ever thought possible because I...
I dare to...
I'm no longer intimidated by...
I let go of...
I've found...
I've claimed...
I'm free because...

ACTIVITY
Visualizing Your Perfect Self

Our human tendency is always to wait until things get better, until we find or create what we want, until the tests come back clean, in order to enjoy our life. Living in the moment sounds good, but the truth is we all live continually in either the future or the past.

In this practice, imagine the perfect scenario, the ideal picture of what is most meaningful to you right now. Imagine you have perfect health, all the money you could possibly want, your children or grandchildren healthy and happy, your work blossoming — in other words, imagine that everything is as good as it gets for you in this moment. This isn't the reality of life, but for this practice let yourself dream and see what scene appears in your inner vision. Is it working in a penthouse office selling your artwork to international buyers? Are you on vacation at the beach telling your grown kids stories of when they were babies? Are you a professional photographer, with state-of-the-art equipment, ready to create the million-dollar shot?

1. Close your eyes and, placing your hands over your heart, settle into a light meditation.
2. Imagine a scene that is perfect.
3. As you imagine this perfect scenario, where are you and what are you doing? Whom are you with?

4. Examine in detail what you are wearing and the environment you are in.
5. Examine the look on your face and the expression in your eyes.
6. Write down or draw what you've envisioned.
7. Gently relax and open your eyes.

As you record your vision, remember the look on your face and the expression in your eyes. Describe your expression in language that is as exact as possible. For example, *I looked deeply peaceful and truly alive with a smile of such confidence and love that it seemed to light up the entire room.* This look — this special look that you imagine you can have only at some imaginary time and place when things are perfect — is actually the true look of Spirit as it shines out into your life.

Instead of waiting for the impossible, which is always some future date that will never come, you can look closely at this special expression and experience the feeling of absolute happiness that is available when you allow your true Self to emerge. You register this lasting happiness in your body.

Your look is a one-of-a-kind joy that you are intended to use right now and in all ways with all people. This is your empowered spiritual self showing you how to soften your eyes and your smile and let the beauty of your genuine nature make itself known. *As your true Self shines through your eyes, you can see your Spirit Light — the light from within.*

Each chance you get, look in a mirror and re-create your expression from the visualization and recognize your Spirit Light shining forth. Here are two examples of what this visualization can look like.

My Perfect Self: Sue Ellen

I am standing in front of a lovely ivy-covered cottage set in the foothills of a range of mountains; the perfume from the many roses fills the autumn air. From this vantage point the ocean in the distance looks brilliant red-gold as the setting sun strikes the water. As I turn away from that scene, I step into the foyer of the cottage, and just beyond, in the main hall, a welcoming fire and the smell of fresh-baked scones beckons. Today is the first gathering of twenty women going through Spiritual Crisis.

My Perfect Self: Ruth

I am invited to be the keynote speaker. I am quite excited, as I have much to share. The atmosphere is informal; I am dressed in a lavender pantsuit and wearing a silver leaf studded with tiny amethyst stones on the lapel of my jacket, with matching amethyst earrings. My hair is cropped close to my head in its most beautiful silver. We sit in a circle just away from the fire, sipping cups of tea while we each take turns giving a bit of our own history and how we came to be in this wonderful gathering. Two hours have passed very quickly and the workshop is over. The women express their gratitude and are clearly impressed with the tools I suggest for self-empowerment and personal transformation. My face is radiant as if lit by some inner glow. I feel deeply contented, loveable and loved.

SPIRIT LIGHT

Spirit Light is the love and warmth that flows through our eyes. To invoke Spirit Light, we can create a mental image of shining a brilliant beam of light into the world and into our most challenging situations to facilitate positive change and healing. *Because this light is of Spirit, it is the power to love, which means it has the power to heal.*

This Spirit Light can be expressed through our hands as well as through our eyes, and we often forget it is available to use whenever we choose. We naturally use Spirit Light when comforting someone we love. We use it in reiki and other hands-on healing techniques, as long as we are touching our deep heart and are genuinely centered in this loving space.

We want to use Spirit Light on ourself for healing, too. Spirit Light is strengthened when our words and actions are aligned. When we put our hands over our heart, for example, we are calling on our Spirit Light to bring healing to our heart and our immune system, which is governed by the heart center.

I've also used Spirit Light in the form of a band of light that I imagine surrounding people who are having trouble understanding each other's real intentions. I learned the healing power of this practice when a dear friend asked me to help her with a difficulty she was having with her boss. My friend asked me to tune in to a meeting they were having at exactly 1 PM; I was delayed and tuned in to the meeting ten minutes late. But after spending a little time surrounding her and her boss with a beautiful wide ribbon of light, I felt that at least a truce had been reached.

My friend later confided to me that the meeting was going miserably, and she had about given up, when suddenly she and her boss began to talk in a more reasonable way, as if they suddenly understood that they both wanted the same result. She told me she had looked at her watch, and it was 1:12.

Spirit Light is the genuine beam of healing light that flows from us when we are at peace with ourself and the world and are aware of ourself as part of the Great Universe. Spirit Light is the look that great spiritual teachers use with students whom they intend to open and enlighten in specific ways. We all theoretically receive this energy when we attend a meditation retreat or a spirituality workshop or receive a direct teaching from an individual spiritual teacher. Obviously, the higher the quality of energy from the teacher and the more directly it is received by the student, the greater the impact. In Eastern cultures, this process is called *shaktipat*. It is recognized as a spiritual transmission of love and wisdom that has profound effect on the recipient.

We can do the same thing through our efforts to ease struggle wherever we find it — near or far. Although our focused power of Spirit Light may not be as fully realized as the great ones, still we are made of the same Divine Love and have the same ability to become a channel of Spirit Light.

ASK YOURSELF

When did I use Spirit Light, even if I wasn't aware of it at the time?

In what troubling relationship might I now practice using my Spirit Light to precipitate healing and positive change?

Am I ready to look in the mirror and turn my Spirit Light on my own physical body for healing?

What do I imagine will happen when I do this?

12 O'CLOCK THOUGHTS

To use our Spirit Light, we need to understand what breaks the energy connection to Spirit. When we are thinking one thing, doing another, and saying something else, there is no connection with Spirit. For example, if we tell our partner that we're pleased with what they did to help us, but at the same time we're aware of an old grudge that we're still harboring, then there is no energetic connection to Spirit — no Spirit Light is generated. This accounts for all the empty pleasantries that we exchange but that generate no inner buzz or hum that indicates we're linked inside. The way to clear old grudges when we become aware of them is to practice 12 o'clock thoughts.

A 12 o'clock thought helps us stay in energetic alignment, since it asks us to punctuate every thought with a positive ending. This is an important way to bring our thoughts, feelings, beliefs, attitudes, and actions into alignment, into congruency. When we are in alignment, the energy flows smoothly through our energy lines and centers. When we say things that don't fit with what we believe, or are negative and judgmental, the energy in the channels of our body slows down. When we live completely out of congruency with spiritual beliefs, we have sluggish energy and sometimes our body begins to break down into illness. To bring strong, clear energy to our body, we should practice having only 12 o'clock thoughts.

ACTIVITY

12 O'Clock Thoughts

Just as both hands of a clock face directly up when at 12 o'clock, so, too, in this practice do we symbolically look up at the sun, the Creative Word of God, the source of light, to draw positive energy into our body, our life, and our earth. Healing requires that we eliminate negativity as much as possible and begin to live *as if* we were more positive until *we actually become more positive.*

To create a 12 o'clock thought, imagine including at the end of every negative sentence, thought, or feeling, either expressed or not, a positive and affirming phrase. When we realize we have a grudge or residual anger, we can clear it, which benefits us most specifically.

We can readily imagine how the resentments we accumulate throughout the years weigh us down. We can now clear these energetically in order to restore our Spirit Light by using 12 o'clock thoughts — adding a positive ending that is honestly aligned with our deep heart. For example, in the case of talking to our partner, when we're alone or during any quiet times, we can articulate the old fear or anger and then end it with a 12 o'clock thought that allows us to be congruous. We might remember, *You promised that you would listen and pay attention to my needs, and yet you never make time for me.* Adding a 12 o'clock thought would make it: *You promised that you would listen and pay attention to my needs, and yet you never make time for me — although I realize it's a process and I need to stay steady in my request.*

❧ ATTITUDE SHIFTS ❧

1. I can renew and regenerate my life. That is my true potential. It is only my self-critical personality mind that tells me otherwise.
2. Spirit operates outside linear time, so I don't need time to set things straight.

3. My body is always intrinsically whole and complete. Even if I have a physical organ removed, energetically all my organs and systems are always present.

4. My body is always seeking to find balance and to heal, and I can tap into this will to heal.

5. My body is surrounded by its perfect reflection, my Template of Perfection, that is continually helping my body heal.

6. I imagine myself as perfect, complete, and happy in this moment. This is what turns on, and keeps on, my Spirit Light.

7. Spirit Light is a genuine beam of healing light that is available to me when I simply place my hands over my heart.

8. I can also cut off the beam of Spirit Light by staying in negative thoughts or by being out of alignment with my true Self.

9. Twelve o'clock thoughts are the easiest way to stay positive and to shift my attitude.

CHAPTER THIRTY

Love Is the Way

The sky-drum plays
All by itself in my head,
Singing all day long
"Allah, Allah,
Allah"

— Hafiz

Whether our life is busy or empty, happy or sad, it's important that we assume more responsibility for what we really feel. For example, if we finally verbalize that we are having serious trouble with our partner and aren't sure the relationship will last, we've lifted the symbolic tree limb from our inner flow by acknowledging what is true. Whether or not our feelings about the situation change, we have taken the emotional pressure off our body and no longer need to pretend to ourself that everything is all right when it's not.

We benefit from listening to our words, trusting what is happening, and remembering that all healing happens from the inside out — from Spirit to our body and our relationships. We can allow ourself to blow away illusion, resist avoiding what we're afraid to feel, and claim our right to a clear view of our life.

There is nothing so terrible that we can't bring it out into the light of day; nothing so gruesome, so painful, or so off-putting that we can't bring it out into the sunshine. This is the time to honor our life journey, not focus on our mistakes. We must look to the big picture of our life and find what is good.

We need to resist pretending, whatever that means for us: perhaps we need to stop telling ourself everything is fine and instead listen to that nagging inner voice that tells us we're not doing what we intended to do with our life, or perhaps we need to silence the self-critic that tells us continually it's our fault that we're sick or without a real love in our life. Neither false bravado nor undue doom and gloom are called for. Nothing is written about our future — not our healing and not our death. We create our future each day through our beliefs, attitudes, and choices.

ACTIVITY
Recognizing What Is True

When you identify what is disturbing to you — whether you think it's silly and trivial or earth-shattering — you actually free up the flow of inner energy so you settle down and slow down. It is extremely important to accept that *no action is required* when you seek clarity of your feelings. *We don't verbalize our feelings because we're afraid to make them real, since in our mind that means we'll need to take immediate action.* There is nothing to change or do right now, except to get clear with yourself about your true feelings. This alone expands the inner flow of energy within, so your body, mind, and emotions have less clutter to deal with in the healing process.

1. Name the problem or challenge you're facing.
2. Ask Spirit to allow you the clarity to identify what is really true beyond your anger, fear, or grief.
3. Put your hand over your deep heart as you repeat the elements of the situation as you sense it truly is without shading it.

4. Separate your awareness from any need for action until you feel it is appropriate to take action.
5. Sense inside in which of three ways you are being guided:
   A. Red light — take no action.
   B. Yellow light — energy is changing, but proceed slowly.
   C. Green light — you know what to do, so do it.

MOTHERS AND DAUGHTERS HAVE A DEEP BOND

Here is a very real and marvelous story of healing. I do want to say, however, as a preface, that while this healing is spectacular, it's not to suggest that every healing ends this way or is suppose to. I do believe that healing is about touching our spirit with love to awaken its knowing and then the rest is up to the Divinity that made us all.

I imagine that there must be a magical conversation between the Creator and our spirit. Both our spirit and beyond are made of the same energy, and yet our particular spirit is for the moment connected to guiding our life. I think of Spirit as having a foot in each camp — our life and the bigger picture.

Late one night I got a phone call from a woman I didn't know who introduced herself as Suzanne; I still don't know how she got my unlisted phone number. It was 10 PM, and Suzanne had that frantic tone to her voice that tells us that something terrible is looming.

Suzanne told me between gulps, sobs, and numbed-out silences the story of her two-year-old blond-haired, blue-eyed daughter, who had collapsed at her second birthday party and been rushed to the hospital. At the hospital the doctors told Suzanne that the child had a virus in her heart, and she would probably need a heart-lung transplant to live — and it was doubtful that even that would succeed because it was so difficult working with a child so young.

We can easily put ourself in this woman's place and imagine her shock. There was no long illness to prepare her for a crisis — it just arrived out of the blue. Suzanne had no idea what to do, but she felt inside that she should not sign the papers authorizing the heart-lung transplant. She felt there was another way.

I never try to dissuade a person from a decision they've arrived at. My job as a healer isn't to choose the path a client is inclined to take, but to reinforce and add healing to the direction they have chosen. Slowly Suzanne calmed down; we began to talk about options and about the power of love and of prayer and the healing that she might bring to her daughter. In her distress, Suzanne completely doubted that she could in any way help her daughter. But just as we have heard the story of a woman picking up a car to free her child, so we can pull ourself together when we absolutely have to.

I got quiet and drew to me the little girl's life energy field. I asked Suzanne's daughter whether she was intending to stay in this lifetime. It seemed the child's spirit hadn't decided, so I felt we had a fighting chance to keep her here.

I taught Suzanne to put her hands over her heart — I taught her the Healing Art of Loving Touch. I talked her through exactly how and when to do it and why it was effective as a healing tool. She was invoking the energy of Divine Love as she put her hands on her child and asked for healing energy to pour through her hands to her child. I told her to call me through the night if things deteriorated, and I too would work on the little girl. It was a long night.

Suzanne called me several times a day over the next few days, giving me reports of the child's vital signs. We held our breath. Several days into the ordeal, she called me to ask if I had a sense of the little girl's determination to leave or stay — was it still up in the air? When I asked the child's spirit, I felt that she had definitely decided to stay. I told Suzanne that, while also reminding her that nothing is ever set in stone. But it was an indication that Suzanne and I took very seriously. We prayed it was true.

The child's condition continued to improve, and eventually she was able to go home. Slowly, over the course of months, she rebuilt her heart and its function. Today the child is a preteen and a beautiful young girl who, it is interesting to note, is very involved in helping others. Her mom is certain she's an angel in disguise. Her doctors called her "the miracle baby."

What made the difference was that she received the best of all care at the physical level and equally meaningful care at the emotional and spiritual levels. Suzanne became a conduit of Divine Love, and through all those who were loving and praying for her, the child did indeed decide to stay.

Indeed, mothers and daughters have a bond that can hold us in this Earth plane even when physical illness might seem to be taking us in another direction.

Suzanne was certainly willing to look clearly at what was happening with her daughter, and she recognized that she needed to do everything within her power to bring together those who could help. Then what actually gathered the collective energy of all of Suzanne's helpers was Suzanne and her absolute belief in the fact that there was a way — and that way made use of both the art and the science of healing.

As we wonder how we, too, can both quiet our mind and awaken our spirit in order to bring maximum power and energy to our own situation, we come to the powerful and essential component of quiet time alone with ourself and Spirit. We call this by many names, but let's explore it as meditation.

MEDITATION

Showing Up Without Going Anywhere

Meditation is both an Eastern religious practice and a mystical Christian one. When we want to quiet our mind and settle down with greater inner focus, we can practice meditation. There are many different types of practices: some focus on the breath, some focus on an absence of thought, and some focus on a particular thought or koan in which the mind gradually slows in its eternal effort to make sense of the world. A koan by its very nature is unsolvable through our ordinary linear mind.

Meditation will probably not enlighten us in the foreseeable future or prevent the onslaught of worrisome thoughts. But by doing it we find new understandings of what we feel and why, as well as how to stay steady within the ongoing stories we tell ourself.

Meditation practice disciplines us to show up without needing to get anywhere, accomplish anything, or become better at something. We already are all we need to be. Sometimes meditation gives us the experience of dancing with the love of the infinite and the great teachers and teachings, whereas at other times, sitting on our meditation cushion or in a chair, we sink into past heartache and fear.

All of who we are, however, is what we explore in meditation. We don't separate out the good and the bad, the evolved and the pedestrian. We sit with all our components and discover how they come together. Healing, as we've said, is about unraveling what we've assumed was our totality in order to get comfortable with being who we are.

Sitting in meditation, we come to terms with our tendencies to judge, hurt, ignore, repudiate, and destroy ourself and each other. We also have times of experiencing peace, softness, forgiveness, and acceptance. Day after day, we slowly carve a winding path of awareness through the crevasses and canyons, the mountain gorges and snow-capped peaks of our thoughts and feelings, until we realize life isn't a problem and doing more doesn't provide a solution. Being more in touch with Spirit allows us to rest, to slow the mind's struggle as we make sense of bad experiences, and finally just to be more available in our everyday life.

Meditation is a process that enhances our devotion to become more aware of Spirit, and it also perhaps reflects our devotion to a special teacher, master, guru, or guide whose teachings carry us along the sacred path. It is wonderful to have a special teacher, but whether or not we do, we can sit in our sacred healing room and find relief from suffering and confirmation of our true nature.

We each hold different beliefs: we may believe in a single God as a Christian; we may hold the understanding that we are one with the grand luminosity of the Universe (the eternal Light of all that is) as a Buddhist; we may honor God through all the various forms and manifestations as a Hindu; we may serve the one God as the unknowable Source as a Jew; or maybe we honor Allah as the one true path. It makes no difference — for religions are different paths up the same mountain to direct awareness of our Divine nature and our oneness with the Source of Love within our own deep heart.

In meditation, we explore our return to love through our understanding of its significance as both the unifying emotion that bonds us together as living beings and creatures and as the means to elevate and maximize our healing energy. Truly, love heals all.

ACTIVITY
A Simple Meditation Practice

1. Sit comfortably on a cushion or meditation pillow on the floor or in a chair with your hands resting comfortably in your lap.
2. Close your eyes and place your hands over your deep heart, which is the essence of your spirit and can be imagined to be located in the center of your chest. This is the heart chakra or energy center.
3. Breathe normally and relax the muscles in your body, calling on those that feel especially tight to relax.
4. Imagine placing your thoughts and worries in a bowl and putting the bowl on a bookshelf or table nearby.
5. As you breathe, imagine that you are following your breath from your mouth down into your deep heart space and allow it to take the shape of a lotus flower.
6. With each breath, allow the lotus to open more and more, inviting you to be present with your true Self.

7. Ask that all health and well-being flow into your body and that your life become an instrument for healing and support, both for yourself and for others.

8. Sit quietly for a designated period of time, continuing to focus on your breathing.

9. Slowly bring yourself back fully into your body and open your eyes.

10. Rest for a few moments before continuing with your day.

11. You may want to write down any thoughts or feelings that come to you. Keeping a meditation journal is a meaningful way to gather your understandings, questions, and concerns. You can use any of these ideas as the beginning point for your next meditation.

ATTITUDE SHIFTS

1. When I identify my true feelings, I free up the flow of healing energy in my body.

2. Identifying my feelings does not mean I have to take any immediate action. All I have to do right now is get clear.

3. Meditation is an excellent practice for learning how to simply "be" with my feelings rather than having to "do" anything about them. Five minutes a day will make a difference in my healing journey.

CHAPTER THIRTY-ONE

Stepping into the Center of Our Own Life

There is a saying about enlightenment, that it is the product of:
one part physical study of awareness,
one part mental application of truth,
one part Cosmic Kiss.

— Mentor

As we heal our body and right the emotional and spiritual imbalances that have held us captive, we face not only ourself in the mirror but also the generations of women who have come before. What did we inherit from them? What language and what instincts? What head-sets and heart-sets? What ways of seeing the world and what assumptions about life and the inevitability of certain aspects of it?

Growing up, we are often told how much we are like someone in our extended family or a distant, long-gone relative. For me, that person was Aunt Peg.

When I was seven years old, my family traveled home to Philadelphia, where we had aunts and uncles to visit. The reason for the trip was that my Aunt Peg had been diagnosed with advanced breast cancer and wanted to have us by her side. She was a remarkable woman whom people found easy to love. She had an unending list of friends. I remember sitting quietly in her room one sunny winter morning on that trip and realizing I didn't know what to say. She rested comfortably in bed, and I remember thinking how beautiful she looked with her soft white nightgown and impressive long red nails. She was something special to see, with the pillow framing her dark hair and dark eyes — she was also something special to me. This was the last time I saw her.

What is this invisible bond that holds us to the women of our past — both those we loved and those we feared? The bonds that speak to our tend-and-befriend energy are indeed intense and become more so as we age. In our twenties, our mothers and grandmothers hold center stage, but as we get older we are called to witness the lives of women who have come before, in the more distant past. We also ponder our own contributions and what others will say after we're gone. What perspectives will our children carry — for what will they blame us, for what will they applaud?

Personally, I find myself more and more interested in studying some of the old grainy black-and-white photos that have been passed to me for safekeeping — the ones resting in the box marked *ancestors*, which had been stowed in a far corner of our attic along with a yellowing wedding gown and old movies of the children when they were young.

In the last several years I've taken down the boxes and enjoyed poring over the old pictures of women with stark expressions and strange hairdos. I've chosen some of these photos to put on a table in our living room: my mother and her mother and her stepmother, as well as several aunts, including my Aunt Peg. I want to remember my roots.

Once in a while it is good to stand back to gain a refreshed perspective when considering our connections to the women in our life, past and present. When we're up close in the middle of family dramas, we tend to see only faults and struggles. With some distance, we can reflect on what might have been and perhaps on what can be that will create a different set of memories with our daughters, granddaughters, and stepdaughters.

Some of the most important women in our lineage aren't necessarily blood relatives. We pull from many different periods of our life to create the circle of women whom we feel close to today.

BERTHA'S STORY

Bertha was a longtime resident of the small New England town in which my husband and I live. She and I often crossed paths at the local restaurant, where everyone showed up for good home-cooked food and local gossip. I guess she was probably in her seventies or eighties; she would never tell me, but the trouble she had walking suggested she'd been around a long time. She wore a collection of clothes that looked like she might have gotten dressed in the closet — so lacking in any apparent effort to make things match that I often wondered if she indeed dressed to be intentionally outlandish.

Yet she was extraordinary. Over the years, as I got to know her, my admiration for her grew and grew. By all accounts she had had a difficult life, with little going right or allowing her to enjoy any ease at all. But she was a survivor.

Bertha was a folk artist at heart and spent her time in a little cabin tucked high up in the hills around our town. She crafted original miniature houses; some were replicas of regal old mansions, some were imagined, and other designs were copied from magazines. She used bits and pieces of everything — from bailing twine to random pieces of cloth — to decorate her little houses, which came complete with upholstered chairs, doors that opened and closed, and porch swings that moved as if swayed by a soft summer breeze.

About two years ago Bertha's normal routine was interrupted by a lengthy stay in the hospital, and when she again appeared, she was obviously much thinner and had the look of someone beginning to fade. She announced to me very matter of factly that the nice young doctor who had cared for her told her she had cancer of the pancreas. She said this without an apparent emotional reaction. I wondered if she comprehended the meaning of that diagnosis.

Soon she was again talking about her little houses, only this time she leaned across the table and in great earnestness asked me if I had any ideas about what she could do with them if she wasn't around. "It seems a shame," she said, "to have them forgotten like my little cabin will be."

My immediate reaction was to look around for someone else to step up to this task. I had no idea who might want these little houses, who might buy them, or even where to begin to look for customers. It looked like a lot of work, and as I mentally checked my schedule to see what time I might manufacture — I realized there wasn't much.

Still, I wanted to help her. At the time I would not have thought of Bertha in terms of my lineage — although I surely do today. We developed a meaningful, if unlikely, friendship that carried us both into the final few weeks of her life.

After several trips to the hospital, Bertha decided she didn't want chemotherapy because she had no way to get to the hospital and because, she said, "I've lived a good life and am not afraid to die — I just don't want to hang around if I can't make my little houses."

Through God's Grace, we managed to get her homes placed in the local historical society, and we even sold a few. The local paper published a wonderful, caring article on Bertha and her houses, and she was so pleased that in some way her talent, and I think her life, felt validated — finally. She was proud as punch of her success.

Bertha was taken by ambulance to the hospital the day the paper was due to come out, so we got some advance copies and rushed a stack to her bedside so she could enjoy them and pass them out to the medical staff. She had wanted pizza for her celebration ceremony, and even though she was in the hospital, she still wanted her pizza party. So in came the pizzas, and she held court from her hospital bed. Her son, his wife, my husband, and I stood around while others came in to laugh good-naturedly at her jokes and applaud her success with her houses.

By the next afternoon she had slipped peacefully into a coma, and over the next few days, it was clear she was getting ready to leave. One afternoon, as I stood by her bed looking out her hospital room window at the beautiful blue sky and tall hemlock trees, I turned around and stopped, struck by what I saw. As I gazed over her sleeping body, I could clearly see-sense a shimmering blue-and-silver light hovering over her. I realized that I was sensing her Spirit preparing to leave her body. I remember thinking how peaceful things seemed — nothing unnatural or in any way out of the ordinary. This is what life is all about — the coming in and the going out.

Her time was getting close.

On the following evening, what would be her final day on Earth, her immediate family — which at this point included my husband and me — stood around her bed. As I gently stroked her feet and legs, which were terribly swollen and I'm sure painful, she began to call out for her mother.

I moved around to the front of the bed as she continued to call out, "Mama, Mama." I didn't know what kind of relationship she had had with her mother, but in that moment, I realized that Spirit was calling me to be her mother's stand-in. I took her face in my hands; although her eyes were closed, I could feel her distress. I imagined that she was calling out to her mother for comfort at this most difficult time. I leaned down close to her face, and I said softly, "Mama's here and Mama loves you."

I repeated the phrase over and over and over, until she quieted and seemed to settle. I like to think that she found in my genuinely felt reassurance the support she needed to take the next step of her journey. I knew then, as I am reminded daily, that both in living each day and as we continue our journey into Spirit, it is always — and only — our loving that in the end counts for anything.

We all have opportunities to play this role of Mama in some way with someone in our life — a someone who lights up our world and reinforces our conviction of the Grace and the Presence of Spirit as our faithful and eternal companion.

My time with Bertha was a gift I will not soon forget.

OUR SPIRITUAL LINEAGE —
THE CIRCLE THAT NEVER BREAKS

As we engage our healing energy of loving, we know deep inside that this powerful force allows us all to be Mama for others. Whether or not we are actual mothers, we clearly embody the mother energy for others of all ages.

We have discovered how having a quality life is closely tied to being a loving human being and seeing our life as worthy. We have nothing and no one to live up to. We are our own woman. There is no one mold we are to fit into and no one way to live. We make it up as we go along, and so a valiant heart, a vivid imagination, and a yen for exploring ideas seem the very best tools for our journey through Earth School.

As we call to mind and heart all the women in our life — the mother and surrogate mothers, grandmothers, great-grandmothers and great-great-grandmothers, sisters, daughters, granddaughters, stepdaughters, and surrogate daughters — we form an imaginary circle. We also include in our spiritual lineage those mother and sister figures who are close friends, the ones we know stand strong with us.

The women in our circle are part of our life, both the ones we've shared our life with and those we've only read or learned about. Their silhouettes seem to appear in silent parade at the times we need support, protection, solutions, and sisters to celebrate with.

Our efforts to heal our body, mind, and connection to Spirit help other women who also want to embrace their lives with greater inspiration and commitment, whether they recognize our gifts to them or not. Because our healing also illuminates the path for our daughters and their daughters, we are called to live our very best life.

Indeed we are being called to forge a strong and unbreakable bond with the important women in our life, and this requires that we explore, face, and forgive old ties that may still be fraught with fear, anger, pain, loss, or betrayal.

We need to reforge bonds with those women who have stood on

the periphery of our life and whom we want to draw closer — if possible. Our attempt at reshaping old problematic relationships is similar to the way a blacksmith works on a flame-orange horseshoe precisely placed on her anvil. While she knows where and how to strike the metal — to shape it — sometimes it breaks in spite of her best efforts.

We are likewise called to shape relationships where we can, drawing from them a new inner freedom and permission to go ahead with our life even if we are unable to bring life back to those relationships. Whether or not troubled relationships can be repaired, we have done our part by calling them back to us and either reshaping them or allowing them to go. We have in effect neutralized the energy between us and others so we can release unwanted emotions and stand true with the women we have called to be with us in our circle of healing.

ASK YOURSELF

Am I ready to call together my lineage of women, biological and spiritual, with whom I am ready to stand now in my life for healing and celebration?

Whom do I call?

Whom am I ready to forgive and invite back into my circle who has left or departed this earth?

Which women outside my bloodline do I acknowledge as family?

STEPPING INTO OUR CIRCLE

Now is the time for all of us who are participating in our own healing through the words and practices in *Spirit Heals* to recognize our role in this circle of women we have called. In this chapter's Activity (page

285), we will imagine walking into the center of our circle in order to claim our power and our heart's desire.

What might we claim? We might claim our faith in our healing, our joy in finding something to feel good about, our good fortune in patching up a relationship, and our steadiness in moving on from a relationship that is over.

We're so used to stepping down and standing down. Now, in our circle, we step up and stand up for our healing and our passion for living and contributing in the ways dearest to our heart. As we prepare for this ceremony, we will find that entering the circle is a powerful and memorable experience. May it have an impact for each of us.

This ceremony is based on the power of speaking our name out loud. What is in a name?

Our name has power and magic. It is the way we've been known as a child in our parent's home and as an adult moving into our own home. Our name is the way we've been called to appointments, to jobs, and to marriages. We may have changed our name so it feels more relevant and authentic, but still it represents our body, mind, and spirit — that which is unique in this lifetime.

We can be proud of our name because no matter how we came by it, it has served us well, carrying us through the decades of our life — through the triumphs and the disappointments — ultimately bringing us to this special moment of healing.

Whether our name is long or short, composed of one ethnicity or several, we come together today in celebration of each of us — as we show up, called by our name, to honor the journey we've walked and to lay out the healing journey we intend to continue to explore.

A name is only temporary, yet for this lifetime it holds the love and energy that is the product of all the years we've spent on this Earth. There will never again be someone with our name who carries our particular set of dreams, goals, and opportunities. We are precious in all the solar system, complete, whole, and beautiful.

ACTIVITY

Step to the Center of Your Circle

1. Find a quiet place to hold your ceremony where you will not be disturbed.

2. Put on soft and appealing music, light some incense, or merely turn the lights down.

3. Imagine a circle on the floor, and picture one by one the women standing around it whom you've called to witness your special experience.

4. Place a candle, flower, or other symbol of your healing in the center.

5. Imagine you now stand at the edge of the circle, close your eyes, and say a short prayer or invocation out loud.

6. Walk slowly to the center of the circle and feel the power of standing there silently for several moments.

7. Now speak your name five times, repeating the following words out loud:

   I SPEAK MY NAME knowing that I speak for all women who have come before me in my family or clan as I celebrate my life and my healing.

   I SPEAK MY NAME and know that echoes of my presence are sensed down through the ages past and through the hearts of those who will follow me. My name brings healing, hope, and heartfelt compassion to those women who follow my example into their own futures.

   I SPEAK MY NAME so that others who were or are unable to speak their names fully or with pride may receive the power of my loving and healing intention — that they too may find the freedom of mind, body, and spirit to enter the new season of their own life wherever they are in this wide world.

   I SPEAK MY NAME and put my hands over my heart, knowing I've said yes to my life and to my healing.

I SPEAK MY NAME and know that I honor my name and all it draws to me in the way of goodness and blessings of the Universe.

8. Say out loud what is in your heart and fully take in its significance. Really hear your words of power, intention, and praise for your healing journey.

9. Look around and imagine thanking each woman you've called.

10. Slowly walk back to your place at the edge of the circle.

11. Imagine that each woman now takes the hands of those standing next to her, forming an unbreakable circle of love and healing for you.

12. Offer your final blessing.

13. Slowly open your eyes.

After you have done this ceremony on your own, you may want to gather a circle of the actual women in your life and do this ceremony again. This creates immense energy for you. Also, you heal through this ceremony because many thousands of women will also be performing this ritual as they read *Spirit Heals*. Although we'll be in different locations and doing this ceremony at different times, it's still important to recognize that we are not alone. We stand together as women who are healing through the power of love.

Our shared intention to care about each other surrounds us all with a mantle of grace and well-being. Our circle will reach around the world, empowering and healing all the women it touches. Through doing the ceremony, we receive all that is most useful and immediately relevant for our own healing and our happiness.

A FINAL WORD

While we have reached an ending, we are also at a new beginning. We have come to the end of *Spirit Heals*, but its heart, which we each carry with us, continues. This is a watershed place in your healing and in your empowerment. You are not the same woman who began this journey when you first opened the pages of this book. You may have wavered, but you've kept going. You've read and considered the Attitude Shifts, Activities, and Ask Yourself questions. You've journaled and thought and prayed and asked to know Spirit. And so you've arrived at the finish line — and as in all meaningful endeavors, it is also the new beginning. Well done!

Listen — and you will hear the sound of all our voices speaking our names. The music we hear is the unity of our hearts and the possibility for ourself, our children, and our world to truly heal.

❧ ATTITUDE SHIFTS ❧

1. I carry the emotional and spiritual imprints of the generations of women who went before me.
2. To effectively forge stronger bonds with the important women in my life, I must explore and forgive whatever is in the way.
3. By claiming my name as a representation of all that I am and all that I can be, I can take my place at the center of the circle of women who support my healing journey.
4. Now is an opportunity to change my name or claim the one I have because it holds power and magic.
5. As I stand in the center of my circle of supportive women, family, and friends, I claim my life and my healing.

ACKNOWLEDGMENTS

Spirit Heals comes from and through many people's hearts and wise thoughts. Clients and professionals alike have shared stories, ideas, healing practices, and their own special journeys with me over the past twenty-seven years, all of which have helped to form the very foundation of my understanding of healing.

Additionally, Spirit, both within as my Source and inner direction and as the enlightened teachings of Mentor and Sri Sathya Sai Baba, continues to hold me in a steady place of holiness through which I seek to learn and grow as a human being.

I want to especially thank the following people who have contributed to the book in meaningful ways:

My Stillpoint staff of loyal and dedicated people, who continue to show up in marvelous support of this amazing Stillpoint vision of spreading love in the world:

Phoebe Price — a Stillpoint graduate and teacher, who continues to inspire both our teachers and students with her effectiveness and compassion. She handles effortlessly the myriad details that cross her desk each day in helping us stay connected to our graduates, clients, customers, and students.

Eileen Woolbert — whose fingers dance across the keys in designing our materials, updating our website, handling our grant accounting, and all the other details that would sink most women.

Mary Ann Brody — also part of the accounting team, who offers us her warm smile and effectiveness in keeping our accounts up to date.

Yvonne Freve — who shares her love and insight not only through managing our database but also by guiding our beautiful *Women Moving Through Breast Cancer* program.

Ann Holmblad — who opens doors for us through her grant expertise and as a trusted member of our travel team to school and events around the country. She is a most amazing woman who is always available to help no matter what hour of day or night.

Pat Garvey — my trusted right hand in our Stillpoint School program and beyond in all the ways we seek to expand our reach. She is a sister, friend, and trusted ally whose loyalty and love have always sustained me.

Debra Boudrieau — amazing editor, helper, and managing director. Her complete dedication to helping me put this book together is nothing short of awesome. Her intuitive insights about what to add and what to subtract have provided essential assistance through the complicating process of creating this book. A deep and heartfelt thank you.

Errol Sowers — my dear husband and life-mate who stands beside me during all the ups and downs, offering ideas, solutions, and possibilities. Your love holds me in the center so I can listen to the words of Spirit and share them with others. Your support throughout our many years together is the thing I count on most.

To the wonderful people at New World Library who saw the possibilities for this book and helped guide me to its conclusion, a huge hug of appreciation — especially to Georgia Hughes, editorial director, whose great intuitive takes have helped shape this book and offered guidance and direction for its completion; and Jeff Campbell as developmental editor, who meticulously edited every line for clarity and continuity — a beautiful job. Thank you to Kristen Cashman, managing editor; Tona Pearce Myers, interior designer and typographer; and Tracy Pitts, cover designer, for their combined effort in making this book so lovely to hold. To Munro Magruder, marketing director, whose knowledge of publishing and amazing insight into marketing avenues to generate attention for this book are so deeply appreciated; and to Monique Muhlenkamp, publicist, whose savvy understanding of promotion and sensitive handling of the book has helped it find the light of day. Finally, to Marc Allen, owner and friend, I thank you for the opportunity to participate in New World Library's publishing work.

NOTES

PART ONE

Page 1, *My dear, this world, its laws*: Hafiz, "The Earth Braces Itself," *The Gift: Poems by Hafiz the Great Sufi Master*, trans. Daniel Ladinsky (New York: Penguin Group, 1999).

Chapter 1

Page 3, *All living entities and all energy fields*: Mikio Sankey, *Esoteric Acupuncture: Gateway to Healing*, vol. 1 (Inglewood, CA: Mountain Castle Publishing, 2004).

Chapter 2

Page 11, *Be content with what you have*: Lao Tzu, in Ronald S. Miller, ed., *As Above So Below* (Los Angeles: Jeremy P. Tarcher, 1992).

Chapter 3

Page 17, *There is more to life*: Mohandas Gandhi, in Ronald S. Miller, ed., *As Above So Below* (Los Angeles: Jeremy P. Tarcher, 1992).

Chapter 4

Page 23, *Act as if everything depended on you*: Saint Ignatius, in Ronald S. Miller, ed., *As Above So Below* (Los Angeles: Jeremy P. Tarcher, 1992).

Chapter 5

Page 29, *The art of medicine consists of*: Voltaire, in Ronald S. Miller, ed., *As Above So Below* (Los Angeles: Jeremy P. Tarcher, 1992).

Chapter 6

Page 33, *He makes me lie down in green pastures*: *New American Standard Bible*, Psalm 23, verses 2–6 (Nashville, TN: Thomas Nelson Publishers, 1977).

PART TWO

Page 41, *If we want stillness of mind*: Carol Lee Flinders, *Enduring Lives: Portraits of Women and Faith in Action* (New York: Jeremy P. Tarcher/Penguin, 2006).

Chapter 7

Page 43, *May I be filled with loving kindness*: Jack Kornfield, *A Path with Heart: A Guide through the Perils and Promises of Spiritual Life* (New York: Bantam Books, 1993).

Chapter 8

Page 51, *Freedom is the basic concept and construct of life everywhere*: Neale Donald Walsch, *Conversations with God: An Uncommon Dialogue, Book 2* (Charlottesville, NC: Hampton Roads Publishing Company, 1997).

Chapter 9

Page 57, *You are a human being. What does that mean?*: Eckhart Tolle, *A New Earth: Awakening to Your Life's Purpose* (New York: Dutton, 2005).

Chapter 10

Page 71, *If in the past you haven't experienced love's purity*: Deepak Chopra, *Ageless Body, Timeless Mind: The Quantum Alternative to Growing Old* (New York: Harmony Books, 1993).

Chapter 11

Page 85, *A hero ventures forth from the world of common day*: Joseph Campbell, *The Hero with a Thousand Faces* (New York: MJF Books, 1949).

PART THREE

Page 93, *Some of us are very aware of the way that our moods*: Joan Borysenko, *The Power of the Mind to Heal* (Carson, CA: Hay House, 1994), 29.

Chapter 12

Page 95, *I have heard enough warrior stories of heroic daring*: Oriah Mountain Dreamer, *The Dance* (San Francisco: HarperCollins Publishers, 2001), 80.
Page 98, *DNA blueprints passed down at birth through genes are not set in concrete*: Bruce Lipton, *Biology of Belief* (Santa Rosa, CA: Mountain of Love Productions, 2005).

Chapter 13

Page 103, *The ego is not only the unobserved mind*: Eckart Tolle, *A New Earth: Awakening to Your Life's Purpose* (New York: Dutton, 2005).

Chapter 14

Page 111, *Something unexpected has been placed in my bowl*: Sue Bender, *Everyday Sacred: A Woman's Journey Home* (New York: Harper San Francisco, 1995).

Chapter 15

Page 121, *The word is not just a sound or a written symbol*: Don Miguel Ruiz, *The Four Agreements* (San Rafael, CA: Amber-Allen Publishing, 1997).

Chapter 16

Page 127, *Go ahead, be brave, say it anyway: "I am a writer."*: Natalie Goldberg, *Wild Mind: Living the Writer's Life* (New York: Bantam Books, 1990).

Chapter 17

Page 137, *I give thanks that I now receive the righteous desires of my heart*: Florence Scovel Shinn, *The Wisdom of Florence Scovel Shinn* (New York: Simon & Schuster, 1989).

PART FOUR

Page 145, *Those who wish to change things may face disappointment*: Rachel Naomi Remen, *Kitchen Table Wisdom: Stories That Heal* (New York: Riverhead Books, 1994).

Chapter 18

Page 147, *To find real emotional security, we have to*: Nancy Lonsdorf, Veronica Butler, and Melanie Brown, *A Woman's Best Medicine: Heath, Happiness, and Long Life through Ayur-Veda* (New York: Jeremy P. Tarcher/Putnam Books, 1993).

Chapter 19

Page 161, *My mother's communication illuminated to me life's delicate balance*: Justin Matott, *A Harvest of Reflections* (New York: Ballantine Books, 1998).

Chapter 20

Page 171, *God gives us songs in the night*: *The Holy Bible: New International Version* (New York: HarperTorch, 1993).

Chapter 21

Page 183, *No plant grew higher than my head*: William Least Heat-Moon, *Blue Highways: A Journey into America* (Boston: Houghton Mifflin Company, 1982).

PART FIVE

Page 189, *I cannot dance, Lord, unless you lead me*: Mechthild of Magdeburg, *Mechthild of Magdeburg: The Flowing Light of the Godhead*, trans. Frank Tobin (Mahwah, NJ: Paulist Press, 1998), 59.

Chapter 22

Page 191, *I have come to understand that they key to genuine satisfaction*: Rachel Naomi Remen, *My Grandfather's Blessings: Stories of Strength, Refuge, and Belonging* (New York: Riverhead Books, 2000).

Chapter 23

Page 197, *Some keep the Sabbath going to church*: Emily Dickinson, *Collected Poems of Emily Dickinson* (New York: Gramercy Books, 1982).

Chapter 24

Page 209, *With a single note the nightingale*: Rumi, in Deepak Chopra, ed., *The Soul in Love* (New York: Harmony Books, 2001), 30.

Page 209, *In a landmark University of California study in 2000, six researchers*: Shelley E. Taylor, Laura Cousino Klein, Brian P. Lewis, Tara L. Gruenewald, Regan A. R. Gurung, and John A. Updegraff, "Biobehavioral Responses to Stress in Females: Tend-and-Befriend, Not Fight-or-Flight," *Psychological Review* 107, no. 3, (2000): 411–29.

Chapter 25

Page 217, *I am never upset for the reason I think*: Gerald G. Jampolsky, *Love Is Letting Go of Fear* (Millbrae, CA: Celestial Arts, 1979).

Chapter 26

Page 225, *How do I love thee? Let me count the ways*: Elizabeth Barrett Browning, *Sonnets from the Portuguese: A Celebration of Life* (New York: St. Martin's Press, 1986).

Chapter 27

Page 233, *After the laughter, all the muscles are relaxed, including the heart*: Bernie Siegel, MD, *Love, Medicine, and Miracles* (New York: Harper & Row, 1986).

PART SIX

Page 243, *Hush... Whisper earth's name in a smile, or a sigh*: Mattie J. T. Stepanek, *Reflections of a Peacemaker: A Portrait Through Heartsongs* (Kansas City: Andrews McMeel Publishing, 2005).

Chapter 28

Page 245, *The best and most beautiful things in the world*: Rumi, in Ronald S. Miller, ed., *As Above So Below* (Los Angeles: Jeremy P. Tarcher, 1992).

Chapter 29

Page 255, *Trust is the universal law of attraction*: Gloria Karpinski, *Where Two Worlds Touch: Spiritual Rites of Passage* (New York: Ballentine Books, 1990).

Chapter 30

Page 269, *The sky-drum plays*: Hafiz, *The Gift: Poems by Hafiz the Great Sufi Master*, trans. Daniel Ladinsky (New York: Penguin, 1999).

Chapter 31

Page 277, *There is a saying about enlightenment, that it is the product of*: Meredith Lady Young, *Agartha: A Journey to the Stars* (Walpole, NH: Stillpoint Publishing, 1984).

INDEX

ABOUT THE AUTHOR

*M*eredith L. Young-Sowers, D. Div., is the cofounder and executive director of the Stillpoint Foundation, a global spiritual community and school located in Walpole, New Hampshire. She is also the creator of the Stillpoint Model of Integrative Life Healing, which is based on the wisdom gained from her twenty-seven years of spiritual practice and work with clients.

Her works include *Angelic Messenger Cards*, *Agartha: A Journey to the Stars*, *Wisdom Bowls*, and the *You Can Heal* audio program. She writes a monthly newsletter column and presents a monthly audio teaching series, Connections. A wife, mother, and grandmother, Meredith lives in Walpole, New Hampshire. She offers workshops and lectures throughout the United States. Her schedule is available at www.stillpoint.org.

HOW YOU CAN CONTINUE LEARNING FROM MEREDITH ABOUT THE SPIRIT HEALS WORK

The teachings of Dr. Meredith L. Young-Sowers and her twenty-five-year mission to awaken in people their own internal and intuitive connection with Spirit are the heart of the Stillpoint School and the nonprofit Stillpoint Foundation. Through a variety of outreach programs, Stillpoint strives to bring the message that Spirit Heals to as many individuals as possible.

Our vision is to offer comfort and guidance to all beings who seek to know their true natures as embodiments of Divine Love.

Our mission is to help people explore their spirituality and personal healing so that they may live their best lives and as a result, positively influence their families, their communities, and the world.

If you have been inspired by reading *Spirit Heals* and want to stay connected to the many ways Meredith guides people to explore and experience Spirit-driven healing, then visit our website at www.stillpoint.org. You'll discover many free resources and events to help you.

The Stillpoint School and Foundation
22 Stillpoint Lane • Walpole, NH 03608
www.stillpoint.org • 800-847-4014 • 603-756-9281